Hugh.
3.8.79

W H Hope
1991

# A SUSSEX CRICKET ODYSSEY

over 50 years of recollection
and enjoyment by

LAETITIA STAPLETON

with photographs many taken
by the author

Published by IAN HARRAP
at THE PELHAM : HAVANT

For Bryan

© Laetitia Stapleton 1979

First Published by IAN HARRAP
The Pelham : Havant
1979
ISBN 0950 4448 8X

Printed by Coasbyprint Ltd.,
Claybank Road, Portsmouth,
Hampshire
Made in Great Britain

## LIST OF CONTENTS

| Chapter | | Page |
|---|---|---|
| 1 | Early Memories 1926 — 1929 | 5 |
| 2 | The Silver Years 1930 — 1937 | 30 |
| 3 | The Little Victims Play 1938 — 1939 | 44 |
| 4 | Keeping the Flag Flying 1940 —1945 | 55 |
| 5 | Picking Up the Threads 1946 — 1949 | 62 |
| 6 | The Great Walk Out | 69 |
| 7 | Whither Cricket? 1950 — 1962 | 76 |
| 8 | One-Day Cricket Is Born 1963 — 1972 | 96 |
| 9 | Of This and That | 116 |
| 10 | The Captaincy of Tony Greig 1973 — 1977 | 130 |
| 11 | Two Men Who Loved Cricket | 157 |
| 12 | The Phoenix Rises | 171 |

# LIST OF ILLUSTRATIONS

| | Page |
|---|---|
| Sussex County Cricket Ground, c. 1925 | 7 |
| "Cushions", Tom Burchall and "Cushions" Assistant, c. 1925 | 7 |
| The Sussex XI, 1928 | 24 |
| Pavilion with Extension | 24 |
| Maurice Tate at his benefit match v Middlesex, Hove 1930 | 31 |
| Tommy Cook at his benefit match v Warwickshire, Hove 1937 | 31 |
| Conversation piece. Hastings, 1930. Front row: Duleepsinjhi (reading), A.H.H. Gilligan (back view), talking to A.P.F. Chapman, Mr. Miller Hallett (President 1937 – 1947), Harry Parks (seated): (standing E.H. Killick (in doorway), T.E. Cook (smoking), Jim Langridge (back to camera) talking to Ted Bowley: (at scorer's table) Mr. Isaacs (wearing hat) and Bert Wensley | 31 |
| *Sussex Daily News* cartoon of Jim Parks, senior, to commemorate his benefit in 1939. *Drawn by A.R. Young* | 52 |
| Three Sussex Captains-to-be at Eastbourne, 1951. Left to right, Robin Marlar, David Sheppard, Hubert Doggart. *Photograph by Cynthia Ford* | 81 |
| Sussex XI 1953. *Photograph by John Whewell* | 81 |
| Ted Dexter. *Photograph by Bill Smith* | 98 |
| John Snow by *Juliet Pannett* | 98 |
| Bernard, Duke of Norfolk and Arthur Gilligan on the occasion of the presentation of the portrait of the past Sussex and England Captain, painted by Juliet Pannett (right). *Photograph by Bill Smith* | 112 |
| The Chalet at Hove. Built as a 'temporary tea pavilion' in 1923 | 118 |
| Peter Graves. *Photograph by Bill Smith* | 134 |
| Ian Greig and Paul Parker | 134 |
| Sussex v Kent at Tunbridge Wells, 1971. Tony Greig 8 – 42. Also in the picture: – Greenidge, Bates, Joshi, Michael Buss, Snow, (Graves hidden), Richard Langridge, Denman, Tony Buss, Mike Griffith and umpires E.J. Rowe and A.G.T. Whitehead. *Photograph by Kent and Sussex Courier* | 141 |
| Lavinia, Duchess of Norfolk with the Rest of the World XI team. Arundel Park, 1977 | 149 |
| Bernard Marmaduke, 16th Duke of Norfolk, by *Juliet Pannett* | 158 |
| A.E.R. Gilligan by *Juliet Pannett* | 168 |
| Sussex Gillette Cup Winners, 1978 | 178 |
| The County Ground Hove, from the top of the Arthur Gilligan Stand. Sussex v Gloucestershire, June 1978 | 184 |
| Front cover: The Sussex County Ground today. *Photograph by Bill Smith* | |

CHAPTER ONE

**EARLY MEMORIES 1926 – 1929**

"Would you sign this for me, please?"

A small child in school uniform approaches Sussex and England captain Arthur Gilligan as he returns from lunch. He is handed a picture which shows him wearing a Free Forester blazer. This was to be the first postcard in an album which covers over fifty years. The year was 1925 and the child has no recollections of what he said at the time, but she recalls the excitement of her new possession to this day.

The first major match that I ever saw was Sussex v The Australians at Hove in 1921 when I was accompanied by my Scots Nanny, who knew more about the Highland Games than she did about the Sassenach game of cricket. I can recall little of that day except that we sat at the south-east corner of the ground, but the atmosphere must have been impressive, because, although details escape me entirely, the occasion is still quite vivid. The only concrete memento which remains is a slightly battered postcard of the Australian team. The name 'Warwick Armstrong' seemed to denote strength and leadership to the young child and although this must have been my first sight of my future heroes, Arthur Gilligan and Maurice Tate, it was the name of the Australian captain that made its mark. The next picture in my album shows the 1926 Australian side 'In Jaegar Shirts and Sweaters': this must have been a very early instance of advertising and I doubt if anyone complained.

For several years I was at boarding school in Suffolk, but intense homesickness caused my parents to bring me back to Hove, though my father said, "I fear she may regret it." I never did. I went to Kenilworth House School in Eaton Road, only a few hundred yards from the County Ground. This school was run by Mr. and Mrs. H.T. Wickham. Harry Temple Wickham played for the Sussex Martlets and he also partnered Arthur Gilligan at golf, under the captaincy of another Sussex amateur, J.K. Mathews. 'H.T.W.', as we called him, took the small boys who attended the school to the nets each evening when homework was done and I soon made myself one of this little gang. One day I found myself on the ground during a game which involved 'Sussex Club and Ground'. On inquiring what this meant I discovered that these were young players who hoped one day to play for the county side.

Did my mind fly back to that day in 1921 and Warwick Armstrong's Australian team? Frankly, I do not know.

I watched a few county games in 1924, my friends and I parking our bicycles under the small balcony of what is now the Secretary's office, but was then the pros' pavilion. It is strange, that although almost everything else in the Club has changed, that little balcony is still there.

In 1924 the County Ground at Hove presented a very different picture from the one you will see to-day. The pavilion was about a third of its present size and the original building is quite obvious. The ladies were severely segregated in what was called the 'Enclosure'. Here there were the sort of chairs which I always called 'bandstand' chairs, very hard and uncomfortable, though youthful enthusiasm did not heed such things. The only shelter provided for the female sex was a rather rickety stand, known affectionately as the 'hen coop'; this now stands — just — on the eastern side of the ground and has a section labelled 'BAR'. How people would have thrown up their hands in horror in 1924! The 'cowshed' at the southern end had a high wooden front, painted white, against which the ball would hurtle with a satisfying thud to register yet another four. To the northern end were some nice red brick Victorian houses and there was a tennis club on that part of the ground where the nets now lie. There were only two rather dignified and handsome houses in Palmeira Avenue: I have watched all the others being built, each one becoming less attractive than its predecessor.

Near the main gates, now the Tate Gates, there was the Sports Club with badminton, squash, and cricket nets, also a shop which sold all manner of sporting equipment and many postcards of players of all the counties and of the touring teams. The county players used these indoor nets on wet days in the spring and somehow we wormed our way in to watch. The 'cowshed' and the Sports Club have long since disappeared, the former giving way to the Arthur Gilligan Stand; the latter became a factory for a while, but was later demolished so that the solid and rather sombre phalanx of flats which we see to-day could be built. There are also large blocks of flats at the northern end which did not exist in 1924.

## Early Memories 1926 – 1929

*(left to right) "Cushions", Head Groundsman, Tom Burchall and "Cushions" assistant. C. 1925*

*Hove County Ground in the 1920's*

For some years after I joined Sussex the amateurs and professionals came out from different doors. The former emerged from the centre of the main pavilion under the clock; the professionals from their own dressing-room, which is now the Secretary's office. A.E.R. Gilligan always used to walk down to meet his pros so that they all approached the wickets as a single team: not so every captain, but this was probably the fault of the system rather than of any individual.

Brighton and Hove Cricket Week before the Second World War was a grand occasion. Enormous marquees went up, flags flew and a band played. Teas were provided by the lady members of the Club, and their domestic staff washed up behind the scenes. There were six different sections and since there were always two matches in Cricket Week, each section was host to the teams during this time. Competition was rife as to who could produce the best cakes and sandwiches: years later I was told of one woman who smoked incessantly and always dropped her cigarette ash into the tea-urn; I am thankful I did not know this at the time! Often the tea interval would be prolonged, as on the day when Amy Johnson, back from one of her triumphal flights, arrived on the ground to meet Don Bradman. In 1925 there was still a horse which used to pull the big roller; he wore huge leather bootees, which for many years afterwards were to be found hanging in the groundsman's hut. When the horse retired the Club and Ground used to pull the roller, assisted by any spectators who were ready to join in — and many were. Now all equipment, except the smallest roller, is mechanized and I feel that the young cricketers of to-day would take a dim view of being asked to roll the pitch!

Cricket was a leisurely affair in the 'Twenties. During intervals people would inspect the wicket with what I always suspected was questionable knowledge. Small boys played with bat and ball on various bits of grass surrounding the playing area — never *on* it. Near the hotel, where we seldom went in those days, men would be lying in the sun (which always seemed to shine from May to September) rather the worse for the amount they had imbibed: this was the era of cloth caps and braces and, if truth be told, they were not a pretty sight. The pavilion, on the other hand, was full of men in MCC and other club ties, often these colours adorning their straw hats, whilst the women in the Ladies' Enclosure were nearly always hatted and wore long dresses and gloves. I only wore a hat when forced to do so and was frequently in trouble with our headmistress when she saw me arriving with my school panama slung nonchalantly over the handle-bars of my bicycle.

One of the sights that has disappeared with the passing of time is that of the telegraph boy, who waited patiently at the players' gate until the end of an over and then proceeded towards So-and-So with dignified demeanour or sprightly sprint, according to his temperament, to deliver what we called a 'wire'. These telegrams lent a sense of urgency, not to say romance, to the proceedings. Sometimes the player would stuff the wire straight into the pocket of his trousers and dismiss the youth with a nod of the head. We presumed that this wire was expected. But what did it say? Sometimes the recipient would open the orange envelope and survey the contents with some thought. Had there been a disaster at home? Had a child been born? Had he been chosen to play for England? Or was it just the result of the 2.30? We hardly ever knew, but just occasionally the rest of the team would approach him and shake hands and then we knew the tidings were good. Now radio, the telephone and television have made life more prosaic: everything is known at once and there is little time for speculation; the news-hounds are onto a story almost before it has happened.

Whilst thinking of other days it is interesting to consider the dress of county players. In the time of which I am writing there was a fashion of 'plus fours' for both cricketers and footballers in plain clothes, but once in cricketing garb almost every player would appear in spotless flannels — and they *were* flannels — and equally spotless shirt, the material of which ranged from cotton to rich cream silk. *Clean* cricket clothes were *de rigueur* and I wish that some of our county players to-day would take a leaf out of the old-stagers' book. Modern clothing is so much easier to keep clean that one has little sympathy with the man who, on the first day of a match, arrives on the field with a pair of trousers which look as if their owner had been sleeping in a dustbin. The old Sussex colours were red, white and blue and were worn round the neck and waist of the capped players' sweaters: it was not until about 1929 that the inverted pyramid of six martlets, those odd footless birds of heraldry, became the badge on sweaters: it had always been the blazer badge. Somewhere about this time the Club colours were altered to dark blue, light blue and gold: I have always preferred the original colours and never knew why they were changed.

Before the war many amateurs wore caps that were known as 'fancy hats' and these represented I Zingari, Harlequins, Quidnuncs. Oxford and Cambridge clubs, the Sussex Martlets and others. Men recognize each other by their school or club ties, just as did regiments in battle recognize their colour when it was trooped. Many of the amateur cricketers, who were often very good players indeed, found themselves able to play county cricket from the middle of July until the end of the season and the variety of head-gear lent colour to the scene. There was the occasional man who would wear a different cap for each session of play, though whether this was for sheer comfort, to show how many 'fancy hats' he possessed, or just to confuse the public, I was never quite sure. Yet, however select some of the clubs may have been (and still are) it was the winning of his county cap that made amateur and professional alike feel several feet taller the moment it was placed upon his head, often at a happy little ceremony before a crowded pavilion: from the day this cap was awarded it was almost certain to take precedence over all others. Blazers were never worn outside the ground or apart from flannels and cricket shirt, whilst England blazers were cherished by their owners and every player who gained one was an additional honour to the Club. To-day blazers are worn with mufti just as any old jacket might be: England blazers are seldom seen at all on the Sussex County Ground to-day, though I cannot speak for other headquarters. It seems to be part of modern life to play everything down; as late as the 'Sixties Jim Parks, Ian Thomson and Ken Suttle would wear their touring MCC sweaters, but in 1975 John Snow was accused of arrogance by a stupid (male) member when, on a bitter day, he had stripped off two large long-sleeved county sweaters and had reached his third line of defence against the cold — a sleeveless MCC sweater, in which he bowled. What has become of our national pride and do we no longer 'want to know' when our players gain the highest honours in the game?

Before the Tanoy system came into being any public announcement was hastily chalked up on on a blackboard and this was carried round for all to see by two lads from the ground staff or, perhaps, by two ageing gatemen. The scores from other matches were not given out at luncheon or tea intervals and we bought endless editions of evening papers, which were never late enough to satisfy our curiosity.

I shall always regret that I have no memory of A.E.R. Gilligan bowling at his fastest. During the Gentleman v Players match in 1924 he had received a blow over the heart which prevented him from ever again reaching his old speed: thus the great partnership of Gilligan and Tate was impaired though they bowled together for several years to come. These two had dismissed South Africa for 30 runs that season and this is still the lowest score to be made by a Test team in this country. Gilligan continued to be a valuable all-rounder and his fielding at mid-off was an example to county cricketer and schoolboy alike.

The following winter Arthur Gilligan led the MCC tour of Australia and I cut out the scores of every game. The feeling that I had actually spoken to the captain of the team that was playing on the other side of the world brought the sort of thrill that only those who remember their own youth will appreciate: as yet we had no wireless and we had to rely on whatever edition of the papers would give the latest news. Later I bought *Gilligan's Men* by M.A. Noble, who had captained Australia in England in 1909, and this story of the 1924-25 tour came with me everywhere — to school, to cricket, onto the beach and up to bed, so that it is duly battered and read: very different from the virgin volumes so often found in private libraries.

The first cricketing event of which I have a really clear memory is the game between Sussex and Surrey at Hove in July, 1925. John Berry Hobbs, my first sight of whom this was, needed one more century to equal the record set up by W.G. Grace. By early July Hobbs had already reached 125 hundreds, but the 126th was eluding him. At Hove expectation was at its height and for once I even *wanted* a member of the opposing side to get the runs so that I could feel that I had been part of history in the making. How often are our hopes dashed? These hopes were not only mine but also those of the host of reporters and photographers who had come to witness the record and rush their copy back to London. Maurice Tate, however, had other views and when he had Hobbs lbw for 1 he was a little less than popular. Memory tells me that mid-way through this match a thunderstorm swept over the ground and I distinctly recall sheltering with my bicycle under the balcony and saying to myself "Please, God, let it stop raining, so that Hobbs can bat again!" I see, however, that Surrey won by an innings, so that would not have been necessary, but the recollection of that rain is so vivid that I am sure it must have been so.

Jack Hobbs had not long to wait to satisfy his admirers, who must have consisted of the whole cricket-loving public in England. Against Somerset in August he first equalled and then beat Grace's record — a great feat by a great and modest man. I am sure that this episode in the annals of cricket had some bearing on my becoming a Sussex member the next year. That first season ticket cost 12/- (60p); it was stiff and pink and lived in the top pocket of my blazer, next to the fountain pen for getting autographs and is, therefore, covered with ink. Just looking at it today brings back that first thrill of pride which I had when I realised that now I was a member of that wonderful thing called 'S.C.C.C.'!

On April 1st 1926 I left KHS with real regret and the following day I saw Duleepsinjhi for the first time when he was practising in the nets. Duleep was qualified for Sussex in 1925, but did not play regularly for the county until he came down from Cambridge. I was soon to appreciate the unique batting of this nephew of Ranjitsinjhi, particularly his late cut with which he seemed to encourage, rather than hit, the ball between first slip and the wicket-keeper, so that it sped to the boundary in a flash. Duleep, like so many of his race, was rather remote and I was a little in awe of him: others laughed and joked when we got their autographs, but Duleep's innate dignity never permitted him to do this.

Almost the whole of the Easter holidays was spent watching the county players in the nets and when they had disappeared for rest and refreshment trying, however feebly, to emulate their achievements. Looking back on those days I can see how fortunate we young people were in having Mr. W.L. Knowles as the Sussex Secretary. Our tickets did not give us permission to practise in the nets and it was entirely due to his turning a blind eye to our activities that we enjoyed so many happy hours on the County Ground, the highlight of our day being when Tate, Bowley or Jim Parks — or one of the other players — would send down a few balls to us or give a bit of advice. Mr. Knowles and his assistant, dear old Billy Newham, both of whom had played for Sussex, smiled benignly on our efforts and, provided that we did not get in anyone's way, were content to let us pursue our hearts' desire.

The Sussex team as I first remember it was:- A.E.R. Gilligan, (capt.), A.H.H. Gilligan, Colonel A.C. Watson, L. Williams, Bowley, Tate, Cook, Wensley, J.H. Parks, Jim Langridge, 'Tich'. Cornford, George Cox, senior, backed up in the holidays by the Rev. F.B.R. Browne, R.A. Young, G.S. Grimston, C.H. Gibson and, of course, Duleepsinjhi. All the professionals were Sussex men and the amateurs nearly all had close county connections. In 1929 Tommy Cook wrote in a sporting journal: "We of Sussex, all Sussex born and bred, seem to have a county spirit that can never be so strong in teams of mixed counties and nationalities. This county spirit seems to give us a will to win stronger than the incentive of the £2 bonus." These words have especial significance fifty years later.

It is hard for the younger cricket followers of to-day to realise the rigid separation which existed between amateur and professional before, and for some years after, the war. The amateurs had often been at school and/or University together, had possibly played hockey or rugger for the same club and may even have married into each others' families: the professionals, whom I shall always regard as the salt of the earth, were mostly country boys whose dual love was cricket — and their county. They gave of their best at all times and would invariably say that the proudest day of their lives was that on which they gained their cap. Quite recently some of the old Sussex professionals whom I have met have said that they regret the passing of the genuine amateur who could add so much to the game, but who has been squeezed out by the financial position of so many would-be cricketers today. Looking at the old scorecards it is interesting to see that in olden days an amateur would have 'Mr' or his rank before his name; then 'Mr' was dropped and the amateur's initials preceeded his name, whilst those of the professional came afterwards, thus: 'A.E.R. Gilligan', but 'Tate, M.W.'. A curious distinction.

During the Easter holidays of 1926 Maurice Tate had a coaching job at Harrods and I got round my mother to take me to see him in the sports department where nets had been set up: but it was Tate, the England cricketer, as much as Tate, the coach, who drew people to that part of the famous London store. Lots of small budding England players did, of course, have the honour of being bowled to by the large and genial man, but one day the tables were turned, and a 14-year-old bowled Tate with a googly! Harold Larwood commented, "He has perfect action and the ball is a natural googly." The name of this boy was Maxwell and he was about to go to Brighton College, but I never heard of him again. How transitory is fame!

During the General Strike I started at my new school. I had been so very happy at Kenilworth House and had only been forced to leave because I had outgrown its teaching facilities. I always kept in touch with KHS and continued to join their cricketing activities at the County Ground. I never settled down to school again although I did express a wish to get my cricket colours before I left. It was at this new school that I met Juliet Somers, now Juliet Pannett, the well-known portrait artist. We became friends and have remained so ever since. We watched cricket together during our school days and later after she had gone to the

Art School: round the edges of her scorecards were her lightning sketches of our favourite players: I am only sorry that neither of us kept them. Later she did a series of Sussex cricketers for the *Sussex County Magazine* and this included pictures of Tate, Bowley, 'Tich' Cornford and the rest.

In mid-May A.W. Carr was made captain of England: I was outraged and heart-broken. "I think it's rotten chucking A.E.R. out," I wrote in my diary, but my enthusiasm was such that I was soon making out my own forecast of the probable England side. It is, perhaps, an indication of how many players were automatic choices that my own list differed from that of the Selectors in only two instances: I had put J.W.H.T. Douglas and H. Howell, whereas the Selectors had preferred A.P.F. Chapman and F. Root. There was a wealth of high-class batting and bowling in 1926 and those who were left out like Hobbs' Surrey partner, Andy Sandham, were very unlucky. In Sussex Ted Bowley, J.H. Parks, John Langridge and Tommy Cook were, over the years, forced to sit back and watch others gain England caps when, at another period, it is almost certain that their own chance would have come.

In a year that was not especially successful for Sussex I recorded the achievements of Gilligan and Tate with an eagerness that should, I suppose, have been direct to my schoolwork and I was not ashamed of my heroes. Gilligan, despite being absent on many occasions as a Test Selector, made four centuries, whilst Tate (playing for England against Australia this summer) completed the 'double' yet again and was top of the averages. People to-day tend to think of Maurice Tate mainly as a bowler and they hardly realise what a useful batsman he was. For some time he opened the innings with Bowley although he, himself, would have preferred to go in lower down the order and have a good slam at everything. Altogether Tate made 17,086 runs for Sussex and that is no mean feat for an opening bowler.

One highlight of this summer was when George Cox, senior, took 17 wickets in the match against Warwickshire, when the fine old son of Sussex received a rapturous ovation: I can still see the headlines in the press. Seventeen wickets in a match was something anyway, but at the age of 53 it was truly remarkable. For Cox, there must have been the added delight that this happened on the Horsham ground only a few miles from his birthplace at Warnham. George Bernard Shaw is supposed to have said: "I loathe being called George." Not so George Cox, nor his son, nor, I suspect, the late George Street, little George Duckworth, the Lancashire wicket-keeper, nor any of the other 'Georges' who have graced the cricket-field throughout the ages. George Cox retired at the end of the following season; he had played for Sussex for thirty-two years, having first appeared for the county in 1895; despite his age many thought that he was capable of continuing for several years more. He had made 14,353 runs and had taken 1,810 wickets for Sussex, the latter being a record then, but later to be beaten by Maurice Tate. One can only quote what the *Sussex Daily News* said at the time: "The Sussex eleven will seem strange without his sturdy figure, his broad Sussex smile, and that easy swing of the left arm, sending in those wily slow balls to baffle generations of batsmen." The only man older than Cox who was still playing county cricket was W.G. Quaife of Warwickshire — and *he* was born in Sussex! Two years later George Cox was made county coach, whilst his son, forever 'young' George, joined the ground staff. At the AGM in 1938 Mr. G.S. Godfree spoke of George Cox and said that he had been made a Life Member of the Club: "For 42 years George has been assisting the county and has never given us a moment's anxiety." Could there possibly be a better tribute from a county to one of its most respected players?

Shortly after Cox's great feat I saw Duleepsingjhi get his maiden century against Hampshire at Hove and this was followed by another in the next game against Surrey at Eastbourne. Skipping school, I also managed to see P.G.H. Fender make 61 not out. "Awfully good batsman," was my brief comment. Another laconic statement reads, "Tooth out. Wensley 107 v Lancs."

August came and holidays at last. We travelled to Hastings on one of those marvellous 10/6 tickets which allowed you to go anywhere within a certain area for one whole week. That first year at Hastings we saw Woolley make 104 and yet Sussex won.

From now on Hastings and Eastbourne cricket weeks came to be looked forward to more and more. The train journey to Hastings was long and entailed an early start. Brighton Station used to be filled with cricketgoers — and players — soon after 8 a.m. Slowly the train wound its way eastward, leaving the main line at Polegate for a detour to pick up the Eastbourne contingent and stopping at Hampden Park in each direction: it was all very frustrating and by the end of the week I had almost developed a 'thing' about Hampden Park, which was but a tiny halt. The journey to Eastbourne is far less tedious, whether by train or car and the Saffrons is a beautiful ground surrounded by trees which create the typical English cricket scene. The red brick Victorian town-hall clock strikes every quarter of an hour and you can eat your lunch on the edge of the croquet lawn, watching exponents of an even more leisurely game than cricket coaxing their varied coloured balls through the narrow hoops. Eastbourne Cricket Week was a very social affair and a large part of the non-playing area was — and still is — taken up by club tents, deck chairs, potted plants and tables weighed down with food and drink, whilst frequently a military band played throughout the afternoon. It was all very colourful, but members of Sussex C.C.C. began to complain that there was little room for *them*. We used to sit on the roof balcony above the small pavilion and since the players left this to go for lunch it was a great venue for taking photographs. Over the years we received great courtesy from the men of all counties, though an exception was George Duckworth, whose autograph I tried to get for a small boy, but Duckworth refused. One of my Eastbourne memories is that of a match against Yorkshire in 1928. Harry Parks, in speeding round the boundary to save a four, tore a muscle and his brother, Jim, came on as substitute. This was right at the start of the match and I wrote that night: "Gilligan consulted W.A. Worsley (father of the future Duchess of Kent) and it was agreed that Jim might bowl. This against MCC rules. Much discussion between umpires etc. before play was resumed." Men could make a gentleman's agreement in those days and one heard less of being 'competitive', whatever that may mean where good sportsmanship is concerned.

Sussex finished only 10th in 1926, but positions in the County Championship were somewhat put in the shade by the wonderful news that on August 18th at the Oval, England had beaten Australia and had regained the Ashes. Great was our joy. I have a magazine picture of that famous side, signed by every member of it:- A.P.F. Chapman, (capt.) Hobbs, Sutcliffe, Tate, Hendren, Larwood, Strudwick, G.T.S. Stevens, W. Rhodes, Geary and Woolley, with Sandham as 12th man. What a side to remember!

Only ten days after their defeat the Australians were at Hove. We arrived at the ground at 7.30 a.m. and already there was a long queue. (To-day it is a queue of cars). I doubt if the gates opened before 9.30, but when they did we made a mad rush. There was a Mrs. Knights, getting on in years, and she asked me if I would run ahead and put a cushion on her special place. This I gladly did. At the end of the season she gave me *The Game's the Thing* by M.A. Noble and she inscribed it: "To my Sprinter. Australian Match 1926." We had managed to get our own seats as well, took endless photographs and got countless autographs. In my diary

I wrote: "Sussex fielding very good. Woodfull's drives in front of the wicket are impressive. Bardsley slow to watch." The latter made 118 not out and was largely responsible for this match being drawn. On the third day I saw for the first time a batsman being dismissed in one of those infuriating ways: Bardsley made a drive, Macartney was backing up, but George Cox deflected the ball onto the stumps as it passed him and Macartney was well out of his crease. He had been out for a duck to Arthur Gilligan in the first innings, so it was certainly not his match.

After the season was over the cricketers went their respective ways and a gloom descended on our lives. There was, however, some compensation in that the MCC was sending a team to India during the winter months. This was rather more of a social affair than anything else, for Test matches between the two countries were still in the future. Arthur Gilligan, who was to captain the side, had, whilst the 1926 season was in progress, written a book called *Collin's Men,* this being an account of the 1925-26 winter tour of Australia. Before he left for India I had written to tell him how much I had enjoyed his book and I sent him a mascot to take with him. I cannot now think what that mascot was, but I believe it was a very small teddy bear! My delight knew no bounds when I received a letter from Marseilles. The writing-paper was headed P & O S.N. Co. S.S. . . . (but the name of the ship is not there). Gilligan wrote:-

Dear Miss Repington,
Thank you very much for sending me a mascot to take to India. It is very kind of you and I hope it brings us luck.
I am glad you liked 'Collin's Men'. We've just arrived here after 24 hours in the train and it's so hot.
Thank you again for your kind message.
Yours sincerely,
Arthur Gilligan.

My friends were very envious of this letter and I have always thought it was extremely kind of the England captain to reply to one of his young admirers.

Soon the glossy magazines were full of pictures of MCC being entertained lavishly by their Indian hosts. At cricket MCC were indubitably superior, but when it came to a day's shooting the positions were reversed. It is unlikely that any member of the party gave a thought to the word 'conservation' for the World Wild Life Fund had not been heard of and they slaughtered their panther, sambhar and Jamnagar buck with clear consciences. All but one. Many years later Bob Wyatt, who was a member of this side, told me that he had been so nauseated by the killing that he had vowed never to kill any living thing again. But one picture shows A.E.R. Gilligan and Major Chichester-Constable, with their Indian bearer behind them and the day's 'bag' at their feet, portraying an age long past.

The MCC visited the home of the Maharajah of Patiala, who played for the tourists on several occasions, and that of the Jam Sahib of Nawanagar — the great Ranji himself. A regiment of lancers which formed a guard of honour for MCC were inspected by Ranji and the Maharajah of Kapurthala.

So ended my first season as a member of the Sussex County Cricket Club. I finished the diary by saying: "Welcome 1927 and may it bring Sussex many cricketing victories." I knew that cricket was going to give me pleasure for some time ahead. For how long, not even I could have guessed.

If future Aprils were to bring joy each September from now on was to bring depression as, one by one, our heroes vanished from our sight, but soon a narrow shaft of light began to pierce the inevitable gloom when a new annual event became part of my personal calendar. In 1927 I was invited to play in a match in aid of the Royal Alexandra Hospital for Children in Brighton. A Ladies' XI took on the 'might' of the Club and Ground, but — indignity of indignities! — they had to play left-handed! The day was organized by Lady Eva de Paravicini, whose husband, H.F. de Paravicini, had been President of Sussex in 1924, and by Miss Zoe Caillard, the Appeal Secretary. Admission was free, but a collection was made for the Hospital and Zoe Caillard tells me that the rules about women entering the Committee Room were so strict that she and her fellow collectors had to be chaperoned when they went in to lay their heavy tins on the table! Those of us who had been asked to play were almost intoxicated with excitement. Here we were playing in the same match as Maurice Tate (always ready to join in), Jim and Harry Parks, Jim Langridge, Reg Hollingdale, Jim Cornford and others, whilst, in 1936, Arthur Gilligan led the side against us. Each year as this day approached my pulse beat a little faster, but I was always a victim of nerves: once, however, I made an unforgettable (for me) 48, but the thought of seeing 50 under my number on the scoreboard that had recorded the scores of so many famous players so completely overwhelmed me that I was bowled next ball by Jack Nye, the young fast bowler who, it was thought, would be the successor to Maurice Tate. One reporter called me "quite a stylish batsman" and another wrote: "It was Miss L. Repington who held up the Club and Ground's quick success. In company with Miss D. Gadsby, she batted with a proficiency equal to that of a stalwart of the game, whilst her pulls to leg and her on drives brought the ready applause they demanded." I hope that no one will wish to deny me my tiny moment of (near) glory.

There were far fewer overseas cricket tours than there are today and less coaching posts to be had. Before flying became the automatic method of getting from one country to another a journey to South Africa or India, let alone Australia or New Zealand, was almost out of the question, except for the official sides. Bowley and Wensley and later Jim Langridge certainly coached in New Zealand and Tommy Cook did so in South Africa, but, of course, they went by sea. It was interesting to learn that little Eddie Paynter, the Lancashire and England batsman, had never flown until, at the age of 75, he went out by air to Melbourne for the Centenary Test in 1977. Most cricketers had to stay at home, play football to keep fit, pick up what odd jobs they could find and even go on the dole. In the slump of the 'Twenties and 'Thirties cricketers were envied by their friends for having even a summer job and also for the fame and glory this sometimes brought in its train.

I had joined the Brighton Foot Beagles. By a fortunate coincidence Lance Knowles, the Sussex Secretary, who had always been so kind about my cricket enthusiasms, was also Master of the Beagles. Maurice Tate, when not overseas, was often out with them and over the years we got to know him quite well. He was a sort of Peter Pan figure, in the sense that he was the man who refused to grow up. This sometimes got him into trouble with the authorities and many years later his dismissal by Sussex was one of the less happy incidents in the history of the Club. My beagling cuttings show pictures of Tate either leaping a five-barred gate, taking a stream in one gigantic stride, disentangling himself from a barbed-wire fence, or, equally characteristically, reclining in the hay, with, of course, his pipe.

The beagles met on Tuesdays and Saturdays, but there were days when hunting was called off because of snow and ice, or, more tragically, because of foot and mouth disease. There had to be an alternative interest and we turned to association football. The reason for this is not far to seek. Throughout the summer we had watched Tommy Cook play cricket for Sussex; fielding as he did at third man, close to where we sat, he had often been the subject of Juliet's sketches. We knew that he played soccer for Brighton and Hove Albion and had gained an England cap in the 1924-25 season when he played at centre-forward against Wales — a rare distinction for a Third Division player: on March 5th, 1927, he was awarded his football benefit in the game against Gillingham, which Brighton won 3–2. There was a very good spirit between the cricketers and the footballers and each were to be found watching the others play. Generally one of the Albion players acted as 'baggage man' for Sussex during the summer. First it was goalkeeper, Sid Webb: it was his business to see that the cricket bags and suitcases were loaded onto one or more taxis at the ground, put on the train and delivered safely to the hotel or at the ground where the next match was to be played. When the match was in progress he would carry out the duties of twelfth man, but, as far as I know, he never played, except to come on as substitute fielder. At the start of the 1930 season Webb was married to a local girl and was presented with a clock by the then captain, Harold Gilligan, which was inscribed, "To Sid, with appreciation and good luck, from the Sussex XI, May 1930". When Webb left Sussex his place was taken by Bobby Farrell one of the Albion forwards. Now, of course, all players have cars and the office of baggage man has become obsolete.

In the Christmas holidays it was arranged that I should have some cricket coaching in the nets at the Hove Sports Club. There was not a county player in sight, but there *was* the enormous thrill of playing where 'they' had played and acting out my part as Gilligan, Tate or Tommy Cook. My coach was H.P. Chaplin, always known as 'Bertie', who had first played for Sussex in 1905, the year that the Sussex Martlets club was founded, and who had been captain of Sussex from 1910–1914. One day Bertie said that I played well, but that I must not attempt Hobbs' strokes! I was also coached by Mr. (later Sir Alan) Saunders, but it is Bertie I remember best, and although he rated me unmercifully when I played badly, I appreciated his firmness. More coaching in the Easter holidays, but by April the county players were mustering for regular practice at the indoor nets. One year my diary said:- "Tate let me bowl (to him) most of the morning," and next day — "Tate let me bowl, then bat." How kind these men were! Soon the nets were completely taken over by the great players, but we did not mind. Now that they were back in action we were happy again.

Sussex, if not exactly challenging for the top position, was an extremely attractive team to watch, so that fifty years later R.E.S. Wyatt would be writing to me saying, "I always enjoyed our matches against Sussex, which was considered a very sporting

## Early Memories 1926 – 1929

county." Arthur Gilligan had a fine team to lead, but he would never play a man, whatever his other qualifications, if he could not field. Gilligan's Sussex was renowned throughout England for superb fielding and this was entirely due to the insistence of the captain that fielding practice was quite as important as batting and bowling. We had the reputation of playing cricket in the right spirit and, win or lose, doing it with dignity. In 1928 H.J. Henley was writing that "although Sussex were beaten at Lords yesterday they went down with the flag flying. And it is better for a side to die pluckily than to go to their doom in an agony of fear." As recently as 1972 Brian Johnston showed that he had not fogotten the old Sussex when he wrote in the *Sussex Centenary Handbook* . . . "the point about Sussex was that they were *fun* to watch and play against . . . Their fielding was brilliant and their batting had a dashing air about it with some welcome rusticity low down the order." These comments warm the heart to-day and I sometimes wonder if we have not grown too concerned with finance and 'winning something' and have forgotten about the fun.

The Sussex County Cricket Club has always been famous for family connections and I have been lucky enough to have known most of the members of these families. I just missed the Relf brothers, Albert and Robert, but Albert was coach when I became a member in 1926. I did not see Ranji play, but I certainly saw and greatly admired his nephew, Duleepsinjhi: I did not see Fred Tate play either, but his son, Maurice, was part of my youth and I saw him throughout the greater part of his distinguished career. Arthur and Harold Gilligan were in action in my early years and they were soon followed by Jim and Harry Parks, Jim and John Langridge, Charlie and Jack Oakes, whilst George Cox's son, 'young' George, gained his county cap before the war. It is almost beginning to sound like a closed shop and just to confuse the public still more we had 'Tich' and Jim Cornford, who were not related. Even when there was no blood relationship new connections would be formed as when Tommy Cook acted as Wensley's best man and when Tate and Wensley became godparents to Tommy's baby son, Roger.

During my first season I had made visits to Hastings and Eastbourne, but 1927 brought my first journey to Horsham, to what must be one of the loveliest grounds in the country. It is sad that county cricket is no longer played on this ground, where the bowler had to be held up every time a train passed above the level of the sight-screen: at one corner of the field stood the cottage inhabited by groundsman Oakes, whose two sons were to become sturdy members of the Sussex side in 1935 and 1937, but whose careers were grievously interrupted by the war.

The informality of the pavilion at Horsham enabled us to mingle freely with the players and one day R.E.S. Wyatt of Warwickshire came to sit with us: he told us lots of cricketing stories and then promised to send us each a signed photograph. We returned on the Monday — was it half-term? — and Wyatt then promised us one of his bats when Warwickshire met Sussex the following year. School was distinctly flat after such glories. Next year my mother invited Bob Wyatt and G.A. Palmer to dinner — and, of course, Juliet came too. The cricketers were probably rather amused by their starry-eyed admirers and it was a completely crazy evening, with Wyatt signing the roll of bread beside his plate: I kept the roll for a long time and why it never went mouldy I shall never know. By this time it was clear that Bob Wyatt was an up and coming player and Arthur Gilligan had thought a lot of him when they had toured India together, whilst Wyatt pays tribute to the help that A.E.R. was to him in his early days. From a Sussex point of view it is interesting to note that Wyatt and Ted Bowley, the Sussex opener, played their first Test match together at Old Trafford in 1929. R.E.S. Wyatt was to become captain of Warwickshire in 1930 and at the end of the year was invited to captain England in the final Test against Australia. From 1949-53 he was a Test Selector and was Chairman of Selectors in 1950, whilst in 1977 he was the senior England captain to attend the Centenary Test at Melbourne.

In 1927 Maurice Tate did the 'double' yet again when he took the wicket of H.J. Enthoven in the Bank Holiday match at Hove. Tate was in fine form this year and later in the same month he was partly responsible for what Sussex rightly regarded as their greatest victory of the season. On the Saffrons ground at Eastbourne they defeated Lancashire, unbeaten by any other side that summer, by an innings and 196 runs. The century-makers were Arthur Gilligan and Harrow schoolmaster, R.L. Holdsworth: the bowlers who secured success were Tate and the Rev. F.B.R. Browne, always known as 'Tishy' (after the racehorse), because of his extraordinary bowling action in which his arms and legs became inexplicably entangled. I well recall the big crowd gathering before the little pavilion to acclaim the Sussex skipper, who was persuaded to make a short speech, then, as was so characteristic of him, he called for three cheers for the losers. It was after all this excitement that Tate and 'Tich' Cornford were involved in a car smash near Peacehaven on the way back to Brighton.

Comford was unhurt, but Tate was thrown out of the car, mercifully only to bruise his knees.

This September Juliet and I went on our first visit to the Oval for the time-honoured fixture between the Champion County and The Rest. Our expectations were high, only to be utterly shattered when it rained all day. What I had to show for the expedition was a copy of Dudley Carew's *England Over*, which I bought at the Oval bookstall and which I have always treasured, not least for its graphic account of a catch made by Tommy Cook at Hastings in 1926. My mother inscribed it for me, "The only nice bit of a thoroughly disappointing day when there was no cricket at the Oval owing to rain. Sept. 10th. 1927." Incidentally, whilst we were watching the rain pour down at the Oval, Cook was scoring a hat-trick for Brighton against Millwall.

In the spring of 1928 I persuaded my mother to allow me to leave school, for once April came work seemed impossible. The headmistress was very annoyed: the games mistress just said, "What a pity!" For me there were no regrets, only complete happiness in my newly-found freedom. At the beginning of this season an extension to the old pavilion was opened by Lord Leconfield, Lord Lieutenant of Sussex and President of MCC: Juliet and I had already sampled the upper storey of this two-tiered stand, but I had no idea that I should be sitting in much the same place on summer days over fifty years later! The new building had an immediate effect on the professionals, who were removed from their old, inadequate and cramped surroundings to what must have seemed a comparatively palatial establishment and with hot water laid on: for years, however, until a more modern heating system was installed, a chimney used to belch forth smoke and grit from 5 p.m. onwards, to the murmurs of "Bath time!" from those within smut reach. The amateurs had always had their own dressing-room in the main pavilion; it was a large, rather sombre sort of place, a bit like the reading-room of a London club. Around the walls were huge sofas and arm-chairs, all upholstered in leather and with brass studs to hold the fabric down. An enormous table stood in the centre of the room and on the walls there was a fine series of drawings of old-time cricketers by A. Chevalier Tayler, dated 1905, these men looking old-fashioned and disapproving even then of their modern counterparts. What their views are as they gaze down from the walls of the members' tea-room to-day I should just love to know! Outside the amateurs' room was a small balcony and a few chairs — enough for the three or four amateurs who might be playing on

FRONT ROW (left to right): Jim Langridge, A.H.H. Gilligan, Maurice Tate, A.E.R. Gilligan, Bowley, W.L. Cornford
BACK ROW: Richards, Wensley, Jim Parks, Harry Parks, Hollingdale

Bryan on Pavilion roof, June 2nd 1978 — The extension was built 50 years earlier in 1928.

either side. As time went by the professionals were allowed to enter this island of privacy, for they had nowhere else from which to watch the game. For the next few years the professionals walked down the flight of steps which had sprung up between the new and old pavilions, but it was not long before the amateurs began to walk along the narrow passage which connected the two dressing-rooms so that the captain might lead his team, as one body, onto the field: as they came along we could hear the skipper's cry of "All aboard!" from where we sat. The division was rigid, however, where accommodation at hotels was concerned and when we stayed at Hastings at the Robertson Hotel the professionals were at the nearby Albany (both hotels bombed out of existence in the blitz), but the amateurs were housed in regal splendour at the Queen's.

Ladies were strictly barred from the old pavilion, still for a long time yet to be called the 'Men's Pavilion', but this worried us not at all. We 'bagged' the gangway seats, next to the gate through which every player would have to pass and this opportunity of having all the well-known cricketers so close meant that we got to know them all by sight as time went by. There was an elderly gateman, whose name I never knew, who opened and shut the gate for every player as he came and went. This fine old chap was of military bearing — surely he must have been a sergeant-major — with a neat grey beard and he always wore a hat which he would raise to us with ceremony as we arrived each day. He was courteous to everyone, even when preventing some erring female from passing over the forbidden line: no roving small boys would ever escape his eagle eye without the necessary ticket. Another familiar figure, whom older members will remember was old 'Cushions', who went round the ground with his 'Threepennyworth of comfort'. He was part of the pre-war Sussex scene and for many years travelled to all the Sussex grounds, always accompanied by his cushions.

Luckily for Sussex Arthur Gilligan recovered from the 'snow blindness' which he had contracted whilst ski-ing in Switzerland and Duleep was also pronounced fit after a serious bout of pneumonia, so both were at net practice when the teams got together, with me in close attendance. Sussex had a good season this year, moving up to seventh. The Bank Holiday match against Middlesex in August was, as ever, a tremendous attraction, with Bowley, Duleep and Tate all getting centuries, but the Sussex score of 496 was beaten by Middlesex, with Patsy Hendren and E.T. Killick replying with their own hundreds. "By tea-time double rows in front of pavilion and cowshed," I wrote in my diary.

The West Indies, captained by R.K. Nunes, had been awarded their first series of Tests against England in 1928 and they came to Hove straight from the last of these at the Oval. Again I wrote, "Huge crowds. Last seats roped off for West Indies and their friends. Constantine sat next but one to me." We were a little cross at having our special seats reserved for others, but it was obviously the right thing to do. Little did I know that the slight Trinidadian sitting so near me was, in 1962, to become 'Sir Learie', and in 1969 'Lord Constantine' — the first black peer of the realm. On this occasion Sussex beat the West Indies decisively by an innings. Soon after my return from Scotland this autumn I heard of the death of A.J. Gaston, 'Leather Hunter' to all Sussex members and a well-known figure at the County Ground. He prepared the little handbook called *Sussex County Cricket 1728-1923-25,* which contains a wealth of information for all lovers of cricket around the county. He had been a great supporter of the Club, touring the villages with Mr. Knowles in a never-ending search for talent.

After my father's death my mother became secretary to an old friend, Alderson Horne, who owned the Westminster Theatre in London. Often I would go to first nights at this or other theatres, travelling up from Hove on a special 'theatre' train, for which the return fare was 6/- (30p)! After I had left school my mother went to live in London, but for a while I remained in Hove with friends: in this way I managed to get the best of both worlds for my mother had a flat within walking distance of Lords. Of course I went to watch Middlesex, with Hendren, J.W. Hearne, Durston, Price, Lee and the amateurs such as F.T. Mann, Nigel Bruce, G.O. Allen, H.J. Enthoven, Ian Peebles, R.W.V. Robins, G.T.S. Stevens and R.H. Twining. It is surprising that after 1921 Middlesex did not gain the highest honours until 1947. I also went to see Surrey at the Oval where I watched Fender, Hobbs, Sandham, Peach, Strudwick, Ducat, E.R.T. Holmes and D.R. Jardine, but nothing would change my loyalty to Sussex, despite the undoubted drawing power of the two London clubs. After my first visit to Lords, which was to a game between MCC and Yorkshire, I wrote, "I prefer our own ground. Lords is all stands and very ugly!" What arrant heresy from one who claimed to live for cricket! A few days after this I was back in Hove, but only to pack and leave, as I thought then, for good, My mother had decided that it was impracticable for me to have two homes and my diary says woefully:- "Packed for London. It's rotten leaving

## Early Memories 1926 – 1929

Sussex." I was duly told off when I started to arrange my cricket photographs on the drawing-room mantelpiece and these were immediately banished to my own room.

Being in London made it possible for me to go to the 'Varsity Match at Lords, but here my allegiance was not involved for my father had been at neither, but at Sandhurst, and I had only the slightest inclination towards the Dark Blues. I also went to the England v The Rest Test Trial, in which our friend, Bob Wyatt, was playing and I was able to speak to him in the luncheon interval and this made me feel very important. I saw the dark, sleek-haired Sutcliffe, with his bronzed complexion, make 91, the short stocky Leyland 76, our own Maurice Tate 79 – all for England, whilst for The Rest P.G.H. Fender, who, with his little black moustache and his silk scarf, could never be mistaken for anyone else, made 100.

South Africa were the tourists this summer and Maurice Tate made 100 not out against them in the second Test. Cameron of South Africa was carried off unconscious after being hit by a ball from Larwood, the demon fast bowler of the 'Twenties and 'Thirties. *Wisden* says:- "The unhappy incident had dampened everybody's spirits and all real interest vanished." As I write today the pundits are greatly concerned about the injuries which may be inflicted by what are now called the 'speed merchants', but, looking back, one can see that history is merely repeating itself.

From London I also went to the Essex ground at Leyton for the first time and found it a bare, grassless place. The game turned into something of a farce for Sussex batted on till nearly 5 o'clock on the third day getting nearly 500 runs, the 202 by Duleep was wasted and Jim Parks broke a finger. My diary blames both captains, but mainly the Essex captain, H.M. Morris (no doubt prejudice here), who had agreed to stop early on the last day because Essex had to travel to Bradford. Now times and even numbers of overs in the final hour are strictly laid down, which prevents such antics.

Towards the end of the 1929 season Arthur Gilligan had to relinquish the captaincy because of illness and his brother, Harold, took over. This produced an unusual record for the Gilligan family, since in the same month their brother, F.W., was also captain of Essex: it is doubtful whether any three brothers have captained county sides in the same month before or since. I was surprised to discover that Harold played more games for his county than did Arthur; however, as captain of England in Australia and India, A.E.R. had been more in the public eye, though A.H.H. (we called him 'Ah-ha-ha') led the MCC tour of New Zealand in the winter of 1929-30. In November 1930 the *London Evening News* was running a series called 'Queer Story of the War'. Arthur Gilligan wrote to describe how, when serving with the 11th Bn Lancashire Fusiliers in 1915, he found himself holding a part of a line south of Ploegstreet and was doing a little sniping. As he replaced a brick in the sniping position it was hit by a German bullet. He had slight injuries to his eyes and lip, but thought little of these. "To my amazement," he now wrote, "last Wednesday morning, exactly 15 years after, I saw, when looking into the mirror, a piece of brick, about a quarter of an inch long, protruding at the corner of my eye, just above the eye-lid. My doctor removed it and found that it had worked its way to the surface. It was certainly a strange memento of the war." And a lucky escape for the future Sussex and England captain.

Towards the end of 1929 my mother became resigned to the fact that I should never be happy in London and that we should have to return to Hove. I had enjoyed my nights with her at the theatre, but my heart was on the other side of the South Downs. I found a maisonette in Hove in an old-fashioned house, but it had big rooms which would take our large furniture, all our books and my own *lares et penates,* which were increasing every year. The new home I went to in November 1929 remained mine for the next thirty years.

I was delighted to find myself back in Sussex and to have my home within about seven minutes walking — or two minutes cycling — distance of the County Ground. Even when there was nothing happening friends and I used to haunt the place. The head groundsman, Tom Burchell, was a great character with a good sense of fun: his assistant, Beach, was a thin, quiet man, who seldom spoke unless it was necessary, but he was by no means unfriendly; the third groundsman was Bert Prior, a short stocky, cheerful little fellow, with a tribe of children always at his heels. We often watched the 'square' being prepared and pitches being marked out for club matches, but I never understood wickets and their strange ways and still less why they behave so unpredictably. Once, when I was still at school, I had been watching Burchell as he got out the County Club's flag in preparation for the next day's game. "Would you like this at the end of the season?" he asked. I was thrilled. Tom Burchell was as good as his word and I had the flag for many, many years, even in my more lunatic moments picturing it draped over my coffin in the manner of a military funeral. Eventually it was the flag, not me, that the moths (if not the rust) consumed! If this sounds a trifle mawkish a true story may help to put the matter into perspective. One day in 1976 head groundsman, Peter Eaton, told me how a young boy had met with his death in a tragic accident. This boy had been devoted to his cricket and so his parents had requested to have their son's ashes scattered at the southern end of the ground: Peter told me that they know the exact place and come often to visit it, bringing with them sprays of flowers. A sad little tale, but one that I can well understand.

## INTERLUDE

Supposing Durston went in first and carried out his bat,
Supposing Sutcliffe's hair rose up and Waddington's lay flat,
Suppose a Surrey partisan imagined Hobbs was Peach,
Supposing Parkin lost his voice and Wooley made a speech,
Supposing Fender took the field without his old silk scarf,
Supposing Tate looked solemn and Hearne was heard to laugh,
Supposing Carr was cautious and Mann renowned for blocks,
S'pose Lee and Dales got reckless and broke pavilion clocks,
Supposing Strudwick stood quite still, that agile wicket-keep,
Supposing Hendren slept at slip and slumbered in the deep,
S'pose Douglas gave up gardening and became a rapid hitter,
Suppose our skipper won the toss and Chapman dropped a sitter,
Suppose the Oval 1/- seats were filled with sleek top hats,
And O! suppose that Warner came to Lords without his spats.

(Author unknown)

CHAPTER TWO

## THE SILVER YEARS 1930 – 1937

I have called this chapter 'The Silver Years' because I am still waiting for the golden era. In 1932, 1933 and 1934 Sussex were runners-up in the County Championship and only once (1936) came lower than seventh. This was due to good leadership and to the fine type of professional cricketer the Club possessed. The Sussex pros were dedicated to the game, proud to belong to Sussex and, above all, not money-conscious in the way that nearly all sports players are to-day.

During this time the county had five different captains and in the judgment of some this constant change of skipper would sound an unsatisfactory state of affairs, but it was, in fact, the hey-day of the county's history, not to be approached again until the early 'Fifties when, in somewhat similar circumstances as regards the captaincy, Sussex so nearly reached their goal.

After only one year Harold Gilligan passed the leadership to Duleepsinjhi, who had obtained residential qualification for the county through the kindness of his uncle's friend, Dr. W.G. Heasman. Having completed his studies at Cambridge University, where he had gained his Blue as a Freshman, Duleep was free to devote his summers to county cricket. In his first season as captain he made nine centuries and brought Sussex from seventh to fourth and the following year from fourth to second. At the end of this successful season (1932) a Complimentary Dinner was given at the Grand Hotel for the 'Sussex County Cricket Team' and – wonder of wonders! – ladies were invited to attend. My first meeting with Duleep had been in the Secretary's office when I was buying my season ticket: he had just been handed a letter addressed to 'The Captain and Members of the Sussex Cricket Team'. I had longed to know what it contained and whether captains often get communications of this sort. It was like the telegrams: one never knew if the contents were pleasurable or not.

Duleep played for England in 1929, 1930 and 1931 and went with Harold Gilligan's side to New Zealand in 1929-30, but when

*Maurice Tate*

*Tommy Cook*

*Conversation piece. Hastings 1930. FRONT ROW: — Duleepsinjhi (reading), A.H.H. Gilligan (back view) talking to A.P.F. Chapman, Mr. Miller Hallett (President 1937 –1947), Harry Parks (seated): (standing E.H. Killick (in doorway), T.E. Cook (smoking), Jim Langridge (back to camera) talking to Ted Bowley: at scorers' table, — Mr. Isaacs (wearing hat) and Bert Wensley.*

the All India party came here in 1932 Duleep refused to play against his own country. Towards the end of the 1932 season he was taken ill and in light of past illnesses this was viewed with dismay by those who knew him: it was a shattering blow when, in the following February, it was announced that he would play no cricket the following summer. Duleep did not play cricket again and his departure was a grievous loss to Sussex: his batting had always been a joy to watch and he had an eye just that fraction of a second quicker than most Europeans. His 333 for Sussex against Northants in 1930 is still the highest individual score made by a Sussex batsman and his partnership (on the same occasion) with Maurice Tate of 255 for the 6th wicket also stands in the books asking to be bettered. Duleep returned to his own country and in 1950 was appointed Indian High Commissioner for Australia and when that was over he went back again to India to become Chairman of the All India Council for Sport. He died in 1959, a great loss to cricket everywhere.

R.S.G. Scott led the side in 1933: again Sussex were runners-up and this time a dance was given in their honour at the Regent Dance Hall in Brighton in November, but in 1934 yet another captain had to be found and Alan Melville, a South African and an Oxford Blue, who was considered by many to be second only to R.E.S. Wyatt as an amateur batsman, was, by general consent, invited to lead Sussex. The foundations that Duleep had laid and which Scott had maintained were carried forward and for the third year in succession Sussex came second. After two years Melville's business commitments forced him to return to South Africa and A.J. Holmes took over until war came.

Before the war and before the arrival of the Welfare Association a player received his benefit by being given one particular match, although collections would be made during Sussex Cricket Weeks at Horsham, Hastings and Eastbourne. The man concerned had to pay all expenses of his benefit game — players, gatemen, umpires, scorers, printers, scorecard sellers and many more — and he took the profits. The English climate encouraged a wise man to take out a pluvious insurance. Those held in the highest esteem by the Club were given the August Bank Holiday match against Middlesex, for, in the days before everyone owned a car and continental holidays were not taken for granted, the Sussex coast would be full of summer visitors and large numbers of these would crowd onto the cricket ground so that there was hardly an inch to spare, even on the grass outside the boundary ropes. Before the war the public greatly outnumbered the members who regarded themselves — and were regarded — as the *élite:* now the pavilion is packed to capacity on big match days, whilst the public seating is half empty. The man whose benefit it was had the privilege of leading the team onto the field, followed by his captain and fellow-players. In my opinion we have lost something of the sense of occasion to-day when raffle tickets are sold throughout the whole season and no special match is allotted to the player, but possibly more money is made so one must not complain. Amateurs, naturally enough, did not receive benefits, but Sussex had a large number of men who were happy to give up any spare time they had in order to play just for the love of the game. The great majority of these were service men on leave or schoolmasters on holiday and it was natural, good players that they were, that they should enjoy turning out for their county. The pros in no way resented the inclusion of the amateur provided he was worth his place in the side, but there were times when a little nepotism was indulged in with some resultant ill-feeling. This was understandable for the professionals were paid only a weekly salary with match money in addition, so that the inclusion of a non-regular player meant that the pay-packet of the professional, already meagre by any standards, fell considerably.

During the period of which I am writing in this chapter, Tate, Bowley, 'Tich' Cornford, Wensley and Cook all had benefits and of these five only Tate and Bowley had the Bank Holiday match. Certainly the crowds were there for Tate in 1930 for he had always been immensely popular. Players from both sides went round the ground collecting for him and people were generous. He let me photograph him at the start of the day and my picture shows him in typical stance, rain-coat and baggy trousers, hat and pipe in hand and — more unusually — what looks like a white carnation in his button-hole! As so often happens on these special days the object of all the jubilation did not do too well; probably he was over-anxious to please his supporters; he made a 'duck' and 5 and took only 3 wickets. G.O. Allen and Ian Peebles wrecked the Sussex batting and Middlesex won by 9 wickets on the second day, thus depriving Tate of the final day's gate.

It may not be out of place here to look ahead to the last few years of Maurice Tate's career. Year after year he had captured over 100 wickets and even when the ball failed to get a wicket he would throw up both arms towards heaven in utter amazement that the fates could be so unkind. He had played for England on numerous occasions and partnered Duleep in that record-breaking partnership, to which his own contribution was 111. In 1931 he and Wensley bowled unchanged (apart from one over from Jim Langridge) throughout the Leicestershire innings, each man taking 5 wickets: again in 1932 Tate bowled throughout an innings, partnered this time by Jim Cornford: Tate took 5—9. In 1934 against Gloucestershire, in the absense of Alan Melville, he captained an all-professional side: this was the first time in the history of the Club that a professional had led the county. Tate declared at 406-8 and then Sussex dismissed their opponents for 101 and 167. Shortly afterwards Tate again led Sussex to victory, this time against Northants. John Marshall says in *Sussex Cricket* that many people regarded Tate as something of a playboy and were surprised at his astuteness when put in command. I knew Tate for thirty years and never felt that he was a playboy; he was a man who was full of pretty innocent fun, who loved life and especially cricket, who may have talked more than was always wise, but who was really a man who was still a boy at heart. John Arlott calls him "the happy cricketer" and one cannot think of a better phrase to describe him.

In the Australian tour of 1930, when Woodfull was captain, a wonderful gadget appeared on the Sun Terrace of the Brighton Aquarium. This was a huge scoreboard, sponsored by the firm of Johnnie Walker, which gave ball by ball commentaries and full details of every Test match. It showed the field of play and the direction in which each shot had been made. On one side were the names of the England team, on the other those of Australia. It was, indeed, a perfect out-size scorecard, with the playing area displayed in the centre. Having discovered this wonder (remember I had no wireless as yet), I became glued to the spot for hours on end. I was there when Bradman was out for 254 in the Second Test at Lords and the cheers that went up must have been heard past the Royal Pavilion and away up the London Road. Those were the days of vast scores and Australia made 729-6 declared, but I never noticed the time pass and was completely enthralled. When the Australians returned in 1934, again under Woodfull, this scoreboard was once more in operation and much of my time was spent being mesmerized by its movements. Four years earlier it had been hot, uncomfortable and very tiring to lean hour upon hour against a concrete balustrade: now one could pay 6d. for a seat. On the Saturday I 'watched' Ames get 120, but Wyatt made only 35, much to my disappointment.

At the end of 1930 we had our first wireless at home. 'Wireless' — was there ever such a misnomer ? — brought a new dimension to life and even to-day I find what we now call 'radio' preferable to

## The Silver Years 1930 — 1937

T.V. in many ways, for it leaves you free to use your imagination. I find Test Match commentaries supermely well done on sound and, like many others, I often turn down the T.V. sound and use my radio. The first note in my diary about listening to cricket on the wireless concerns the Test Match against New Zealand at the Oval in 1931, when Duleep made 109 and Sutcliffe 117.

In February 1931 it was announced the Reg Hollingdale, the fast medium bowler, was leaving Sussex to join the Greenock (Glasgow) club. He had come onto the ground staff at the age of sixteen, but had never quite reached the heights; he did. however. make 4,061 runs for Greenock and took 574 wickets, then, in 1932 he made 79 against another Scottish club, Grange, and no doubt this innings was partly instrumental in the premier Scottish club inviting him to become their professional in 1938. Hollingdale and his wife, Phyllis, were happy in Scotland, but he hardly made his fortune, for, in 1934, when playing for the Scottish professionals against the Scottish amateurs each pro was paid 2/6d! They agreed to pool the money and winner take all. The following year Hollingdale played for Scotland in a 2-day game against South Africa at Broughty Ferry: he took 5-35 and was paid £1 a day. In 1938 he played again for Scotland, this time against Yorkshire: the late T.D. Watt, then Secretary of the Scottish Cricket Union, said that he would see that Reg was paid. After this 3-day match he was 'presented' with 5/— at Waverley Station, presumably, his wife suggests, for a taxi home! Ten years later Hollingdale was asked to umpire the Scotland v Australians game in Edinburgh, a match in which Don Bradman played. Reg was offered £1 which he declined and after much consultation the two umpires were given £2 each for a 3-day match. Did Hollingdale ever wonder why he left Sussex ? After the war he went as coach to Fettes School where he spent 30 very contented years and in *The Fettesian* of September 1975 he and his wife received a warm tribute which indicated how much they had been appreciated. But this is looking far ahead: I was to meet Reg Hollingdale again in Edinburgh in circumstances which could never have been foreseen the day I read that paragraph in the local paper at the beginning of 1931.

For one reason or another potentially good players left the Club to seek employment elsewhere. One of my photographs taken in 1927 shows a group of 'Nursery' players; the names written below are:- Jim Langridge, Feltham, Eaton, H. Parks, Hollingdale, Tuppin, Rist, Waghorn, Pearce and Richards. When I look at this picture I feel rather sad, for so few of these men made the grade: looking, once again at the young cricketers on the staff to-day, I wonder if their future will be any brighter. Cricket is a bit of a gamble and it is not easy to foretell who will come to the top. Jack Eaton, a fine reserve wicket-keeper, grew tired of living in the shadow of 'Tich' Cornford, whose health and form remained remarkably good, and left to play club cricket; George Pearce, who, but for his deafness which was a great handicap in the field, might have become a good fast bowler, left to build up his own excellent butcher's business in his home town of Horsham, whilst Jim Hammond, one of those who was always losing his place in the side to the occasional amateur, played for Sussex for one year after the war and then went to coach in Holland — the first indication I had that the Dutch knew anything about the game. Later Hammond was on the first-class umpires list for two years before going as coach to Cheltenham College, where he stayed until 1960.

Maurice Tate's benefit was followed by that of Ted Bowley in 1931 and there could hardly have been two more different men. Tate was the complete extrovert whilst Bowley was so grave that one wondered whether he had ever learnt to smile. When he came back to the pavilion from batting it would be impossible to tell from the expression on his face if he had made nought or a hundred. The shy, quiet, almost austere Bowley overawed me almost as much as did Duleepsinjhi: he left Sussex in 1934 going as coach to Winchester College where he remained for 20 years. He lived to a ripe old age and when I saw him again long after he had ceased to play a strange feeling of nostalgia came over me.

During the winter of 1932–33 I listened eagerly to the early morning commentaries from Australia. Our set was not portable; it was not even transportable, and I had to get up at some unearthly hour on bitterly cold mornings and come down to an icy room (no central heating in 1932) where, wrapped in a rug and drinking endless cups of tea and eating ginger nuts, I listened anxiously for the latest news from across the world. There was a great magic about this: do we all take too much for granted to-day? Reception was often bad and the air would be rent with all manner of ear-splitting atmospherics, but there was no doubt about the Australian roars of disapproval which could be heard distinctly in England on sets of all shapes and sizes long before the English sun had risen. By February we had won the Ashes, but this was not an entirely joyous tour. Larwood, and to a lesser degree Bowes and Voce, became responsible for perpetrating what came to be know as 'leg theory' or 'body-line' bowling, an event which caused considerable ill-feeling between the oldest cricketing protagonists. During the previous summer John Langridge had already suffered at the hands of Bowes (whom I had described as 'awful!') and he has the scar on his face until this day.

In 1934 'Tich' Cornford's benefit came round. He had taken over behind the stumps when George Street was killed in a motor-cycle crash at Portslade in 1924. In my fifty (plus) years of watching Sussex cricket there have been only four regular wicket-keepers until the arrival of Arnold Long from Surrey in 1976. Dare I say "I spy strangers!"? 'Tich' was one of the many Sussex men who really enjoyed his cricket and his broad grin was a never-ending source of encouragement to those around him. In their early playing days Tate and Cornford — the great bowler and the tiny wicket-keeper — who were close friends, shared digs in Lorna Road, Hove, which to-day is the location of our local post-office. A man I met recently was highly indignant that no blue plaque adorns the humble little house.

1936 brought the benefit of Bert Wensley. This sound, dependable all-rounder may seldom have hit the headlines, but he was part of the back bone of a fine team. His 9th wicket partnership with Harry Parks at Horsham in 1930 is still a Sussex record. He always wore a cream *short*-sleeved shirt which billowed in the wind as he bowled: there may have been others who had short-sleeved shirts, but I do not remember them until, quite recently, Jeff Thomson, the Australian fast bowler, adopted the same style. Matches were played for Wensley, as usual, around the county and one at the Dripping Pan, Lewes, was billed in a strangely archaic manner:— "Wickets will be pitched at 11.30 a.m. and stumps will not be drawn until 6.30 p.m. so that there will be an opportunity for people to witness some of the game after work." What happened if the game were over at tea-time does not appear to have been worked out. At the end of the 1934 season Sussex "dispensed with the services of Wensley" — in other words he was redundant.

It was not until 1936 that I bought my own car and I was delighted when I passed my test at the first attempt. The car was a small, pale blue Singer with a grey hood and a 'dickey': it cost me £12 and the Road Fund Licence was £1.13.0! John Langridge and his wife, Nina, can still picture this funny little vehicle arriving at county grounds in Sussex, at Lords, the Oval, Portsmouth and elsewhere.

Throughout all my cricket watching there have been days of joy and days of sorrow. Amongst the former was the record partnership between Duleepsinjhi and Tate and in the same year Jack Hobbs made 106 at Hastings and Dempster 167 for the New Zealanders the following year. In 1934 the Australians were once more at

Hove. They made 560 and Kippax, who made 250 of these, was mobbed as he came off the field, four policemen having to help him in. In this game Bradman made only 19, but I wrote:— "A marvellous day. Although the Australians hit all over the place it was wonderful to watch and the crowd was great."

In 1935 an innings of 162 earned George Cox his county cap and in 1936 I saw Joe Hulme make 114, the young Denis Compton 80 and the 'ever-young' Patsy Hendren 75 in the Middlesex match at Hove, but that evening my diary records:— "R.P. Northway killed in car crash. Bakewell critically injured." I recalled the accident to Tate and Cornford and could only be thankful that no great harm had come to either of them. Another joy was the defeat of the Indian touring team by Sussex in 1936, the hero of this game being James Langridge who took 7-47. This Whitsun I was again at Lords where I saw Sussex defeat Middlesex by 210 runs and it was always a triumph to beat them on their own ground. In 1937 the match against Northants was noteworthy for the fact that play went on until 7.18 p.m. — an event unheard of in the history of the Club and we won by an innings and 128 runs. This same year when Lancashire came south they made a huge score: Paynter hit 332, Washbrook 108 and Oldfield 92. The joy, for me, was a brave 115 from George Cox, junior, but Sussex suffered what was only their second defeat of the season. Scores, generally, tended to be much higher than they are to-day: I sometimes wonder if this is because modern fielding is, on the whole, considerably improved.

Then there were days of sorrow. I find that in 1930 I was actually *bored* with a game between Sussex and Notts. I thought that this had been excessively slow and complained about so much depending on first innings points. Despite a variety of systems over the years, no perfect way of allocating points has yet been devised.

In 1933 I had another moan. We may have regarded Lancashire as a stolid side, but this time Sussex, not Lancashire, were the offenders and I wrote:— "Harry Parks was ghastly — 1½ hours for 1 run! Jim Langridge is 100 not out, but that has been in hours." This was not the Sussex I loved. I have never been one to want sixes off every other ball, but I hate a game which just stands still.

In 1934 our second place in the Championship, which we could no longer win, depended on the result of the game against Yorkshire: it was drawn, but Sussex managed to get the necessary 5 points:— "A marvellous day's cricket. Awful to think it ends tomorrow." "Look the last on all things lovely," I wrote with youthful tragicalness the following evening.

If there were days of joy and sorrow there were also days of fustration and, one, indeed, of sheer fury.

1936 was the year in which Sussex embarked on a duel with Notts. 'Duel' is the right word and by the end of the game pistols and seconds were almost required. The first two days showed no sign of the ructions to come. On Monday A.J. Holmes celebrated his birthday with 107 which was, at the time, his highest score: Melville made 125 and Sussex declared at 327-9. Tuesday was one of those rain-interrupted days, so trying to performer and spectator alike. Eight Notts wickets were down in the second innings and suddenly the skies lightened and at 5.30 play re-started. I can only quote what I wrote, as I felt, that night. "Even then it seemed we'd never get the wickets: Tate was no use, but the minute Jim Hammond came on he disposed of the last two men and it was 6.15. We had to get 9 runs to win. The awful ten minute interval was taken and at 6.25 Notts sauntered onto the field, following closely by Cook and Jim Parks. Behind them came Harry Parks, Holmes and Wensley, padded and ready as they sat on the pavilion steps: never had anyone seen such a sight. Jim and Tommy hit at everything. It wanted two minutes to 6.30 and the umpires drew stumps. The uproar was tremendous, umpires and Notts boo-ed to the echo. A frightful example of bad sportsmanship." It 'transpired', to use the word of the *Morning Post,* that the Nottinghamshire players walked off the field, pleading that it was raining. The press went to town. 'Irate Reader' wrote to the *Sussex Daily News,* 'Lt. Col.' in the *Morning Post* demanded 'Abolish the Championship', whilst another letter-writer claimed that the game should go to Sussex. A cartoon showed the fielders, all armed with umbrellas, heading for the pavilion, whilst batsmen and umpires remained in the middle. This was entitled 'NOT(TS) CRICKET!' The row rumbled on for several days, the secretaries of both clubs writing frantic letters to and fro. Eventually an apology was extracted from G.F. Heane, the Notts captain, and his Committee said that although Mr. Heane was within his rights they did not uphold an action which marred the good feeling hitherto existing between Nottinghamshire and her oldest opponent in county cricket. A.J. Holmes, himself, would have preferred to let the matter drop at once as it was obviously embarrassing, but when Sussex lost at Portsmouth the following week, R.H. Moore, captaining Hants, told the *Sussex Daily News* how much he and his team had appreciated Holmes' sporting declaration. The *S.D.N.* wrote:— "It is seldom that one sees a crowd gather in front of a pavilion on a cricket ground raising three cheers for the losing side. That happened at the United Services ground at Portsmouth at 5.54 last evening. Spectators crowded in front of the pavilion to clap their two batsmen who had pulled them through; they clapped Sussex, too, and then an elderly gentleman in the pavilion called, 'Three cheers for the gallant losers'!" These cheers must have warmed the heart of 'Sherlock' Holmes and it only shows that it is not always quite so important to *win*.

By the end of 1936 things between Tate and the Club were turning a trifle sour. At the next AGM a few remarks about him were made and someone said, "The side will not be lacking in character and conversation so long as he is present." Underneath this rather sarcastic remark there seemed to be a direct dig at Tate from the platform. It was not long after this that there was an attempt to remove the feeling of uneasiness amongst the players which was said to be one of the causes of the team's indifferent form in the previous year. At an informal dinner to the players it was announced that Tate was to be rested. Poor Maurice was bitterly hurt and upset, claiming that he was as fit as ever and could bring a doctor's certificate to prove it. The idea seemed to be to rest Tate in away matches and play him at home as he was still the Club's greatest draw. The paragraph in the paper ended:— "Sussex cannot afford to do without him yet." The word 'yet' was rather sinister. What one thinks of now as the 'Tate Row' was coming to a head and towards the end of the season of 1937 it was obvious that he would play no more. One London paper headed an article:- 'Tate will not watch Matches: Too Heart-breaking, he says.' There is a picture of Tate, pipe in mouth and as big a grin as ever, digging in his garden at *Wanaka*. Now 42, he had not heard whether or not he would be engaged the following April and with this doubt in his mind he could not make plans. Possibly, from Tate's point of view, it was unfortunate that the team had once again begun to play well together and the Committee was loathe to change it. His old friend and skipper, Arthur Gilligan, was forced to explain to Tate that it would be absurd to alter a side which was playing as well as Sussex. Arthur said that Maurice had taken this in the best possible way, as everyone knew he would. But people took sides. At the annual dinner of Shoreham C.C. Mr. H.W.G. Tingley suggested that "if Tate were sent to Central Europe to teach cricket he could stop war." Even I, watching very much from the sidelines, could sense some discontent still in the Sussex team. From this point in the season they began to go downhill and one almost believed they were unhappy for Tate.

Tommy Cook had his benefit in 1937. Three years before,

there had been demands from journalists that Cook should be selected as a member of the side to tour the West Indies, but this never came to pass. One day in 1932 Cook made a superb catch to dismiss Mercer of Glamorgan (another man who was Sussex-born) with the sun in his eyes and at a terrific height. He rolled over, his cap came off and when he appeared with the ball clutched firmly in both hands there was a roar of applause from the crowd for it meant that Glamorgan had to follow on and so probably he had won us the match. I wonder if this was the catch about which George Cox told me years later. Cook's mother, who always sat in the back row on the roof with Mrs. Jupp, leapt to her feet and cried above the din, "He's my son! He's my son!" Tommy's mother was one of his staunchest supporters. In his benefit year he made 106 in the first match of the season which was away to Worcestershire, then I saw him at the Oval in a fine partnership with Jim Langridge, but one drive by Cook maimed a sparrow, which Surrey captain, Errol Holmes, carried tenderly into the pavilion, but the poor thing died. As far as I know it was not stuffed and exhibited as was the one which met a similar fate at Lords. Strudwick, now turned scorer for Surrey, was reported to have said of Cook's sparrow, "It must have been a fledgling. The ground sparrows are used to dodging the ball."

Cook got his 1,000 runs this year and on the Bank Holiday there was a collection for him which brought in £74.13.4. This was said to be a record at the time, but I cannot verify this. But Cook was being dropped for the odd match here and there and my suspicions grew that there was something wrong. During Eastbourne Week this happened again. I met Cook at Brighton Station and he was deeply depressed, saying that he had bought a new bat 'just in case'. Now there was a rumour that Cook was to retire. I tackled Mr. Herbert, the Club's masseur, on the subject, but he remained tight-lipped then suddenly he rounded on me and asked, almost angrily, who had told me that. To this day I have no idea, but once a rumour starts it soon spreads around and it was hardly surprising that the team was unsettled.

Cook's benefit took place during the Warwickshire match at Hove on August 11th. The sun shone fitfully, but collections of £47 and £38 were considered good by 1937 standards. Tommy had football as well as cricket supporters and it was estimated that his benefit would come to over £1,000, which sounds little enough to-day, but was excellent at the time.

Even allowing for the uncertainty about the futures of Tate and Cook in 1937, the county was once again going great guns: they were doing so well that when I called on Ernest Raymond, the novelist, at his home in Haywards Heath, he inscribed his book *The Marsh* for me:— "To Laetitia Repington, August 17th 1937, the year Sussex nearly won the Championship. Keep hoping." I still am.

Susssex could finish no better than fifth, but the real heroes of the summer were Jim and John Langridge, who each scored 2,000 runs, whilst Jim also took 100 wickets, and George Cox only just missed the 2,000 mark. Above all, Jim Parks (now senior) set up the incredible record of 3,003 runs and 101 wickets, an achievement performed with the quietness and modesty of this great Sussex cricketer.

Immediately the season was over came the announcement that 'Tommy Cook Says Farewell to Sussex', and it was made known that at the beginning of the season, Cook had asked the Committee not to renew his contract as he wished to take up a business career in South Africa. Cook had a fine record for Sussex, scoring over 20,000 runs and taking 80 wickets. He had always been a fine fielder and one of the most attractive batsmen in the side. With his quickness of foot and eye nothing delighted him more than to jump down the wicket to the slow bowlers when he would punish them unmercifully. As with all who take their lives in their hands there would be the occasional disaster, but that these disasters were few is shown by the fact that Cook was never dropped from the side for indifferent play between 1922 and 1935 — a record not to be found in the books, perhaps, but a very satisfactory one all the same. In the July of 1930 Cook had made his highest score of 278 at Hove and a local clergyman wrote to the papers:— "I noticed that Tommy Cook wore his sweater whilst scoring the first 241 runs of his innings against Hampshire; and this on a moderately warm day! Surely this is a cricket curiosity, if not a record."

Sussex played matches for Cook at Haywards Heath, Lewes, Rye and at Ditton Place, Balcombe, where the county cricketers took on Mr. A.B. Horne's XI, called 'The Ducks'. I saw Cook on the County Ground the day before he sailed for South Africa, but felt shy and could think of nothing to say — it was like seeing someone off on a train. I only saw him once again.

This September the ground was full of ghosts. I called on the Tates and the whole family was just back from a mushrooming expedition so we all had tea together. By October the English papers were full of what they called 'The Sacking of Tate!'; 'Tate Told he's not Wanted'; 'Cricket is Cruel to Stars'; 'Only 42 and

Fit as Ever'; 'Sussex Committee Blunder' — and so it went on. I was never embroiled in the inner workings of the Club and am, therefore, in no position to apportion blame, but over the years I have seen players, who have served their county faithfully and well, go in a welter of bitterness. Surely things could be done otherwise. Maurice Tate continually referred to his 'firing' and was very low in spirits. It was suggested that Northants was interested in having him, but nothing came of this. Fortunately for all concerned, Captain T.W.E. Brinckman invited Tate to tour the Argentine with a side which he had organized: Tate was taken ill with pneumonia on board the *Arlanza* and then suffered from a severely poisoned foot so that he played no cricket and these illnesses were, doubtless, due as much to his unhappiness as to anything else. We called on Mrs. Tate to ask her how he was and she reassured us, but confided that he cried every time he packed to go abroad. He was always a great family man and a devoted husband and father.

CHAPTER THREE

## THE LITTLE VICTIMS PLAY 1938–39

In the spring of 1938 I wrote to the Cricket Correspondent of *The Times* and he replied to what he called my 'lament' with an article which occupied a full column of the newspaper. His opening paragraph ran thus:— "There are always those who prefer the ancient to the modern, who like to live in the past with their tendency leaning towards yesterday's hero, whether he be a singer of grand opera, a preacher, or a cricketer. Their particular idols will remain for ever unchallenged by those who were unfortunate enough to be born at a later date." He was right to speak of my lament for I had written to regret the disappearance of so many well-known cricketers who, at the end of 1937, had left the first-class scene for good. There was Hendren, that tough, chunky little Middlesex batsman, speedy fielder and one-time captain of Brentwood F.C.: there was George Duckworth, another small, stocky man: I bore him no ill-will for the autograph incident at Eastbourne. Then there was the great Andy Sandham, great in character and performance, but small and slight and quiet as a man, a worthy partner to Jack Hobbs for Surrey, who, but for the consistency of Herbert Sutcliffe, would have played for England far more often than he did. Larwood, too, the demon bowler of those years before the war, controversial as so many fast bowlers are, began the body-line uproar in Australia: lithe and wiry he was, looking almost too frail to be the purveyor of such fearsome deliveries. Finally there was Sussex's own pair, Maurice Tate and Tommy Cook, without whom, for one member at least, the county would be a great deal the poorer.

Sad as these swan-songs were there were more sinister events afoot to which I gave but little heed, but on February 20th 1938 I heard Hitler speaking for over an hour and a half at the opening of the Reichstag: I could understand only parts of what he said, but I well remember the raving, ranting, fanatical voice of the man whom, shortly, and with typical English humour, Richard 'Stinker' Murdoch, was to nickname 'Old Nasty'.

Notwithstanding the general unease at world happenings, the

## The Little Victims Play 1938 — 1939

Club's AGM took place, as usual, in the Music Room of the Royal Pavilion. The *Sussex Daily News* stated that a record had been created in that 250 members were present: Mr. Alex Miller Hallett was elected President for the second year running. The need for a fast bowler was stressed and Mr. G.S. Godfree explained how Mr. W.N. Riley and Arthur Gilligan had been scouting around the county. Dudley Bass, a young man living in Manchester, but who had birth qualifications for Sussex, was expected to be the answer to this prayer, but like so many others before and since, he disappeared into that limbo of cricketing souls and was seen no more.

At this meeting there were several remarks about Tate and it was said that there was no ill-feeling between him and the Club, but I knew otherwise. The blame for his retirement was put on the Selection Committee. There was genuine regret expressed at Cook's departure for South Africa and only a few days later I had a letter from Cook. In this he showed every sign of homesickness. He wrote:— "I suppose the boys will soon be at practice again, and I believe the weather is quite good. I have not played cricket since November and really do not even feel that I want to. I have quite a nice hotel (the *Prince Alfred* in Simonstown) and business is quite good. I hope to get home in about three years time, that is, of course, if war does not break out before then. I shall try to arrange it so that I am there for some of the cricket season." He then wrote of visits he had received from E. Davis of Glamorgan and Len Hopwood of Lancashire, who dropped in and spent an hour or two. He drove the two men back to town and they insisted on singing all the way! Obviously Cook had been a good host. He was following Brighton's fortunes in the Third Division and also said how much he looked forward to seeing the MCC in South Africa the following summer.

Meanwhile I wrote that "Hitler yesterday brought off a coup in Austria, the German troops crossing the frontier and taking possession. Schüssnig, the Austrian Chancellor, resigned." A couple of days later Tate and Mrs. Tate came to tea to look at my cricket photographs and cuttings. Despite the gloom it was impossible to feel depressed when Maurice was around; he was even funny about his very painful foot, which looked horrible and was still terribly swollen. Tate was a little bitter about one or two people who had not visited him in hospital in the Argentine, but it was part of his nature that he always had to have a little grumble about something and one did not take it too seriously.

Before the opening match of the season I heard — on the radio— speeches at the British Sportmen's Club Luncheon to the Australian cricketers. Don Bradman's was excellent and he began by saying (Anzac Day) that Australia would stand shoulder to shoulder with England if the need should ever arise in time of war. There was tumultuous applause.

During the first game of 1938 Mr. Miller Hallett presented silver salvers to Jim Parks for his world record of the year before and also to Jim and John Langridge for being the first brothers to score 2,000 runs each in a season for the same county. Both replied with little speeches, Jim Langridge saying that he thanked them for "this fine piece of work" and that he hoped that Jim Hammond's 'friend' (he had just had a burglar) would not come and relieve him of it.

By early May the poor little Singer car had finally broken down and I had to pay 3/5 per day to go to Horsham Cricket Week. Tate sat in his car most of the time shunning the limelight of the arena which he knew so well, but one day he and 'Tich' Cornford came to sit with us and Maurice began to chatter again as he had done in the past. We also talked at some length to the father and mother of Jim and Harry Parks; at Horsham everyone sat together in the pavilion, which was very tiny, and there was always a very happy and friendly atmosphere.

Back at Hove, A.J. Holmes, who had been out of the side for several weeks, returned and made 133 not out against Notts, which was to be the highest score of his career. Jim Wood, though making only 7, lent such valuable support that he was roundly applauded. Runs are always relative to the situation and a quick 50 — or less — is often worth more to a side than a laboured century. Next day 17 wickets fell and Wood got his county cap, though Sussex lost.

June was full of cricket, for Worthing Week followed directly upon the Notts game and Charlie Oakes made 148 not out. On the Thursday I had a change of venue and went to Southwick Green to watch Southwick C.C. v S.P.B. Mais' XI, with Christopher Stone, the first 'disc jockey' and fellow-broadcaster of S.P.B., playing in the latter's side. Mr. Stone wore brown crepe-rubber-soled shoes, one of the bowlers had a coolie hat, yet another a sort of tuxedo, whilst an admiral's wife was knitting as if her life depended on it. A very different scene from that on county grounds, but the villages are the cradle of all cricket in the land.

Because of hay-fever I have seldom been to Tunbridge Wells, our fixture with Kent always falling in what is, for me, a fatal month. This year, however, I went for the first time and have a vivid recollection of Frank Woolley and the rhodedendrons. Woolley

## The Little Victims Play 1938 – 1939

at the age 51 made 162 and it gave me particular satisfaction to see this fine player at his best. Sussex hardly shone except for Hugh Bartlett's 62 not out; he twice put the ball over the hedge onto the railway. Bartlett had made his debut for Sussex the previous summer and was already proving himself to be an outstanding player. Tate, now working for *Reynold's News* and discussing the forthcoming 'Timeless Test' at the Oval, wrote:— "I should like to see H.T. Bartlett, the Sussex amateur, have an opportunity to show his worth against Australia. Bartlett is a left-hander who has improved immensely this season. If he is bang on form he can turn a match completely with hitting that, if not Jessopian, is certainly full of power and spirit." Tate gave his team for this match as Fagg, Paynter, W.L. Hammond, Ames (or Gibb), Whitfield, Bartlett, Compton, Verity (or Goddard), Bowes, Wright and Farnes. Of Tate's selection only Paynter, Hammond, Compton, Bowes and Farnes were on the official Selectors' list.

Meanwhile Hugh Bartlett continued on his way with centuries at Hastings against Northants and Kent, thus supporting Tate's claim for his inclusion: he was becoming a real box-office draw and I believe that loud speaker vans went round Brighton and Hove when he was batting and on hearing the news people would flock to the ground. I say "I believe" because I never heard them – I was already there!

The first day of the Gloucestershire match at Hove turned out to be an important one in my own private life. A friend called Bryan Stapleton suggested that he should come to cricket with me and this surpised me not a little since I had no idea that the man whom I had met a few times when he had been on leave from his ship had any interest in the game. Now, having been married for nearly forty years, we seldom miss a match.

We had a marvellous evening's cricket, especially from S.C. Griffith, who replaced 'Tich' Cornford behind the stumps in this match; he hit three sixes into a Palmeira Avenue garden and two others as well: Jim Hammond also hit out at everything and even Jim Cornford, not renowned for his batting, reached double figures.

As has always been the case during a Test match I was torn between listening to the radio (and to-day watching T.V.) and supporting Sussex. This time it was the Fourth Test against Australia and on the Wednesday I listened to England getting 223, starting off with a disaster when Hardstaff was run out; next day I was back with Sussex, who were in one of their incapable moods and were all out for 195 against Lancashire and lost by an innings on the second day owing to a complete inability to bowl. It was during this match that I first heard a radio at cricket and next day I wrote up the result of watching and listening at the same time. Talk about being schizophrenic! That article appeared in the *Journal of the Cricket Society* in the spring of 1978. Forty years on!

The Edrich-Compton era was now in full flow and at the end of the first day of our meeting with Middlesex I wrote that "they (Compton and Edrich) are batting and will no doubt make 100 each on Monday." But not so. Jack Nye had a devastating spell and took 5-11, but Sussex fared badly and Jim Parks was out first ball, whilst Harry Parks had his face cut open by a ball from G.O. Allen and fell on his wicket. Middlesex won what I described as "a grand match." I have always enjoyed a game of fluctuating fortunes: such a contest makes the dull days — and there *are* some — all worth while.

During the Bank Holiday fixture I introduced myself to Dudley Carew, who was on the ground and who signed the book I had bought at the Oval eleven years before. Another interesting meeting this summer was at Hastings when I sat next to a man who told me he was F.G.J. Ford of Cambridge University and Middlesex, a cricketer of days before my time for he was born in 1866! He had very definite theories on the lbw rule and told me that it was he who had persuaded MCC to introduce the new one. I am not entirely sure that Mr. Ford's claim was correct; in any case Bob Wyatt, writing to me in 1976 said:— "I'm afraid the game has lost a lot of its beauty owing to the accent being so much on defence and the alteration of the lbw rule in 1935 which restricts the off-side strokes." Wyatt, himself, was the only county captain to vote against the new laws and so, would have found himself in direct opposition to F.G.J. Ford. The people I am sorry for are the umpires who have had to administer all the changes over the years with such scrupulous impartiality.

After this I was glued to the 'Timeless Test' which afterwards became known as 'Hutton's Match' for he made 364 runs. Meanwhile the anxiety about the German problem that had lain more or less dormant most of the summer began to be apparent to us all. In this atmosphere there was a strange visit of a German Police football team and already the atmosphere was sufficiently edgy for there to be loud boos when the team arrived at Hove Station! leaflets were handed out saving:— *"Wir wollen nicht Fascimus hier."* ("We do not want Fascism here.") The next day England reached 903-7 dec., Bradman slipped when fielding and was carried from the field with an unspecified injury: I wrote:— "I do not like timeless tests" and on August 24th "I was relieved when this one drew

## The Little Victims Play 1938 – 1939

to a merciful close at 3.40 when England won by an innings and 579 runs." Thus the series was drawn and Australia kept the Ashes.

During the final Sussex game of this season, against Yorkshire, Bartlett was presented with a gold cup, apparently given for the quickest hundred on the ground during the year. Mr. Miller Hallett handed it over to Bartlett who said a few words. This turned out to be the biggest joke of the summer, for there had been some confusion and the award was for the fastest 50: Bartlett had scored his in 57 minutes but the next day Cox hit a splended century and *his* 50 took only 33. *The Sussex Daily News* wrote:- "The crowd spent the tea interval trying to make head or tail of the muddle and then rain put a stop to the argument and to the day's play as well." I believe that there was a bit of ill-feeling over this cup, but by this time Bartlett, who was not playing in the last match, had taken it home, so it could not be presented to Cox publicly. The previous year it had been won by Jim Parks and he, too, had had to come and fetch it. He told me that little Jimmy used to present it to him every time he beat his son at cards, so it had had its uses besides being just an ornament.

All these weeks whilst we had been filling in our scorecards international affairs had been moving fast. On September 11th I woke up to find that "the news is pretty girm." Poor Juliet, whose marriage was fixed for October, was dreadfully distressed. Her fiancé was in the Reserve of Officers and would be called up in the event of war. Bryan, too, was commissioned in the Royal Naval Reserve and the same would apply to him. On September 14th it was announced that the Prime Minister, Mr. Neville Chamberlain, would fly to Berchtesgarten to see Hitler, but I remember thinking, "Why souldn't he come to see us?"

Negotiations now started between the leaders of Great Britain, France, Germany and Italy, which ended in Chamberlain's return to England, bearing the famous bit of paper which, he declared, meant "Peace with honour" and "Peace in our time."

So Juliet was married to Captain (now Major) Pannett at the little church at Newtimber at the foot of the Sussex Downs, but a fortnight later mock air-raid warnings were being sounded; a horrid, eerie wail which, before any of us were much older, was to become part of our daily lives. I had another jolly tea with the Tates; Maurice, yet again, talking cricket all the time as if nothing else mattered. We got out a large trunk of photographs which told of his cricketing tours around the world.

It was not until the following March that the country realised that it had merely gained a respite from Hitler's antics, but I was more interested in the fact the Bryan had come back to Hove. I took him to see the Tates and he and Maurice hit if off at once, sitting one on each side of the roaring log fire whilst Tate reminisced in his own way, mainly about the foot. Eventually off came his shoe and sock and the toe was exhibited; then the whole family came in and there was another of those wonderful Tate teas.

Bobby Farrell, Sussex 12th man and the Albion's outside-right, had played his last game of football and was considering becoming 'mine host' at a local public house. An understanding having been arrived at between Bryan and me, I happened one day to tell Farrell how sad I should be to leave the town where I had been for so long. He sympathised and said, "Still, if you've enjoyed yourself when you were young, that's all right." I certainly had, and I have often thought of the simple philosophy in those few words.

At the beginning of 1939 the Albion had a benefit match for Dick Meades, the masseur, but it was poorly attended. This was sad, for Meades had done so much good work for Brighton and also acted as masseur to the Sussex team after the retirement of Mr. Herbert. Many friends of mine went to him for minor ailments and he cured my back at a time when I had developed a bad attack of fibrositis. He was succeeded, both with the Albion and with Sussex, by Sam Cowan, another kindly man, who was masseur until his early death in 1954.

A short visit to an aunt in Felixstowe gave me a chance, on the way home, to watch Sussex playing Essex at Chelmsford. I travelled back to London with John Langridge, Cox and Hammond. We discussed the possibility of war and Hammond drew diagrams of barrage balloons round the edges of my crossword. We all shared a taxi to Victoria Station, for which the men insisted on paying and I stood them all coffee!

August 7th was the Bank Holiday and after much delay for rain Edrich and F.G. Mann (son of F.T. Mann) fairly went for the Sussex bowling. Edrich made a fine century and Mann finished with 88. Next day Middlesex were out for 328 and it soon dawned on people that they did not want to get us out and so obtain first innings lead, because if there was no result on the first innings the match would be considered as 'abandoned' and would not count in the Championship, thus the Middlesex percentage would not be lowered, as with 3 points it would. The Sussex innings became a farce when 5 wickets were down for 60. Middlesex missed stumpings and run-outs, dropped catches and generally deported themselves most oddly. The crowd got thoroughly fed up and called out,

"Play cricket!" and "Put the umpires on to bowl!" Sussex lost 9 wickets and it was 5.45. Middlesex did not claim the extra time and the game was abandoned amidst booing.

In 1937 my mother had met Rosalind Twining, wife of R.H. Twining, whose autograph I had got in my 'teens. Richard Haynes Twining, educated at Eton, kept wicket for Oxford University and afterwards joined Middlesex, for whom his highest score was 135 when, with J.T. Hearne, he helped his county beat Surrey and so retain the Championship in 1921. He played at intervals until 1928, was President of Middlesex 1950-57 and President of MCC in 1964. This year Rosalind, Dick and Dickie, their son, were staying at Eastbourne for Cricket Week and I joined them on the Saturday when Sussex were playing Worcestershire. It was a lovely, scorching summer's day: even those in the pavilion were shedding as many garments as was comfortable with the times. I went back to the Twinings' hotel for lunch and there was a sudden decision to bathe. We lay on the beach looking out to sea and saying that it was quite, quite impossible for there to be a war. With war only two weeks away what a dream world we all lived in, that August of 1939! I saw Dickie only once again: it was at his home in South Kensington and he was dressed in the uniform of an officer of the Welsh Guards preparatory to going overseas. Captain R.C. Twining was killed on April 9th 1943 with the First Army in Tunisia: his mother died over twenty years later and Dick, who was born in 1889, wrote to me not long ago to say that he simply cannot understand cricket to-day.

In a few days none of us could behave like ostriches any longer. "A miserable day with the European crisis becoming worse and worse," I wrote on August 24th. Bryan had returned to sea and was heading for the Far East, so I had my own worries. Next day, "News no better and all the black-out *in situ*, pavement kerbs whitened. Heard that West Indies have cancelled the remainder of their tour. Due here tomorrow."

When 'tomorrow' came never have I seen such a deserted cricket ground: general opinion was that West Indies had done a cowardly and unsporting thing in returning immediately; Jim Parks said, "It's breaking their contract." He was the one to suffer as the collection (for his benefit) would have been at least £50. A match called 'President's XI v Captain's XI' was substituted for that of the touring team. "We are carrying on and keeping the flag flying," announced Mr. Knowles. It was a noble effort, but more members might have turned up, if only for Jim Parks, who had served the Club so well. Those who did come were asked to support the tea

52                     *A Sussex Cricket Odyssey*

tent and I remember wondering if it, like the world about us, was in danger of falling around our ears. The match, which, hardly surprisingly, was not a great draw, was limited to two days. Hugh Bartlett captained the President's side, but they were defeated by 8 wickets. Mr. Knowles received a letter from the agent of the West Indies touring team, which ran as follows:- "Mr. J.M. Kidney, the Manager of the West Indies team, has asked me to confirm his telegram to you advising the sudden return of the team to the West Indies owing to the international crisis. The decision was only taken hurriedly at 11 o'clock this morning, as the team found themselves faced with the option of accepting accommodation immediately or having to wait for an indefinite period should there be an outbreak of war, and as they had already received intimation that some of their remaining fixtures might have to be cancelled owing to the present emergency, it was felt that the decision to

Jim Parks takes his benefit in the Sussex v. Yorkshire match to-morrow.

return was forced upon them by the circumstances. Mr. Kidney wishes me to express his regrets for the suddenness of this decision, but feels sure you will realise the necessity for taking it. I am to convey to you his kind regards. Yours truly, A.L. Jupp."

The Mayors of Brighton and Hove gave the luncheon to Sussex which had been planned for both the teams and the Mayor of Hove (Councillor A.W. Hillman, J.P.) said that he was very disappointed that the West Indies had let Sussex down so badly. The Mayor of Brighton (Councillor J. Talbot Nansen, J.P.) suggested that "the failure of the West Indies to keep their agreement would certainly give the impression that we were not putting up a united front." These were, of course, the emotions of the moment, which, I think it is fair to say, most of us shared. With hindsight one realizes that the Manager of the West Indies took the only course possible.

In the circumstances Jim Parks' benefit match against Yorkshire was a curious affair and seemed quite unreal. A *Sussex Daily News* cartoon explained how he had taken over 700 wickets for Sussex: how his highest partnership was 368. A large crowd certainly turned up for the first days of the benefit match, trying to forget the crisis; Sussex made 387 with George Cox getting 198 in his own best manner. The collection for Jim Parks came to £75, whilst the Queen of Holland and the King of the Belgians were offering to mediate and Poland was accepting their offer. But there was little doubt that things had gone too far and the fact that Sussex were all out for 33 in the second innings and that the last first-class match on the County Ground for nearly seven years was won by Yorkshire, was of interest only to the statisticians.

On September 3rd I was meeting trains and shepherding evacuee children to the waiting 'buses, so I was unable to hear Chamberlain's historic announcement at 11 a.m., but we all knew that we were at war.

On September 14th the *Athenia* was torpedoed, then two British tankers and *H.M.S. Courageous* was sunk. On the day that I noted "all this frightful sinking of merchant ships," Jack Nye was married in Hove. My cutting shows the happy pair, smiling a little self-consciously, and each holding at the end of a piece of string a small carboard box: these boxes look like containers for sandwiches at a day's cricket, but were, in fact, gas masks, which, from now on we were supposed to carry everywhere, though as time went on I fear we did not. At the beginning of October Germany announced unrestricted warfare on merchant ships. I felt so depressed that I took myself over to see the Tate family. They had been storing apples in the loft and the younger son, Michael, insisted that I take some home. Next *H.M.S. Royal Oak* was sunk and there was a daylight raid on the Firth of Forth. I worked on the distribution of Ration Books under the chandelier in the Royal Pavilion where, in happier times, the Sussex AGM had been held. I had a letter from Jim Parks saying he was very sorry that all my arrangements had been upset and he trusted that "things will soon clear up, and that your marriage will not have to be postponed." Although Bryan had written to me from Singapore the day war broke out I did not receive this letter until October 31st. Correspondence from now on was censored, so I could never be sure where he was, though over the months we came to develop a code of our own.

CHAPTER FOUR

KEEPING THE FLAG FLYING 1940 – 1945

Bryan came back to U.K. in March 1940, and was called up immediately, but before being appointed to a ship he stayed with us and on March 19th we became officially engaged. I took him again to see the Tates, where, besides Maurice, Mrs. Tate, Joan, Betty, Jimmy and Michael, we also found F.W. Tate and his wife, an elderly aunt and Maurice's brother, Geoffrey. I had the honour of sitting next to the great Fred Tate, for ever famous for the catch he dropped in the Test match of 1902 against Australia at Manchester: unfortunately memory fails me about anything we said at tea that day, but I do know that Maurice was trying to get a job with the Air Ministry and a week or so later he wrote to tell me that his name had been registered and they were "considering the position." He said that Betty and Joan had had "good old English measles" and the family wished us both every happiness and they hoped that the danger of war would soon be over. "You know where we live when you are passing," concluded Maurice Tate, "please accept all good wishes and let us know the important day."

Meanwhile Sussex were trying to keep cricket on the map and quite a large programme was arranged, though much of it later had to be abandoned. Bill O'Byrne, headmaster of Claremont School, organized the side which appeared as 'A.E.R. Gilligan's XI' and fixtures were played against clubs and the Services: one day Sussex beat an R.A.F. side which included Flt. Lt. W.R. Hammond at Lewes by 15 runs. The Committee appealed for support and we were asked to pay at least half the previous year's subscription and the response was fairly good. I duly paid 10/- for the duration of the war and still have the pasteboard tickets which we had at the time.

Naturally, we planned to be married in Hove, then Bryan was sent to command *H.M.S. Brimnes,* an armed trawler on anti-submarine duties, which was stationed at the port of Leith in the Firth of Forth. Germany invaded Holland and Belgium, whilst France was about to fall, so we re-planned a wedding in Scotland.

A Sussex-Surrey game had been arranged for Saturday, May 11th, but this had to be put off owing to so many leaves being curtailed. "Blast Hitler," I wrote vehemently, "he would *wait* until the first fixture." Soon the Germans were in Cologne and King Leopold of the Belgians had capitulated, but his Government decided to fight on. Before going north to join Bryan I paid yet another visit to the Tates, but Maurice was out. I felt that he had gone into hiding as he had been turned down by the Air Ministry and Mrs Tate said he was feeling very low and thought he had an enemy. This was, of course, Tate's imagination running away with him again and he later became a Billeting Officer for the Army.

Bryan and I were married quietly in Edinburgh on June 3rd and a few days later we went to look at Grange Cricket Ground where we found Reg Hollingdale — no longer in his white cricket flannels, but in the uniform of the A.F.S. (Auxiliary Fire Service). I had not seen him since he left the county in 1931 so there was much to talk about. In a few weeks Bryan joined *H.M.S. Southern Pride* and on July 1st the Battle of Britain began. We moved to Blythe for the working up of this ship, but after a brief stay there the orders were to procede to Belfast and I returned to Hove, where I found a letter from Mr. Knowles as follows:-

Dear Mrs. Stapleton,
   I feel I must address you thus, your having arrived at the stage of being a British matron. Thank you very much indeed for your kind letter. It is good in these times when one is doing one's best to keep the old Sussex flag flying to get a letter of encouragement such as yours. I still go to the County Ground practically every day and a letter will always find me there. All our lads are serving in some capacity or another, we have not one left — Tom Burchell and Beach look after the ground and old Billy (Newham) aged 80 and myself look after the office. There is quite a lot to do as the Home Guard use a portion of the Pavilion and some of the Ground for training. We have quite a lot of cricket. Soldiers and Home Guard all play a bit. Most of our members have sent 10/- or £1 and we have to keep going as best we can.
   Yours sincerely,
   W.L. Knowles.

I saw my first match of this season on August 31st! It was a game I called Sussex Club and Ground v L.D.V. (Local Defence Force). On September 14th there was another called Sussex XI v Brighton Clubs in aid of the Spitfire Fund. Tate came and sat with me and a friend; at last he had a job and was on top of the world. During a short air-raid warning from 12.5 until 12.35 they played on, then, as there were no refreshments on the ground, I dashed home to lunch and back again afterwards, but at 3.30 another raid came and shortly after the siren there were two heavy explosions over Brighton: then the enemy aircraft flew low over the ground, but *still* the cricketers played on. Then the pilot returned, swooping right down: I thought he was machine-gunning and we all fled to the inside of the pavilion; the players fell flat on their faces on the grass and someone yelled to us, "Lie down!" and "Keep away from the glass!" After this there was silence. At length we were herded underneath the pavilion with the boilers, but later emerged to go to look at the crater made in the south-east corner. Soon it was discovered that the bomb had not gone off and the ground was cleared: the other bomb landed on the Sports Club, also without exploding. Arthur Gilligan, Maurice Tate, John Langridge and Spen Cama were all playing this day and Arthur told me how Maurice came up to him, hand to mouth in his usual manner as if to impart some portentous secret, only to say, "Fancy THEM doing that to US!" We all had our particular bomb story, but it always seemed strange to me that mine happened on my much-loved County Ground.

Undaunted, but rather spurred on by this attack, a Sussex XI played the Brighton and Hove District Club Association two days later in aid of the local Fighter Fund. Arthur Gilligan and John Langridge were again playing for Sussex, the latter making 91, whilst Spen Cama led out the Club Cricket side. A keen spectator of this game was Mr. Miller Hallett, one of the oldest members of the Club and still its President, a position he was to hold for ten years.

In the autumn I obtained a permit to travel to Belfast to join Bryan. One day I went to watch football: it was Distillery v Cliftonville, but there were no other women present and I realised that I could not go again. How different this was from the days when I saw Tommy Cook playing for Brighton and Hove Albion!

In December 1940 Bryan was transferred to *H.M.S. Amaranthus* which was sent to Freetown in Sierre Leone: I was unable to follow and came back to Hove to spend Christmas with my mother.

When Bryan was given this command his Navigating Officer was a certain F.G. (Poona) White. Poona, considerably older than Bryan and an R.N.V.R. officer who had spent much of his time in India, was always considered by his captain to have been one of his finest officers. He put up with the hardships of war uncomplainingly and acted as Bryan's watchdog, never allowing anyone into his cabin unless he, Poona, had vetted him first. Imagine our surprise when, after the war, he turned up on the County Ground at Hove! Now, Poona always introduced Bryan as 'my late commanding officer', to the amusement of many. Over the post-war years no one has worked harder for Sussex than Poona White, especially in endeavouring to increase the membership which grew vastly through his enthusiastic campaigns: in 1957 he was made a vice-President.

In April 1941 Betty Tate was married at Burgess Hill and was given away by her father, now Second Lieutenant Maurice William Tate, and of course the whole family was there. It was so odd to see pictures of Tate in soldier's uniform and he looked almost as proud of this as of his daughter's marriage. There was not much cricket to be seen this year, but on May 31st there was Sussex v R.A.F., when Lieut. Tate was out second ball to a good catch by Cpl. L.J. Todd, the Kent player. Wing Cmdr. A.J. Holmes captained the R.A.F. and also playing were P/O A.E.R. Gilligan, Capt. S.C. Griffith and Lieut. H.T. Bartlett. Then there was Sussex v The Brighton and Hove Cricket Association in which Tate and young Jimmy Tate were the only Sussex people playing. As Sussex declared Jimmy did not bat, but he showed up well as a bowler.

Double Summer Time came into force during the war years and this enabled cricket to be played until 7.0 p.m. without much fear of bad light. One day the R.A.F. made 223 and Sussex wanted 8 to win when the last wicket fell at 7.0 precisely: Jim Parks had made 76 and Sgt. Charlie Oakes a century for the R.A.F.

I often went to help Mr. Knowles and old Billy Newham in the office and one day Mr. Knowles said that I was welcome to come to the County Ground at any time I wished. In April 1942 the spring offensive appeared to have begun, but, not to be put off, Sussex encouraged Services cricket in the area by forming a Sussex League, which included Navy, Army, Air Force, Civil Defence and A.F.S. A United Services XI consisted of a side with Alec and Eric Bedser, Alf Gover, Denis Compton and H.P. Chaplin — my old coach! One day I was watching the Club and Ground playing Hurstpierpoint College when "it was a glorious game: just the sight and sound of it all made me feel that life is still worth living." Both Tates, Maurice and Jimmy, played in an Army v R.A.F. game, but the Army made only 57 and were beaten by 10 wickets. There was a lot of cricket in 1942 for Roedean School, the Grand and Metropole Hotels, as well as the King Alfred Swimming Baths, were all commandeered as training centres for officers, so there were many well-known cricketers on hand.

During the Battle of Britain the air was full of ominous sounds by day and night, but still the Police played cricket against the N.F.S. and the Navy made 272 in 2½ hours (the time allowed) to beat the R.A.F.: Tate, now Capt. Tate, led a team against the Home Guard and Sussex played the R.A.F., which could generally muster a good side for no less than nine Sussex players were eligible, plus W.R. Hammond and Leslie Ames. The Army played the Police, who were out for 13, Alec Bedser taking 9—3! I saw Cpl. P.F. Judge of Middlesex and Glamorgan do the hat-trick for the R.A.F. against Sussex and I added, almost casually, "a bomb dropped in Brighton and all took cover for a while." It is extraordinary how quickly one can become accustomed to the most bizarre events. It is obvious that many of these matches were between unevenly balanced sides, but no one minded in the least: the spirit of cricket was being kept alive and I think that this helped when the time came for the game to get back onto its feet again.

The last match of the summer was R.A.F. (West) v R.A.F. (South). I acceeded to Mr. Knowles' request that I sell raffle tickets round the ground. One man signed the counterfoil and the name was 'Gilbert Frankau'. For a moment I thought it was a joke, but, finding that it was not, I told the author how much my husband and I had enjoyed *Royal Regiment,* his novel about the Gunners. Mr. Frankau invited me to Princes Hotel, where he was staying, and where he signed this book for me. He died in 1952, but his wife, Susan, is now one of my greatest friends and his grandson, Timothy d'Arch Smith, who is an ardent cricket enthusiast, later published John Snow's first book of poems.

I helped Mr. Knowles with the typing of the 1942 Annual Report, but he had been far from well for some time, so it was with no surprise, but with much sorrow, that I learned that he had been forced to retire: Sir Home Gordon took over the duties of Secretary for the remainder of the war.

In 1943 there was a game called Sussex Club and Ground v East Sussex. I described this as "a motley collection of players in which I knew only Sunnucks and Keith Wilson by sight." Another day G.H.G. Doggart, then captain of Winchester, played at Hove and showed very obvious promise for the future. Tate captained another Army side against N.F.S., C.D. and Police, then Sussex played S.E. Command, when "dear old Maurice came and sat with us for a while, as cheery and full of stories as ever." One of the cricketing stars of this summer was Australian Keith Miller, based in Brighton with the Royal Australian Air Force; he played several games for 'Sussex', but, naturally, his allegiance changed when our opponents were the R.A.A.F. In one match A.J. Holmes was the only Sussex player on the field: Miller made a century and took 7–36. There was some talk of Miller joining Sussex after the war, but when the time came he decided to return to Australia. In another game against the R.A.A.F. Keith Carmody made 103 by 1 o'clock: he hit all over the place and there were 200 runs on the board by this time. In 1944 Carmody was shot down over Holland, was picked up by a U-boat and imprisoned at Stalagluft 3; he was eventually freed by the Russians and in 1945 played in the last of the 'Victory Tests'.

Early in 1944 Billy Newham died. He had first played for Sussex in 1881 and had helped in the office until shortly before his death. In the spring Sussex played C.S. Dempster's XI at Chichester; there was a Sussex XI v the Club Cricket Conference; Sussex played the London Counties and the R.A.F.: later, when they played the Forty Club the Doggarts, father and son, were in the latter side. A few other games were played, but more and more men were overseas and it became increasingly difficult to get teams together: other counties had their own fixtures, but we were lucky in that so many good players were stationed in the south.

On June 6th 1944 the invasion of Europe began. Our road and most other roads in the town were lined with tanks, jeeps and other military vehicles and there were troops everywhere. I woke one morning and found that they had all disappeared! I shall never know how vehicles of that size and number could have gone so quietly whilst I slept. The D-Day secret had been well kept, but soon the places of these tanks and jeeps were taken by more and more men and materials so that on June 13th I wrote:- "An awful night: could not sleep at all. Motor bikes roared up and down at 3 a.m. and there were soldiers tramping in the empty house opposite." This indicated a further exodus and there were several bumps and bangs which I was too sleepy to contemplate. This night was quickly followed by the first pilotless planes, and what uncanny brutes they were! Now talk was all of Flying Bombs, Buzz Bombs or Doodlebugs, V-1s — or whatever one chose to call them, but as the months passed and winter arrived and then turned into spring there was nothing to prevent the steady progress of the Allies across Europe. At length on May 8th 1945

Churchill told us of Germany's unconditional surrender and we called it VE-Day.

Cricket at once endeavoured to restore some sort of normality to itself and games began to be arranged against Surrey, Hants, West Indies, Northants, the Club Conference, New Zealand, the Forty Club and Eastern Command. On August 14th I paid my full subscription and the pavilion was again for 'Members Only'. Peace became official on August 15th, then came the horrific dropping of the atomic bomb and the war against Japan also came to an end.

A series of five 'Victory Tests' were played against Lindsay Hassett's Services XI in which S.C. 'Billy' Griffith kept wicket for England: there were two wins each and one game drawn which, in the circumstances, was just as it should have been. Everything was now set for a new Championship season in 1946, but in our hearts many of us knew that some things would never be quite the same again.

CHAPTER FIVE

## PICKING UP THE THREADS 1946 – 1949

Whilst waiting for Bryan's demobilisation we gave much thought to his future and hoped that he would be able to work ashore, but with thousands of men leaving the Services at this time our efforts in that direction were almost bound to fail, for the qualifications necessary for a navigating officer are not easily transferred to land, so, in the end, he joined the Royal Fleet Auxiliary Service, which meant continuing to work with the Royal Navy. My mother moved to a smaller flat in the same road and Bryan and I took over the large maisonette which I had found in 1929: we had Nanny to housekeep for us and life, for me, continued very much as before, and that included cricket.

Ever since I was born my home has been filled with books, my father's, my mother's, my husband's and my own: every so often I am compelled to have a discarding process to make room for new arrivals. Thinking that a move was imminent after the war I had sent some of my cricket books to the County Cricket Club and I still have the letter I received from the Secretary, S.C. Griffith. Then, in 1959, when we really did move to buy our own house in Hove, I presented more books to the Library and at the same time took some old photographs of Maurice Tate, drawings by Juliet (Pannett) and my autographed cricket bat to Colonel Grimston for the cricket museum; he was very pleased with these and told me that they had very few pictures of that period. When I see these hanging on the pavilion walls to-day selfishness gets the better of me and I sometimes regret that sudden burst of generosity and wish I had them back: the irony of this is that the Library, under a new Librarian, is now having to do its own weeding out and I find myself buying back my own books, third-hand, from the Club Shop!

No one who is under fifty years old can possibly appreciate the sheer delight with which cricket-lovers the world over greeted the game's return to its old routine in 1947. After six years which had involved civilian and Serviceman alike, those who had survived the conflict began, gradually, to resume their positions

## Picking Up the Threads 1946 – 1949

as before, but there were gaps in the stands which would never be filled and no one reader will know who filled them all, but each will have his own private list. On the field of play, too, there were some absentees, notably Ken Farnes, the Essex fast bowler, and Hedley Verity of Yorkshire, both of whom had been killed, but for those who knew them they live on.

A.J. Holmes had retired from first-class cricket and S.C. Griffith was the first post-war Sussex captain, combining this with the job of Secretary. My first visit to net practice this year was a heart-warming one. Billy Griffith and Hugh Bartlett were the chief amateurs in the side and they were backed up by schoolmaster Robert Stainton, J.A. Dew, P.D.S. Blake, J.H. Bartlett (no relation to H.T.) and a host of others who played only the odd game for the county and, therefore, made no great mark in my memory. Robert Stainton I certainly recall as a strong, forceful batsman, who, had he been able to give more time to cricket, might well have made himself a permanent member of the team: Peter Blake remains in my mind mainly for a memorable catch he made, the ball soaring ever skywards until after what seemed an age it decided to descend – into the safe hands of young Blake. The professionals were back in force, except that Jim Parks had retired. Jim and John Langridge were there as were Charlie and Jack Oakes, George Cox, Harry Parks, Jack Nye (his gas mask happily discarded), Jim Hammond, Jim Wood and Jim Cornford. There was a period when we felt that if anyone called "Jim!" half the Sussex team would come running. Many of these, however, had been reaching their prime in 1939 and had lost seven valuable years which could never be returned to them. They were ready to carry on where they had left off and were joined, in due course, by new and promising young players – talent enough, one would have thought, to take Sussex well up the Championship. But for Billy Griffith things were not so easy as they seemed.

Always hopeful, however, I bought Bryan his first S.C.C.C. tie and we saw Sussex beat Worcestershire at Hove and then followed them to the Oval where Cox, Harry Parks and Charlie Oakes all made centuries as if nothing had changed. The first touring team to come to England after the war was that of the Indians, captained by the Nawab of Pataudi, whose son, 'Tiger' Pataudi, was to play for Sussex in about ten years time. Mankad, Merchant, Amarnath and Pataudi, himself, all helped themselves to centuries off the Sussex bowling and not even a battling 234 by George Cox could rescue the English county from defeat. I noted that "the weather was dreadful. S.W. gale kept blowing bails off. V. cold. How the Indians must hate our climate." We brought a Middlesex-supporting friend to the fixture with that county and, having seen Denis Compton make yet another hundred, he went home happy. Sussex were not so happy and lost by 10 wickets. It was, to say the least, a disastrous season for Sussex, who finished last.

S.C. Griffith had found the combined jobs of secretary and captain too much of a burden; he continued to play but H.T. Bartlett took over the leadership until the end of 1949. At the beginning of 1947 two Trial Matches were held between sides captained by Griffith and Bartlett. The careers of these two men had run parallel ever since their schooldays. They had been in the Dulwich XI together, had gone to Pembroke College, Cambridge, had enlisted in the Glider Pilot Regiment and had both been at Arnhem, where they had shown great courage and were each awarded the D.F.C.

This was the first year since 1939 that we had received the old type of membership ticket complete with fixtures for the whole season. I am amazed to find that I was still paying only one guinea, which was the same as I had paid in 1930, when the increase from 12/- was made. What extraordinarily good value this was!

One day I watched young Jimmy Tate who was having a trial with Sussex, but, sadly, this led to nothing. Another day I wrote in my diary, "a young amateur, Sheppard, scored 50 before we left."

This same year James Langridge was awarded a long overdue benefit in the Middlesex match, but (as captain) he lost the toss, Denis Compton and Robertson, at their best, got their runs between the showers, and Middlesex won by 10 wickets. The collection for Langridge on the Saturday was £196 plus £243 gathered on the Bank Holiday and there were wonderful crowds on both days to do honour to the man who had served his county so long and so well.

The South Africans were the visitors in 1947 and we always looked forward to their coming for they played an exciting brand of cricket, which makes their later exile from the international scene all the more regrettable. This year Sussex made a huge score against them, aided mainly by George Cox and Harry Parks; Alan Melville, who had captained Sussex so long ago – or so it seemed – was now captain of South Africa and it probably gave him special pleasure to make a century against his old county,

## Picking Up the Threads 1946 – 1949

whilst Viljoen made 201. These high scores, rather naturally, produced a draw and the season ended with Griffith and Bartlett bowling, the latter wearing a new Martlet cap. Sussex finished 10th in the Championship.

1948 was an Australian year and how long it felt since the last! It was an eagerly awaited game for Sussex and yet they were deep in the doldrums and made precisely 86. The great Don Bradman made 109, Morris and Harvey got hundreds and the Australians won by an innings. One day I wrote that Sussex were showing no spirit at all, words which harked back to those I had written as long ago as 1937.

This year James Langridge's brother, John, shared a benefit with Harry Parks: this seemed unfair to many of us, but benefits had become so disorganized because of the war that rather than force either man to wait it was decided to make this a joint affair. Each player received £1,930 and it is only just to say that John Langridge had a testimonial in 1953 which brought him £3,825. Harry Parks left Sussex soon after his benefit and went as coach to Somerset.

Some of our batsmen, though sound, were a trifle stodgy, but George Cox was not one of these and after a vintage 165 from this exciting player I wrote, "I'm glad he's such a jolly player." It is possible that the happy, carefree attitude of this son of the old Sussex cricketer may have prevented him from playing for England. It was all or nothing with 'young' George – either 100 or a 'duck'. One year he had such a spell of the latter that it might almost have been termed a 'clutch' and this was cleverly captured in cartoon form by artist Mary Hoad. George, himself, took no offence and merely laughed when the picture was put up in the pavilion for all to see. At one point it was arranged that he should open the batting. What happened? A duck! That evening Cox came off the field and, drawing a crumpled piece of paper from his pocket, showed it to us then and there. 'George Cox Fails as Opening Bat' ran the headline: George found this as funny as life itself; he could never be down for long and always had a tale to tell. Once when sitting chatting with us in our usual seat he related how his young son, Nicholas, watching cricket with him from the players' enclosure, had witnessed Billy Griffith get the dreaded duck. "How unfortunate for Mr. Griffith!" was the quaint comment of the small boy. On another occasion George told us how Nicholas, by now at school at Christ's Hospital, had managed to run someone out from long stop whilst the wicket-keeper was making a daisy chain! So as not to offend

'C.H.', for which I have the highest regard, it must be added that Nicholas was very young at the time and still in the 'Prep'. In the September of 1948 *The Brighton and Hove Herald* printed a letter in praise of George Cox, junior, and I should like to quote this to show how much his cricket was appreciated:-

> Sir, — I would like to say how much I agree with W.D. How in his admiration of George Cox, the Sussex cricketer. As your correspondent says, his fielding is a joy to watch. His clean picking up and swift and accurate returns, which often result in a batsman being run out, are quite exhilarating. Whether he is enjoying success or going through a 'bad patch' Cox's demeanour is always in the very best sporting spirit. I can honestly say that there are few cricketers I would rather watch in any department of the game than George Cox.
>
> (Miss) P.E. Simon

I may add that this lady lived, and for all I know may still live, in Surrey! Miss Simon was right to regard Cox as an all-rounder, for his 'floaters', as he called them, gained him many a valuable wicket.

But 1948 has been another bad season for Sussex who had tumbled back to 16th position, mainly because of a weakness in the bowling: Jim Cornford and Jim Wood had almost bowled themselves into the ground, but with little support.

When I went to see the Sussex Trial Matches in 1949 no other than James Langridge was umpiring and this made me feel very old! I am not sure why this was, except that in my youth the umpires were, of course, so much older than I. Several years later George Cox asked me to bowl to him in the nets, but I "didn't dare, being utterly out of practice, makes me feel very old!" Unwillingly I was having to realise that time was moving on. This same day I commented that young Jim Parks was playing, but that I could not distinguish him on the field. This was, in fact, the year of 'young' Jim's debut in the first team and he gained his county cap two years later; a fine batsman and field at cover, Parks always wanted to keep wicket: he did so a few times in 1958 and the following year took over permanently from Rupert Webb, eventually keeping wicket for England.

It was lovely to go back to Hastings, to the ground I love so well. One year I saw Ames and Fagg get hundreds for Kent, another year it was Todd and Ames. I did not return to Eastbourne until 1948 and then witnessed 310 by Gimblett of Somerset. Scores are often high at Eastbourne. I had not been there since that summer's day in 1939 and I now wrote, "The Saffrons

## Picking Up the Threads 1946 — 1949

ground looks as lovely as ever, but the town itself has bad war scars." It was not only the town that had scars, I thought, as I recalled the last time I had been there with the Twinings and all that had happened since.

Another day I went to Lords and found a notice outside stating that 'Play may be delayed'. There had been rain on the pitch, but we paid our gate money and as members of Sussex were admitted to the Enclosure. Whilst strolling behind the pavilion and waiting for play to begin we met a schoolmaster friend who introduced a certain Fr. George Long. Fr. Long, born in Brighton, was a keen cricketer and had been an Army chaplain during the war: he had wished to remain in the Service when hostilities were over, but, as he held only a temporary commission, the Cardinal, who was his superior, reclaimed him for other work. Now he was running a boys' club in Notting Hill, but he had rejoined the Sussex Martlets and had met Billy Griffith and Hugh Bartlett, both of whom had helped him in his cricketing ambitions, for soon he was made captain of the Sussex 2nd XI, an honour which he fully appreciated. When, in 1966 George Long published his autobiography *All I Could Never Be* he explained how he eventually gained the regard of men like Don Smith, Alan Oakman, Ken Suttle and the young Jim Parks, who became his friends. More of Fr. Long a little later.

One day during the Gloucestershire match in 1947 I had a strange meeting. Walking down the ground I met Tommy Cook; it was almost exactly ten years since I had last spoken to him. I told him that I was married and he hoped that I was happy. We exchanged a few remarks and he told me that he had returned from South Africa to take up the post of Team Manager for Brighton and Hove Albion. The Albion Handbook of 1947-48 gave him a great write-up which ended:- "Tommy's deeds on the cricket field have made him even better known than his career as a footballer. To him go our best wishes for success in his new job." But when I spoke to Cook I could detect some underlying unhappiness, even distress. I never saw him again. It is necessary to carry Cook's story ahead into the January of 1950, when, to my great sadness, I read in the local paper that on January 16th he had died at the Royal Sussex County Hospital: he was only 49. During the war he had been a corporal in the South African Air Force and in 1943 had been seriously injured in an accident in which several of his friends had died and he, himself, had spent six weeks in hospital. It appears that he had never fully recovered from this incident in his life and had been the victim of severe bouts of depression: before his death he suffered from heart trouble and chronic bronchitis. It seemed such a very sad end to the life of one who had played cricket so well for Sussex and who had given so much pleasure to the spectators, therefore, I was glad that, because of my cutting books, I was able to pay tribute to him with an article in *The Journal of the Cricket Society* in 1976. At the beginning of this same year I met Tommy's son, Roger, himself a keen cricketer and fast bowler, whom I had last seen as a little boy of about eleven. Roger told me that he had been to look at his father's grave at the small village of Cuckfield, where Tommy had also been born. It had been in the winter of 1974-75, when England's batsmen were falling to the might of Lillee and Thomson. An old gardener in the churchyard had asked if he could help. Roger told him who his father had been and the old man exclaimed, "Gor! couldn't we 'arf do with 'im in Australia now!" If Tommy Cook had been able to hear how pleased he would have been!

It may be supposed from what I have written that all went on as before in the cricketing world after the war. Insofar as it did so one must thank those people who had endeavoured to keep good cricket alive at a time when the County Championship was, of necessity, in abeyance. I have already explained that many of those who played in calmer times were still on the field of play, whilst new men were appearing to join Billy Griffith and Hugh Bartlett — men like David Sheppard, Hubert Doggart, Robin Marlar, Don Smith, Don Bates, Ian Thomson, Alan Oakman, Ken Suttle, Jim Parks, Ted James and others; these were all at the start of their cricketing careers, guided, no doubt, by the older hands who were to be found in almost every county for several years to come. Despite this apparent continuity the wind of change (a phrase not yet invented) was just beginning to stir at the end of 1949. So far it was only a gentle rustle, but by the time my story ends it will have worked up to a good Force 10-12.

In mid-August 1949 I was off to Scotland and as the Sussex season ended I was concerning myself with the Aboyne Games and the Braemar Highland Gathering. It was sad that, although James Langridge had made twelve centuries, Sussex had finished only 14th and a storm was brewing.

CHAPTER SIX

THE GREAT WALK OUT

The storm which had been ready to break at the end of 1949 burst overhead on May 17th of the following year when, at the AGM held in the splendid Banqueting Room of the Royal Pavilion, the 41-year-old Duke of Norfolk, Premier Duke of England, Earl Marshal and President of Sussex County Cricket Club, 'picking up his cane and his gloves' according to *The Daily Mail,* left the platform and led the historic walk-out of the Committee after a vote of 'No confidence' had been carried. Next day the papers had a field day with headings such as 'Cricket Duke Walks Out' (*Daily Express*); 'Duke Walks Out of Row Over Cricket Captain' (*Daily Mail*); 'Duke and Committee Stage Walk-Out' — 'Uproar at Sussex County Cricket Meeting' (*Evening Argus*); 'Duke Leads Walk-Out in Sussex Cricket' (*Sussex Daily News*); though *The Times* in its usual restrained manner had but a short paragraph headed 'Sussex County Cricket Club' and *The Daily Telegraph* let itself go only so far as 'Sussex Cricket Dispute'.

I was present at this astonishing meeting and can recall the events vividly. For some reason which was never clear a large number of non-members had made their way into the room and I am pretty sure that many of these took part, quite illegally, in the voting which followed. There had been rumblings for some while in the press about Bartlett's captaincy and when the question of who should lead in the coming season was raised the riff-raff (for there is little else one could call them) at the back of the room refused to let the Duke speak.

"I do not wish to ask more than once to be allowed to finish my remarks," he said coldly. He then went on to say that the captaincy was a matter for the Committee and that, as Bartlett did not have the confidence one could have hoped for, R.G. Hunt and G.H.G. Doggart had been appointed joint captains for 1950. Upon this announcement there were cries of 'No!' and 'Shame!' Amidst the uproar the Duke managed to explain that after discussions and letters between himself and Bartlett the latter had sent his letter of resignation. At this point Fr. George Long, whom I had met that day at Lords and who was seated a few places away from me, jumped to his feet and asked if we might see the letters. His request was refused, the Duke saying that it was not for him to read out Mr. Bartlett's letters and he had no intention of doing so. The Duke of Norfolk could be very firm indeed when occasion demanded, but others refused to let the business rest. Mr. A.C.C. David, a preparatory schoolmaster said, "We must have some elucidation. The Committee's decision is disastrous." Fr. Long, too, stuck to his guns and was supported by the 20-year-old David Sheppard who was sitting next to him. Fr. Long wanted to know why the Club's report had praised Mr. Bartlett for the way he had handled a moderate team to the best possible advantage and yet the captain had resigned without the members knowing the full facts. David Sheppard urged Fr. Long to "Read them the rules, George," whereupon Fr. Long produced the small rule book of the Sussex County Cricket Club and began to refer to Rule 8 which said that appointments had to be confirmed at the AGM. The Duke countered this by stating that the matter had been dealt with under Rule 25 which gave the Committee the right of appointment.

By this time there was general disorder, people arguing and shouting their own remarks from every corner of the room, although Mr. David made himself heard sufficiently to issue his challenge. "It grieves me as a very old member of the Club to do this. I shall move a vote of 'No confidence' unless I have an answer," he said. "Then it had better come to a head," replied the Duke.

Now there was that strange hush which comes over a class of naughty school-children which realises it has gone too far. The vote was taken in almost complete silence. Was I cowardly not to vote? I do not think so. I knew so little of what was behind the furore, which in the end turned out to be something even more fundamental than the captaincy. When the counting was over there was a shocked and bewildered conclave on the platform, then the Duke announced:- "The motion has been carried, and as President of the Sussex County Cricket Club I tender my resignation. The Committee will no doubt do the same."

At this point, according to *The Daily Express*, 'pandemonium broke out' as the Duke left the hall, followed by Committee members and three past Presidents, Lord Leconfield, Sir William Campion and Sir Home Gordon. One member grunted, "Mob rule," which only brought forth cries of "Dictators!" from the opposition. Uncertainty reigned in the Banqueting Room and through it walked the lone figure of the Duke of Norfolk's chauffeur, who ascended the platform and with complete dignity removed the Duke's coat which was still lying, somewhat forlornly, over the back of his chair: the chauffeur left the room and immediately drove his master back to Arundel Castle. I have often wondered what thoughts were in the Duke's mind at this time.

The meeting itself was in obvious disarray. It was not until Mr. F.T.K. Wilson, a club cricketer and a magistrate, was invited to take the chair, however temporarily, that any sort of business could continue. Remaining with him on the platform was S.C. Griffith, the Club's Secretary, who, himself, was due to retire on April 30th. Now at last the audience decided to settle down and listen. Frank Wilson made it clear that he was no rebel, but he simply wanted to get things sorted out for the sake of the Club. Some people were still agitating for Bartlett to remain as captain and for his correspondence with the Duke to be made public. Hugh Bartlett said that he had no objection and when asked if he would withdraw his resignation he said, "It is not for me to do any reconsidering, but if it is the members' wish I could be asked." Then he added, "I am deeply sorry that to-day's meeting turned into such a confusion because of me."

There is no doubt that Frank Wilson found himself in an unenviable position, but he handled the situation well. There were those, mainly older members, who considered the vote had been hasty and ill-advised, others wanted the Committee to be asked to return and though this motion was passed many of them had left and only Mr. W.N. Riley, chairman of the Executive Committe, resumed his seat. When Mr. Wilson pointed out that his own chairmanship was unconstitutional Mr. Riley took the chair. He tried to explain that by a genuine error the item concerning nomination for Committee membership had been left off the agenda, but the Committee had arranged a special meeting to go into the question: he said the rules had been revised and were in the hands of the printers. It was clear that nothing further could be done on this day and, wisely giving passions time to cool, Mr. Riley proposed that the meeting should adjourn and reassemble at the Hove Town Hall at 6.30 p.m. on April 17th. This was generally agreed, but David Sheppard pointed out that the professionals would be reporting at the County Ground on Monday and it was essential that the captain should be present. Mr. Riley, however, insisted that the present meeting was in no position to pass further resolutions and that, so to speak, was that. All this could be fairly summed up in *The Evening Standard's* headline:-

'After the Walk-Out: What Now?" and from Arundel Castle the only message was "His Grace has read the newspapers. He has no further comment to make."

I doubt if anyone could have been happy at what had happened. Behind all the argument about the captaincy lay the self-perpetuating attitude of the Committee which had gone on for far too long. E.W. Swanton, writing in *The Daily Telegraph,* said that the AGM had "come as an unexpected shock to all followers of cricket." He also made clear that "in Colonel Griffith alone, as the paid officer of the Club and *ipso facto* member of the Committee, authority constitutionally resides. It is an additional complication that although Colonel Griffith's own resignation takes effect from April 30th no successor has been appointed. Who is empowered to appoint him?" Mr. Swanton also explained that the position of President changes yearly and he felt that many would have sympathy with the Duke of Norfolk "who apparently found himself precipitated into a hornet's nest. Sussex cricket in the minds of games-folk generally has always been the personification of good sportsmanship and surrounded by the happiest of atmospheres." Fortunately, Billy Griffith agreed to remain until his successor was named, for it would have taken several weeks to get out the ballot papers and nominate a new Committee: he thought that the affairs of the Club should be put into the hands of a caretaker Committee.

On April 3rd, therefore, there was a private meeting of the 40-strong Committee at the County Ground, but the Duke was not present. It should be understood, though it was not entirely understood at the time, that only the Duke had resigned at the AGM; the Committee had merely followed him from the room. It may be best to quote here the official statement issued after the special meeting by Colonel Griffith to the press:-

> "The Committee, having been requested by the adjourned AGM to carry on until the Special Meeting on April 17th, met to-day. Careful consideration was given to the unprecedented situation, and as a result the Committee decided to resign and to place the management of the Club for the time being in the hands of the following vice-presidents:- Group Captain A.J. Holmes, A.E.R. Gilligan, W.N. Riley, Sir A. Saunders, J.K. Mathews and E.G. Maltby. This temporary management was given power to co-opt during the interim period."

The chairman of this administration was to be Sir Alan Saunders, who had coached me in the Sports Club so many years before. "It has been a very amiable meeting," stated Lord Leconfield, "I think the future of Sussex cricket is all right." At the very time that these deliberations were going on the players were gathering for their first net practice of the season under their new coach, Patsy Hendren. One of my cuttings shows a group of cricketers shivering in their overcoats and this includes James and John Langridge, Charlie and Jack Oakes, Jim Woods and Jim Cornford: another picture shows a happily smiling Hubert Doggart taking a piece of batting advice from an equally smiling Patsy Hendren. Others, not pictured, who were on the ground that day were David Sheppard, Rupert Webb, Ted James, Don Smith and Ken Suttle. Amongst Patsy's 'colts' one sees such names as Alan Oakman, Jim Parks and Don Bates, all to become well-known names in Sussex cricket in the years ahead and none of them, seemingly, unduly worried about the important talks going on behind closed doors.

As the Hove Town Hall meeting approached the press was busy with conjectures as to the captaincy, *The Sunday Graphic* deciding that "it should not be taken for granted that Hugh (Bartlett) will walk in as a hero." When the great day arrived over 1,000 members, including the present writer, turned up to what must have been one of the largest AGMs ever held. The chair was taken by Sir Alan Saunders and I have never ceased to admire the way he managed what might so easily have been another fiasco. After the events at the Royal Pavilion it was obvious that the first question to be settled was that of the captaincy. When the packed hall heard the suggestion that James Langridge, Sussex born and bred and one of the most highly respected professionals ever to play for Sussex, should take on the role of caretaker captain there was immediate applause and when the vote was taken it was 'carried unanimously'. One could not but feel some sympathy for Hugh Bartlett, R.G. Hunt and Hubert Doggart, but in the circumstances it was surely wise to leave them out of contention for the time being at least and so save all three from further embarrassment. Maurice Tate had captained Sussex on various occasions, but James Langridge was the first Sussex professional to be assigned to this position officially and few could have deserved the honour more. A quiet, modest and reserved man, but with a twinkle in his eye, Jim was an all-rounder whose sound knowledge of the game would be of great value to those he was to lead. Years later his widow told me what help he had given to the young Jim Wood, who, though a good fast bowler, was nervous and unsure of himself at this stage; there is no doubt that the encouragement he had from Jim Langridge made him a better bowler than he might otherwise have been. Langridge, himself, had played against all the overseas sides except Australia and New Zealand and had on many occasions saved Sussex batting from disaster when, going in at number 5, he had stopped a rot. Before he retired he had scored over 28,000 runs and taken 1,416 wickets with his slow left-arm bowling. At the time of his selection as captain he and his brother were busy coaching at their indoor cricket school at the *King Alfred,* now restored to civilian status by the Admiralty and used as a sports centre. When he heard the news Jim was reported as saying, "I am delighted that the honour of the temporary captaincy has fallen to me; whilst skipper I shall do my best to ensure that Sussex cricketing traditions are carried on." Little did Jim Langridge realise that the captaincy was to be his for the next three seasons — until the arrival of David Sheppard.

Once the leadership question had been settled the caretaker Committee's proposals for the reconstruction of the Club were passed, the only issue in contention being whether only Full Members were eligible for election to the new Committee or whether those paying one guinea could also be nominated. When Sir Alan Saunders was asked the difference between three-guinea and one-guinea members, he replied quickly, "Two guineas." This sort of quiet humour was really the keynote to the evening. Everyone seemed determined that Sussex cricket must suffer no further injury. When Sir Alan asked for a unanimous vote that the Duke of Norfolk be asked to resume the Presidency there was no doubt where the heart of the Sussex members lay: every hand shot up and there was another burst of spontaneous cheering. I always felt that it was gracious of the Duke to return after having been treated in such a cavalier manner only a few weeks before, but Bernard, Duke of Norfolk, was a big man and not one to harbour a grudge; he was also devoted to cricket and during his years of Presidency he hardly ever missed an AGM. On this April evening there had been Sussex members who had travelled from as far afield as Liverpool and Somerset and I am sure that they were happy at the outcome. Later Sir Alan Saunders was quoted as saying, "Sussex have shown that they can go to war and can make peace too." Arthur Gilligan paid tribute to Sir Alan when he said that mainly due to his "magnificent handling of the meeting we have taken a big step nearer to the solution of our problems."

I have treated this episode at some length because it made a great impression on me at the time and also because it is an example of how, because the future of cricket is more important than individuals, harmony can be achieved to the honour of all.

The futures of the two men who offered Hugh Bartlett such strong support were very different. George Long, who had done such excellent work as a chaplain during the war and with his boys' club in London, found himself unable to settle to the life of a civilian priest and eventually returned to the lay state: when I last heard of him he was doing welfare work in London. David Sheppard captained Sussex in 1953, later played for England and was captain in 1954 after Len Hutton had been taken ill: he was ordained by the Bishop of London in St. Paul's Cathedral in 1955, became curate at St. Mary's, Islington, in North London and is now Bishop of Liverpool.

CHAPTER SEVEN

## WHITHER CRICKET? 1950 – 1962

A world war does not cease to affect a population when peace is signed or for many years afterwards. I still have my Ration Book dated 1953-54 with its pages for meat, eggs, fish, cheese, bacon, sugar and sweets, also a space marked 'spare' which was never allocated to anything. Each page was ruled in sections and scrupulously marked by the retailer as we made our purchases, but as the book is only partially used I presume that rationing ended early in this period, though National Service went on for several more years and caused the cricketing careers of many to be blighted by its obvious necessity. The 18-year-old Derek Semmence, who had made a century in his first season, had to go off soon afterwards and as late as 1962 Tony Buss was doing his own stint. Some players returned, as did Buss, who is still with the Club to-day, but Semmence came back only briefly in 1968 and 1969 and is now coach at Hurstpierpoint College. The absence of these players was unavoidable, but others have suffered in different ways. Young Peter Ledden, of whom I once wrote that his innings had been the brightest of the day, remained with Sussex until 1968, never got his cap and quietly disappeared. I often wonder what sort of personal grief lies behind these bare words. Seven years of a young man's life is a long time unless it brings some reward and it is good to know that to-day more thought is given to a cricketer's future and that he is advised to qualify in some other sphere in case he does not prove up to county cricket.

Things returned to normal very slowly and as they did so all county clubs sought ways to improve their grounds for the crowds that were expected to flow back over the summer months ahead. At Hove a further addition to the 1928 extension of the pavilion was built, mainly of concrete and later picked out in 'Sussex blue' iron and woodwork; there were new changing-rooms for the players, a special 'look-out' from which they can watch the game and a captain's room, which, I am told, is one of the very few in the country: there is now a VIP space erected above the Committee Room, which has three sides of glass and is like a greenhouse on a hot day. Through the interest which the Duke of Norfolk always took in the Club of which he was President, turves were brought from Arundel Castle Estate to make a banking which now runs from the nothern end of the pavilion right round to the north-east corner of the ground and upon this bank, in front of the cars, deck chairs have been placed for the greater comfort of members. Later the front of the dear old cowshed was pulled down (though it might have fallen down anyway) and a further banking for more deck chairs was made. The Hove ground slopes quite steeply from the South Downs to the sea, but from the third or fourth row of these chairs it was possible to get an excellent view from behind the bowler's arm, with the advantage of having the sun behind you. Sometime in the 'Fifties — I forget exactly when — I deserted my seat in the pavilion and went to sit in front of the cowshed on these new deck chairs. One felt a bit cut off and could no longer see the players come and go at such close range, but the constant chatter in the pavilion was spoiling my day and although women are blamed for this I have found that some men are no less garrulous when they start discussing their war experiences or days in Imperial India.

Throughout this time, when Bryan was often away at sea for long spells, I had a good friend with whom I watched cricket. Hylda Whittome had been evacuated with St. Dunstan's during the war, but when they returned to Ovingdean, near Brighton, she would escort parties of the blinded men to the County Ground and had, of necessity, become a good commentator with a sound knowledge of the game. When there was a nail-biting finish we would burst into poetry reciting Henry Newbolt's famous lines:-

> 'There's a breathless hush in the close to-night,
> Ten to make and match to win;
> A bumping pitch and a blinding light,
> An hour to play and the last man in.'

The idea of 'Play up, play up and play the game!' was not such an outmoded piece of blimpism as it would be to many of the younger generation to-day. Yet, whilst Hylda and I were sitting in front of the cowshed dreaming our cricketing dreams, things were slowly, if almost imperceptibly, beginning to change. Hylda died, after a long illness, in 1972, but before she left the ground she presented the Club with the flagstaff with its yardarm from which fly the flags of Sussex and the visiting teams and there are few more cheering sights than to see these blowing out in the breeze as one drives up Selborne Road.

George Cox's benefit was due in 1951 and a Committee was formed to organize matches for this popular player with various sides throughout the county. The Committee was so successful that, at the end of the season, it was decided not to disband it but rather to expand it into what became the Sussex County Welfare Association. Mr. F.G. White (not to be confused with Poona White) did great work for the Welfare Association until his untimely death in a road accident on the Hove front in 1954; the following year the Duke of Norfolk unveiled a plaque on the new Welfare buildings to Mr. White in the presence of his widow. Other members of that early Welfare Committee were Kenneth Gilkes and Keith Wilson, both well-known for their work for Sussex over many years.

The object of the Welfare Committee was to help the Club raise money at a time when all counties were finding themselves in varying degrees of financial difficulties and, in particular, to assist the players during their benefit year, ever seeking new and attractive ways to bring in additional funds. Previously players had been forced to make their own arrangements and to have the backing of this new body was an immense help, though players still have to work *with* the Association if they wish to get the most out of what is, for them, an important year. The Welfare does great work behind the scenes running raffles, football pools and social evenings; then, in 1977, Norman Hartley and his band of helpers took over the membership from the Secretary, thus leaving him free to carry out other duties.

When S.C. Griffith gave up the Secretaryship in 1950 it was taken on by Colonel George Grimston, whom I had seen playing for Sussex before the war. During his second year as Secretary he collected together a small group which had the honorary title of 'Ladies Committee' and we were each given an official badge. This was a friendly little band consisting of Mrs. Woolston, mother of W.C. Brown, one-time captain of Northants, Mrs. Jim Langridge, Mrs. Keates, myself and one or two others who put in an occasional appearance, with Mr. Roger Green, of Chailey, to advise and someone called 'Frank' to fetch and carry, and with Colonel Grimston calling and sitting in on all our meetings. The first job we undertook was that of retrieving numberless cricket pictures which had been stored beneath the pavilion during the war years; these were thick with dust, cobwebs and even the inevitable spider, from which I fled. On the first day the picture rail had not arrived so we spent the time cleaning, but later we put up each picture with cord or picture wire which was quite a task!

Later a peg-board was provided so that whoever has rearranged things as more and more pictures have come along has had a much easier job than we did in 1951. For years the tea-room in the Ladies' Pavilion had been furnished with cane chairs and tables which had once been orange, but were now very tatty. For days we painted these pale green, the paint having been left over from work on some other part of the ground. I remember having green paint around my finger nails for days and one morning George Cox came past giving us a cheerful wave. "Who do you think you are — Picasso or Matisse?" he called. This Committee remained in being for quite a while and we worked closely with the Secretary, making ourselves available to take on anything that was needed to be done. Once this entailed addressing hundreds of envelopes to members, a chore for which even Bryan, during one of his leaves, was roped in. Colonel Grimston never failed to send each one of us a courteous letter of thanks for our efforts and it was this friendly atmosphere that made the whole thing possible, for women members can be mobilized to be just as useful as men, although at this time none of us aspired to becoming fully-fledged members of the main Committee.

It was in the early 'Fifties that Sussex had their second spell — during my cricket-watching days — of frequent change of captaincy. When David Sheppard took over from Jim Langridge in 1953 he had made it clear to the Sussex Committee that he could give only one year to cricket as he intended to study for the church, yet in that one year he brought the county from 13th to 2nd, a position higher than any they have held since. Later, after Sheppard had been ordained he was familiarly known as 'The Rev' and when he returned to make 113 against Australia in 1956 Hollowood has an amusing cartoon depicting a fearce some-looking Freddie Trueman to whom the umpire is saying, "Watch it, Fred. the Rev's back." I cannot speak for Fred Trueman, but Jim Parks writes that no Sussex cricketer would let slip a swear word in front of Sheppard, so much did they admire him. Parks writes in *Runs in the Sun* that "without any effort he (Sheppard) can bring the best out of any man, and any cricketer who plays alongside him will joyfully do anything for David Sheppard," and again, speaking of Sheppard's virtual retirement from the field, Parks writes:- "He has given his services to a better cause than the game we serve." What finer tribute from one England cricketer to another? Sheppard was the first ordained priest to play for England and this gave the sports writers a new angle for comment: the same year he conducted C.B. Fry's cremation service — a strange transformation of roles. David always took a great interest in his boys' club at Islington and one day he brought a group of these lads to be coached by George Cox in the nets at Hove: this was the era of the 'Teddy boys' so that these budding cricketers all wore drain-pipe trousers and very pointed black shoes which looked oddly out of place. Cox told us that they would have regarded it as frightfully 'sissy' to be seen in white flannels, which in any case none of them possessed, let alone white shoes, yet, despite the 'gear', they seemed to be having a grand time under the kindly eye of their coach and I am sure that they must have gained something of value from that day on the County Ground.

During the final week of David Sheppard's captaincy a party was held which, when it was planned, was hoped would celebrate our winning the County Championship for the first time in history. My invitation read:- "The President and Committee of the Sussex County Cricket Club request the pleasure of the company of Mrs. L.F.M. Stapleton for cocktails at the County Ground Hotel, to meet the Sussex and Surrey Elevens on Saturday 19th August 1953 at 6.30 p.m." Again my memory of this is vague, but I do recall having quite a long conversation with Jim Laker. This match against Surrey was a battle for the honour of being first and all Surrey had to do was to stop Sussex from winning, so on the third day I was writing, "Cricket a flop. Sussex managed to get first innings points, but after that there was never any hope of a finish: thus Surrey become Champion County for the second year running." But this summer had been a triumph for David Sheppard and after play crowds gathered in front of the pavilion, calling for the captain, until he came out onto the roof and made a little speech, praising each member of his team. He looked very boyish and shy, but very happy. Later I had a talk with his mother and promised to send her a cutting about the Welfare Association's presentation to her son. I wonder if I ever did! Having no recollection of this gift I recently made enquiries and the answer I received was as follows:- "Welfare presented David Sheppard with a cake (a joke played on David as the cake was sub-standard)." But there had been nothing sub-standard about Sheppard's captaincy and the gift sounds singularly inappropriate, for Sussex had done better than at any time since 1934.

Hubert Doggart took over from Sheppard and soon *The Daily Express* was hailing this Cambridge Blue as the 'new C.B. Fry': Bob Wyatt, now Chairman of the Selection Committee, announced that Doggart would captain the Rest against the England side led by

## Whither Cricket? 1950 — 1962

*Left to right : Robin Marlar, David Sheppard, Hubert Doggart, 1951*

*Sussex 1953*

*FRONT ROW (left to right): Marlar, S.C. Griffith, Jim Langridge, Sheppard, Duke of Norfolk, John Langridge, Doggart, Cox, Charlie Oakes*

*BACK ROW: Wood, Bates, Oakman, Smith, Jim Parks (Jnr.), James, Suttle, Webb*

Norman Yardley and Doggart did, indeed, play against the West Indians in the first two Tests. At the end of the summer he had to return to his teaching at Winchester College and next in line for the captaincy was Robin Marlar of Harrow and Cambridge University: he remained in charge for five years, leading Sussex to fourth place in his first season, but then having to watch a slow slide downwards until, in 1959, Sussex were 15th. Marlar had been capped for Sussex in 1952, was captain of Cambridge U. in 1953 and was an extremely useful off-break bowler, who took 9-46 against Lancashire in 1956. During the last few matches of Robin Marlar's captaincy I was busy moving house and cricket just had to take second place. Bryan and I are like squirrels and collect everthing, so that it was no small job, but one evening I went to the ground to join the usual party, which included Robin Marlar and Don Smith, the latter in his benefit year. I could not help feeling sorry for Marlar, who was standing as Conservative candidate for Bolsover at the next General Election and we all wished him luck, but he replied sadly, "The public doesn't like failures." I suppose he regretted that he had not been able to take Sussex higher up the Table.

After Marlar's last game as captain, which was against Warwickshire, I wrote in my diary, "Sussex made 374, with Suttle 136, and never looked back, winning by 7 wickets. Marlar went in second wicket down in the second innings and was out first ball, swiping for six and being c and b. He was called for at the end to make a speech, which he did, saying that he did not intend saying good-bye as he hoped to be back again. The small crowd gave him a good reception, for which I was glad." During his cricketing days Marlar had acted as Librarian to the Duke of Norfolk and when he stopped playing, turned to sports journalism and is also often heard on the radio.

During this time there were several notable retirements and these I always wrote about with sorrow in my diary. The first departure of this chapter was that of Jim Cornford in 1952: Jim, who had bowled so hard and so well for Sussex since his debut in 1931 was now leaving with his family for Rhodesia and he took the good wishes of the Sussex members with him. He had taken 1,019 wickets and had never bowled a no-ball! To-day's bowlers should take note of this, although I know that the 'front foot rule' has made things different for them.

In 1953 came the departure of Jim Langridge, one of the greatest of those old Sussex stalwarts, who had first played for his county as far back as 1924 and I had first known him as an uncapped player. When Jim accepted the captaincy in 1950 he probably regarded it as a stop-gap measure, but as things turned out he remained at the helm for three happy years and before his cricketing days were over he had made more than 30,000 runs and had taken 1,500 wickets. If I half close my eyes I can still see him walking out to bat and, as he left the pavilion, always looking up to the sky above as if to ascertain where the sun had reached, or if it was not there at all, he wondered why not! On his retirement from the playing scene Jim became the county coach, a position he held until 1960. Jim Langridge died on 10th September 1966 and 'Mrs. Jim' told me later that, although he had been ill for some time few people had known how serious it was: he had been at the County Ground only a few days before his death and no one had realised that anything was wrong. To the end Jim had shown the courage that he had so often demonstrated on the cricket field. Long after his death I went to visit Mrs. Jim and she showed me, with warrantable pride, the trophies her husband had won and which she keeps in a place of honour in her home for they are part of the history of the Club. There is a silver salver, one of the two which were presented to Jim and his brother, John, when they each made 2,000 runs in 1937. There is also another silver-salver given by Mr. Miller Hallett on behalf of the Club in 1938 "in token of the unselfish patience and self-restraint exercised by him which enabled H.T. Bartlett and George Cox to make their wonderful record scores against the Australians and Yorkshire respectively." There are four cricket balls, each with its silver shield inscribed with the feat performed: 7-19 v Somerset (1929); 7-8 v Gloucestershire (1932); 9-34 v Yorkshire (1934); and the ball with which Langridge did the hat-trick against Derbyshire in 1939. Mrs. Langridge can be assured that all of us who knew and admired Jim at cricket will ever have happy memories of him and it is good to know that she values his trophies so much: I hope that the wives of to-day's cricketers will do the same when their time comes, though sometimes I am doubtful, for values have changed so greatly over the years.

In 1954 Charlie Oakes received a well-earned Testimonial and retired soon afterwards: he had made over 10,000 runs and had taken 449 wickets. First he went to his old home at Horsham on the edge of the cricket ground and later became coach at Stowe, where he is to this day.

In 1955 there was a triple *valete* to be said, when John Langridge, George Cox and Jim Wood all took their leave. It was on the last day of the Somerset match that these three players appeared in their last games for Sussex (though Cox had a game or two later) and I wrote that "It was one of those memorable days. Sussex made Somerset follow on; the latter saved an innings defeat and gave us 18 to make to win." Play had gone on till 7.0 p.m. and the extra ½ hour was claimed." John Langridge and George Cox went forth to do battle for the last time. "Unluckily," I continued, "Cox was caught in the deep from what would have been the winning hit and it was left to Marlar to make it. A good crowd yelled for "John and George and Jim." At length they came, led by Marlar, onto the roof. All four made speeches, of which George Cox's was the best, full of wit and also sentiment. We all cheered and sang 'For they are jolly good fellows!' — And so home.

The record of John Langridge is no less remarkable than that of his brother and he made more runs and centuries than any man who has not played for England; added to this his slip fielding must have been about the finest in the country and resulted in his holding 786 catches: his record first wicket stand of 490 with Ted Bowley in 1933 seems unlikely ever to be beaten. John has never left the cricket world for in 1956 he was appointed to the list of first-class umpires and 'stood' in 7 Tests between 1960 and 1963. He has always appeared to be the ideal umpire, unemotional, watchful, deeply concentrating and so wise in the ways of cricket: he is one of the best examples of how fortunate England is in her umpires, who, mostly ex-players themselves, know the game inside out. I once asked John if he did not get tired, standing as he does for so many hours on end, but he explained that all those years of standing in the slips had been good training and he did not feel the strain at all.

Jim Wood, another of those men whose cricket had been interrupted by the war, had bowled hard with Jim Cornford over many years and had taken over 500 wickets for Sussex: he was yet another of the old type of dedicated cricketer who worked indefatigably and would never give up trying.

George Cox has always been one of the great characters of Sussex cricket and, given a little more concentration and a little less *joie de vivre,* might well have played for England: yet, I fancy, that none of us, not even George himself, would have had it otherwise. On retirement he went to coach at Winchester, replacing Ted Bowley, after which he returned to become the Sussex coach and was, for a time, a member of the Sussex Committee, representing Mid-Sussex. He was laughing to the end of his playing days and his advice to a young pro was, "Don't remain a promising young player as I did, for 25 years." One day in 1954 Bryan had met the scholar-poet, Edmund Blunden, in a busy street in Hongkong and at once these two Sussex exiles found themselves talking of the county, of cricket and, above all, of George Cox. It is even possible that George Cox's ears must have burned across the thousands of miles, for Edmund Blunden was one of his greatest admirers. The three men who had left the team in 1955 had given much pleasure to others by their happy and unselfish play and I am sure that they too, had gained much pleasure.

With the departure of those whom I shall always think of as the 'old' players (although I doubt if they would like to be called old even to-day) Sussex was developing a new generation of cricketers — the cricketers of my middle years and however much one may regret the loss of those one has known and whose play one has admired it is always interesting to find fresh aspirants coming along and enjoyable to conjecture what the future of this or that man may be.

The batsmen I was now watching included Don Smith from Worthing, who was capped in 1950 and who continued to play until the end of the 1962 season, having received his benefit in 1959. Smith, at his best, was a fine batsman and a strong hitter of the ball so that those who saw it will never forget his epic 166 in under two hours against Gloucestershire in 1957, when even the scoreboard could not keep up with the spate of sixes which were hammered into the pavilion; at length an elderly man was hit by one of these and was removed to hospital by ambulance muttering enthusiastically, "It was a wonderful innings," and John Marshall wrote that Don's effort was one of "sustained and galloping fury." By this time the 34-year-old Don Smith was the senior professional and he was having a particularly good season. Twenty years later I was talking to him about this exciting day and he told me how he had visited his victim in hospital. "He only had a broken jaw," said Don!

'Young' Jim Parks was given his cap in 1951 and soon showed promise with the bat and in the field, especially at cover point where his speed and agility won him much applause. One day when Sussex were playing Oxford University between showers of rain the game ended with Rupert Webb bowling in wicket-keeping pads and Jim Parks keeping wicket without, but little did we know at the time that Jim Parks in this role was just a foretaste of the future. It was soon obvious that Parks intended to make this position his own and eventually he succeeded Webb, the regular 'keeper, and went on to keep wicket for England, playing in no less than 46 Tests. Young Jim's mother had died when he was little more than a baby and I had seen his grandparents wheeling him round the ground in his pram, for they would never miss a match in which their sons, Jim and Harry, were playing. I had thus watched the younger Jim from the start of his career and I have never seen a man play any game with more obvious enjoyment. Jim Parks loved every moment of his time on the field, though the end of the story is a little sad.

I always think of Alan Oakman and Ken Suttle together and they were great friends and all-rounders, Oakman the more established bowler, but Suttle a frequent breaker of tiresome partnerships. One of the most amusing sights was to see the tiny Suttle, who was a tremendous talker, in conference with the 6ft 4in ex-Guardsman, Oakman, these little natters always setting up a ripple of laughter round the ground. We thought that Alan Oakman was tall in 1953, but then we had not seen Tony Greig. Oakman fielded in the slips, feet splayed so widely apart that it appeared that he would have difficulty in moving quickly from this stance, but Oakman held his catches well. In 'Laker's Match' (the Fourth Test against Australia in 1956) Oakman took five catches to help the Surrey bowler take 19 wickets in the match. Suttle, who also played soccer for Chelsea and for Brighton and Hove Albion, was always a bit of a humorist and once came out wearing a false 'W.G' beard and another time was attired in a huge cowboy hat. It was nice to think that there could be touches of lightheartedness in what from day to day is a fairly serious affair.

When I first saw Les Lenham in a trial match in 1957 I thought that this young man from nearby Lancing was quite a find for Sussex. He was given his cap in his first year and looked all set for a successful career. In those early days he was a graceful player with some fine strokes and he made 1,000 runs for the season on a number of occasions, but later his batting got bogged down and soon after his joint benefit with Graham Cooper in 1969 he gave up playing to take over the important post of county coach until, in 1973, he became Southern Regional National Coach for the National Cricket Association. This entails a vast amount of travelling along the length of the South Coast of England and Les Lenham is doing a grand job: always friendly and courteous, he must be very popular wherever he goes. Les tells me that his young son, Neil, who is 'cricket mad', is showing considerable promise as a 12-year-old and he is just 'keeping his fingers crossed' in the hopes that there might be yet another of those famous Sussex family connections in the future.

Ted Dexter got his cap in 1959 and needs little introduction to followers of the game, for he captained Radley in 1953, Cambridge University in 1958, Sussex in 1960 and England in 1962. When he arrived in the Sussex side he was very much the man for the moment and his swashbuckling type of cricket began to pull back the ever-dwindling crowds. Dexter was debonair, if somewhat aloof, had also gained a golfing Blue and was a tremendous racing enthusiast (the latter to such an extent that there were times when he seemed little less than ubiquitous). At school he had been nicknamed 'Lord Edward' by one of his masters, a name which followed him throughout his cricketing career.

In 1961 Dexter gave caps to Graham Cooper and Richard Langridge. Cooper, who played football for Hastings United, was an amusing character and an athletic fielder, who made 1,000 runs three times and also bowled off-breaks: as already mentioned he shared a benefit with Lenham and left soon afterwards. Richard Langridge, son of Jim, had shown a desire to play cricket from his earliest days, following his father and the other players whenever he could, absorbing knowledge all the time. He scored 1,000 in the three seasons after getting his cap and for some time was one of the opening batsmen; then, for some reason, his batting powers declined and, for a young man, he was not very fast in the field, but then neither of the older Langridges ever ran fast and there seemed to be an inherent inability to do so. Wisely, I am sure, Richard decided to train as a teacher and finally gave up first-class cricket and is now doing valuable work with deliquent children, and is living happily with his family at Beeding.

These were some of the batsmen of the 'Fifties, but now we must turn to the bowlers. Ted James was given his cap in 1950 and remained on the staff for ten years at the end of which he received a benefit. He was a hard-working county bowler, who deserved greater success than came his way, but he did take over 800 wickets, which is some measure of his worth. When Dexter gave caps to Richard Langridge and Cooper he also gave one to Ron Bell, who, like Suttle, had played for Chelsea and came to Sussex from the Middlesex ground staff at Lords. He was a left-hand bat and slow left-arm bowler, but he went after the 1964 season, possibly because slow bowling was becoming unfashionable. Marlar, as a bowler has already been discussed and his successor as captain, Ted Dexter, also comes into this category. We shall see how Dexter led Sussex into a new era and, since we are here considering the bowlers, it should be remembered that Dexter was more than just a change bowler and he took over 400 wickets. Graham Cooper, too, came into the bowling strength, but the main force of the Sussex attack lay in the strong and capable hands of Ian Thomson and Don Bates, who were given their caps in 1953 and 1957 respectively. The seemingly tireless and ever hard-bowling Thomson was one of the greatest triers I have known, looking backwards, to Maurice Tate and (had I realised) forward to John Spencer. The grey-haired and be-spectacled Don Bates, looking more like a professor than a cricketer, was slightly less powerfully built than Thomson and more prone to that quick bowler's occupational hazard — back trouble. Yet these two bowled for Sussex day in and day out completely unaware of the meaning of fatigue. Slow bowlers were growing more and more rare and the inevitable long run of what were to be called the 'seamers' or 'speed merchants' was nearly upon us, though neither Thomson nor Bates would have claimed to be more than fast medium and they did not indulge in the exaggerated run of the modern so-called fast bowler. It was this marathon that began to be so tedious and which put such a brake on the number of overs bowled in a day: for many people it had already started to destroy the enjoyment of watching the game. There have been suggestions of making laws for limiting the length of the bowler's run (which is, of course, done in Sunday cricket) but I am against any more artificial rules and would merely ask all coaches, be they at schools, clubs or at indoor nets, to do all they can to discourage young boys from this method of attack: in nine cases out of ten it is valueless and the tenth must be permitted to use it if is absolutely necessary to his turn of speed.

When Billy Griffith left it was Rupert Webb who became the Sussex wicket-keeper and he received his cap in 1950. His stay of ten years might well have been extended had not Jim Parks taken over behind the stumps in 1959, but in view of this Webb retired after his benefit in 1960. Even after his official retirement S.C. Griffith made the occasional appearance as wicket-keeper for his old Club and in 1952 he was accidentally hit on the head by a ball from one of the Indians against whom Sussex was playing. Griffith had to leave the field, his place being taken by Ken Suttle, who on several occasions acted as emergency 'keeper: Griffith was taken to hospital to have three stitches inserted and although he returned to the ground it was not to play. The Indian wicket-keeper also became a casualty and Sir Home Gordon pointed out in his article in *The Cricketer* that we had had the unusual sight of four men keeping wicket in one day.

In 1952 a young coloured South African from Cape Town, Denis Foreman, made his debut for Sussex; he also played at outside-left for the Albion. Foreman, a keen, hard hitter of the ball, never achieved as much as he could have wished although he made a lot of runs for the 2nd XI and was given his cap in 1966. I remember talking to Colonel Grimston one day as Foreman passed by. "There goes one of the nicest men I've ever had on the ground," said George Grimston. "He's always ready to help and will do anything he is asked." A year or so later George Cox, when referring to Foreman, remarked that he was "such a good servant" — words very similar to those of the Secretary several years before.

In 1952 *The People* ran a coaching exhibition at the County Ground: here boys were being given encouragement by a group of cricketers which included Alan Fairfax from New South Wales, Joe Hulme of Middlesex and Maurice Tate with his two sons, Jimmy and Michael. The young Michael I had known before the war was now a strapping young man and Jimmy had put on a lot of weight. I believe that it was during this coaching period that Maurice Tate and the Club made their peace with one another, for Maurice had never forgotten his 'sacking' in 1937, and it was good to hear that wounds were being healed.

I am glad to be able to say that the vast majority of the players of whom I have been writing in this chapter were born or grew up in Sussex and even if success did not always come their way they kept the old county spirit alive. They were the players I watched from my new seat in the deck chairs and at the same time debuts were being made by the Nawab of Pataudi, Tony and Mike Buss, John Snow and Mike Griffith, the latter playing his first game for Sussex against Surrey in 1962. He made only 1 but kept wicket extremely well so that I was delighted when I met his father, Billy Griffith, later in the day, to be able to congratulate him on his son's first appearance. This same day George Cox took me into the forbidden territory of the Men's Pavilion to see a plaque unveiled to Frederick William Lillywhite.

Matches and scores may be found in other books, but here I want to tell of a few incidents that occurred on and off the field. I was soon to discover that the wives of cricketers did not always find life fun. Mrs. Jim Langridge once told me that she could hardly bear to come to the ground, much as she wanted to do so, for fear lest her husband might not do well: she should not have been so sensitive, for Jim was one of the most reliable of the Sussex players of this time and his appearance at No 5 frequently stopped a rot. Another wife, Gay Webb, who had watched cricket at Hove since her childhood days, said she had never really enjoyed the game after she married Rupert; she was so anxious that he might drop a catch or miss a stumping that all the pleasure for her had gone. I can appreciate this anxiety, but perhaps it is better if wives are not all that interested in cricket: conversely, I may have been wise to marry a sailor!

It was wonderful to return to Horsham, Hastings, Eastbourne and Worthing when the war was over, but soon the first of these four grounds was dropped from the calendar. In 1951 both county matches at Horsham were finished in two days, resulting in a considerable financial loss for the Club. Most of the matches are now played at Hove, a deliberate policy over the years which is hard on members from the outlying areas, for Sussex has a long coast line stretching from Chichester Harbour to Rye and inland from part of Tunbridge Wells to Rogate on the Hampshire border. On the other hand the Hastings Festival at the end of the season was becoming something of a *bonne bouche* for supporters in East Sussex and in 1950 Hubert Doggart, with Jim and John Langridge and George Cox in his side, captained The South against the West Indians and I saw Clive Walcott make 103.

When Sussex played Glamorgan in 1952 a certain amount of acrimony crept into the game. Sussex had to make 301 to win and though in his enthusiasm Cox got himself run out there was still an outside chance when James Langridge and Suttle put on over 100 together, but after this Webb was out and Glamorgan had won with seven minutes to spare. All the same there had been a lot of unpleasantness over time-wasting: first wolf whistles (which may not sound odd to-day, but were almost unheard of in 1952): next Wilf Wooller, the Glamorgan captain, told Webb, to whom he was bowling, not to waste time by patting the pitch. There have been countless changes in the laws of cricket over the years and the enforcement of 20 overs in the last hour certainly prevents any sort of dilatory gamesmanship of which all counties were guilty at one time or another. The following year when Sussex played Glamorgan at Horsham memories allowed the previous season's happenings to rankle and one of the players told me that there were words exchanged between the two skippers. David Sheppard, who made a century, and Wilf Wooller were — and presumably still are — poles apart in character, and it does not need much imagination to conjure up the situation. I understand that the umpires became so annoyed with the arguments that they threatened to go off to the Carfax (the town square) 'for a coffee' until the differences were settled. Perhaps it was as well that the game was rained off. Again with Glamorgan as opponents in 1956 I had the temerity to write in my diary, "It was the slowest day *ever* in England. 143 runs in 400 minutes." Wondering where I had gleaned these facts I recently consulted *Wisden* and discovered that Wooller had taken 6½ hours to made 79. All the same that word 'ever' worries me a bit.

I had seen John Langridge badly injured by that ball from Bowes in 1932 and twenty years later when Cambridge University came to Hove I was to witness the worst accident that I have seen on the cricket field when John's brother, Jim, was hit by a rising ball from Cuan McCarthy from South Afica, who, it had been said, might qualify for Sussex. McCarthy was well over 6ft tall, with a mop of fair hair; in South Africa his bowling action had been in question and David Sheppard writes in *Parson's Pitch* that this player had said that he had no wish to bowl if his action was considered unfair. Presumably the difficulty had been sorted out, but James Langridge was to suffer. On being hit he fell in an extraordinary way, arms and legs flailing the air and then, suddenly, he was still. It was horrible. He was carried from the field on a stretcher and later we heard that he had been taken to Hove Hospital. The ball had hit him just below the ear with a crack that must have been heard all around the ground. Mrs. Langridge and the 13-year-old Richard were watching from the roof and it must have been an agonising moment for them. I remember that people sitting near by spoke afterwards of how well Mrs. Langridge had behaved and how she kept her head, but everyone was shattered. Only George Cox kept calm and made 127 before indulging in a little foolery, probably to relieve the tension. There was some divergence of opinion as to the validity of McCarthy's bowling: some said 'body-line', but Poona White said, "Nothing of the sort." Next day I left a card of sympathy at the hospital and was told that Jim was 'comfortable' — that curious euphemism that means absolutely nothing. Two bulletins were issued at cricket, the second to say that Langridge was making good progress and would be returning home during the afternoon. How well I remember the enormous relief we all felt! The result of this accident was that Jim became slightly deaf in one ear, but he shrugged this off saying that he found it very convenient at times!

Another serious accident to a Sussex player took place off the field in 1961. Driving home after playing for Oxford University against Sussex the Nawab of Pataudi, then aged 20 and captain of his side, and his wicket-keeper, Robin Waters, were injured in a car smash on the Hove front. I know the place well, drive there frequently and never forget how careful I must be at a spot where an unexpected service road always takes one by surprise. Waters was struck by flying glass, but, though taken to hospital, had escaped bad injury. With Pataudi things were otherwise: his right eye was so badly damaged that doctors at the Sussex Eye Hospital had to operate immediately and when Colonel Grimston spoke to E.W. Swanton he said that they could not guarantee being able to save the eye. I could find out little more when I went to the ground after the week-end and the accident was a disaster for Oxford with the 'Varsity match less than a fortnight away. Fortunately for Pataudi the sight of the eye *was* saved, though never again to be perfect. On the day he left hospital he was telling Harry Carpenter that he could only see a blur and that he was uncertain about his cricketing future as he was to have another operation in about two months time. Pataudi's mother came from New Delhi to be with her son and a man from India offered one of his own eyes! We know now that Pataudi was able to return to the Oxford side in 1963 and was to captain Sussex in 1966, also playing for India against all the major test-playing countries except South Africa, eventually as Mansur Ali Khan. 'Tiger' Pataudi had a droll sense of humour and once pulled everybody's leg by turning up at the ground with a large patch on his brow, saying that he had been beaten up in The Lanes in Brighton.

In 1953 Dick Twining and his wife, Rosalind, who as great friends of my mother had been saddened by her death earlier in the year, invited me to join them in their box at Lords on the Saturday of the Second Test against Australia. These boxes give their owners a chance to entertain and between drinks and superb food to allow their guests to watch the cricket. "Many there with no knowledge of cricket, but friendly enough," I wrote, with a certain amount of disdain, but dear Dick Twining, one of the kindest of men, made sure that I had a seat right at the front of the box and thus an unimpeded view of the field. Tom Graveney made 78, Hutton 145 and Compton 57 and England were all out for 372. Then Hassett was out quickly before Morris and Miller settled down together and it was time for me to leave for a dinner date. Again in 1956 I went with the Twinings to Lords and "what cricket I saw I enjoyed, but places kept being changed and towards the end I was quite unsighted." England were all out for 171, but I had seen Miller again as well as Richie Benaud, the latter taking 5-72.

On May 18th 1956 Maurice Tate died. In 1949 he had been made an Honorary Member of MCC, an honour given to very few and the following year he went as coach to Tonbridge School. In 1952 he and his wife had been hosts at *The Huntsman*, a tiny pub close to Eridge Station, where we had been to see them once or twice, then later they moved to *The Greyhound* at Wadhurst. The coaching at Tonbridge went on until, in the spring of 1956 Tate was offered a job at Butlin's holiday camp at Clacton. One weekend he came home early, felt unwell and went to bed. Shortly afterwards there was a crash: the great bowler's heart had had enough. It was a happy ending for *him*, for he hated doctors and the very thought of illness, but a terrible shock for his family. I heard the news on the radio at 7 a.m. the following morning and felt a deep sense of loss. I thought of those days with the beagles long ago, the jolly 'Tate teas' and all the overs I had seen him bowl. The county season went on — naturally — but many young people now on the ground were quite oblivious of the fact that a new, ever-bronzed ghost was haunting the Sussex turf. The great lover of and writer about cricket, John Arlott, came to the assistance of Mrs. Tate, for Maurice had only just taken over *The Greyhound* and she was in some financial difficulty. With the help and encouragement from Mr. Arlott and her husband's many friends enough money was raised to enable Mrs. Tate to carry on. Meanwhile a sympathetic pilot crashed his 'plane on the rival pub!

May 17th 1958 was a day that Mrs. Tate and her family will not forget. At 10.30 a.m. the Duke of Norfolk opened the new 'Tate Gates'. First there were speeches from Keith Wilson, Arthur Gilligan and the Duke, then Mrs. Tate handed the Duke a gold-plated key with which he unlocked the gates and they walked through together, after which the Duke returned the key to her, saying "Sussex has not forgotten your Maurice." I am not usually emotional, but at this moment there was a lump in my throat.

As ever I followed the winter tours on the radio, but now, thanks to transistors, I was curled up comfortably in bed and even dozing at odd moments, although I will always wake when a wicket falls. During the 1954-55 tour by MCC of Australia it gave me added pleasure to hear the voice of Arthur Gilligan, who was describing the play for the Australian Broadcasting Commission. When he returned home Arthur wrote of this tour in a book called *The Urn Returns,* for MCC, under the captaincy of Len Hutton, had brought the Ashes back to England.

The South African cricketers came to this country in 1960 and in April David Sheppard announced that he would take no part in matches against them because of the South African Government's policy of apartheid — an Afrikaner word comparatively new to English ears, but one with which we are now only too familiar. That night I wrote of my disagreement with Sheppard's action, feeling that cricket, like the monarchy, was above politics. Almost at once people began to take sides and to argue, but it was not until I paid a very brief visit to Cape Town in 1963 that I was able to understand more fully the issues that were at stake. The MCC warned South Africa's cricket authorities that there might be demonstrations against them when they arrived on Easter Sunday, but arrive they did and played their opening match at Arundel Castle undeterred. One other event took place this spring which was to affect the whole of South African cricket in the years ahead. A young coloured South African from Cape Town came to England for the first time in his life, quite independently of the touring team, to act as professional to the Middleton Club in the Lancashire League. The name of the young man ? Basil D'Oliviera.

The Sussex match against the South Africans this particular year was rained off without a ball being bowled.

Gradually the players of my childhood and early youth had all softly — if not suddenly — vanished away and things were becoming very different. It is difficult to pin-point the reason as to why my interest in cricket flagged a little during this time and it always made me feel a trifle guilty. Perhaps it was because I was now what Mr. Knowles had described as 'a British matron', though I heartly disliked the term as it sounded so staid, yet the fact remained that I was no longer in a position to laugh and joke with the players as I had done of old and, after removing myself from the pavilion I knew fewer of them to speak to. Recently, however, a well-known England player, when I mentioned this lapse on my part, admitted that this period in the game's history had not been one of the most attractive, a comment certainly borne out by the fact that fewer and fewer people were watching county matches. Although I hate crowds, especially the modern noise-making mobs, there is no denying that numbers do lend a sense of urgency and importance and this is communicated to the players who, normally, will respond to the encouragement they receive. But no matter how one argues there was probably no single cause for the very slight diminution of my early enthusiasm and we must look rather to the social structure which was changing faster than at any other point in the history of man, let alone of cricket. All the improvements on the ground could not compete with the motor-car which gave Mr. Everyman and his family a freedom they had never known before and they travelled further afield to the country, the beaches, to the mountains and to foreign lands. Then came television with which the planners had not yet reckoned and which has played such a large part in the modern game — a part for good or evil we hardly know as yet.

In the autumn of 1962 S.C. (Billy) Griffith, our one-time captain and secretary, became Secretary of MCC. It often seems to me that this appointment is not unlike that of the captain of a ship. The man in charge has his own work to do, but not only that, he also has a vast number of other people under his command and is also responsible to others who employ him. No man would expect such a secretaryship to be a sinecure, but it is hardly likely that Billy Griffith could possibly have foreseen the turmoil that would come into being during his term of office.

In November the Advisory County Cricket Council abolished the distinction between amateur and professional. This is no place to go into a long debate on the merits and demerits of this decision, except to say that I sometimes think that we have lost as much as we have gained. On September 8th 1962 the last Gentlemen v Players match took place at Scarborough: the words would have no meaning to-day. Now all the men (if not the women) are 'merely players'.

CHAPTER EIGHT

## ONE-DAY CRICKET IS BORN
## 1963–1972

The 'sixties were notable — amongst other things — for the Beatles, Man in Space, one-day cricket and the D'Oliviera Affair. The first three have something in common, the fourth nothing at all. The reason I claim that the first three are connected is the fact that, on the whole, the 'Fifties had been rather dull. People were still readjusting their lives after six years of war; the old ways were *too* old and they were looking for something new. Thus, four young men from Liverpool (short-haired and tidy then) were welcomed with their new form of what was now called 'pop' — no longer 'jazz'; the scientists, reaching ever further with their knowledge, now had ambitions beyond the earth on which they lived: space, the moon, even Mars, all were becoming attainable to them. This reaching out affected everyone, including cricket administrators. Crowds in the 'Fifties had become smaller and smaller and club secretaries were worried. Something had to be done. One-day cricket was, possibly, the greatest revolution since Christina Willes bowled round-arm to her brother, John, early in the nineteenth century, a casual action from which modern over-arm bowling may well have come into being. When the first ball of limited over cricket was bowled a new era had set in.

"In this century there has been no cricket season so important to the first-class game as that of 1963, and none which held out better prospects of stimulating cricket." So wrote Gordon Ross in his introduction to the *Playfair Cricket Annual*.

When Rothmans sponsored their International Cavalier games, staged in great part for a television audience, it quickly became obvious that this sort of cricket had its own following, but it was just for fun and there were no outright winners; the fun had to suffice. Later when Sunday cricket was official Rothmans were, understandably, somewhat at variance with the authorities and perhaps it is fair to say that they never received credit for what was, after all, their original idea, but that is another story. Now the Gillette razor-blade people thought up a competition on knock-out lines similar to those of the F.A. Cup, which captured the imagination of the cricketing public from the very start and the stimulus alluded to by Gordon Ross came to life: from now on almost every Gillette Cup match would find crowds of visiting fans arriving by car, coach and train to join the home supporters, and all wearing coloured favours, be-badged hats, tee-shirts, pullovers and scarves, so that there should be no doubt whatever where their allegiance lay. How different from the sober cricket of my youth! But who am I to say that it is less good: certainly the enthusiasm is there. No one has come up with anything better than the Gillette Cup so that, with the rest, I have found myself caught up in the general excitement. Only now, when there are so many one-day competitions that the County Championship is in danger of being squeezed out, do I view the new trend with misgivings.

The crowds grew bigger and bigger on Gillette Cup days: I did not attempt to bring a car to the ground and we were thankful for seats which we now booked (£1 for the season!) at the back of the cowshed: for years we sat here, monarchs of all we surveyed, until the cowshed was at last pulled down and on its site the 'Arthur Gilligan Stand' was erected — an unattractive piece of architecture which has some rather uncomfortable seating for members on its roof.

Sussex won the Gillette Cup in the first two years of its being played and have just gained their third victory. They have three times been the losing finalists. Ted Dexter, the Sussex captain found one-day cricket greatly to his liking and supported by Richard Langridge, Oakman, Suttle, Parks, Lenham, Cooper, Thomson, Tony Buss, Snow and Don Bates, he got Sussex off to a whirlwind start so that in 1963 and 1964 we were able to fly the victor's pennant from Hylda Wittome's flagpole at the County Ground.

In the first year we even defeated the West Indies in the one-day game when Thomson, Tony Buss and Bates shot out the tourists for 177. Sussex were the undoubted one-day champions and we were cock-a-hoop. As time went by others learnt what had been apparent to Ted Dexter all along — that in this kind of limited over match it is essential to set a defensive field from the start. There was an enormous crowd for the first Gillette Cup at Hove, far in excess of anything we had seen, even on Bank Holidays, since the war and it showed that people will come to watch a game when they are sure of a result: my only criticism is that there should be more incentive to get wickets: in this case, however, all 20 fell.

Soon the drawing power of the new limited over game was apparent, but at the AGM in 1965, which was held in the Long

*Ted Dexter*

*John Snow by Juliet Pannett*

Room at the County Ground, there was some discontent because it had been decreed from Lords that members should pay at the gates for future Gillette Cup matches: this had been arranged by the Advisory Cricket Committee and Sussex, although disagreeing, had been out-voted. From this time onwards everyone had to have a 'cup tie' ticket to enter the ground.

The International Cavaliers' games had shown that Sunday was too valuable a day to be lost to cricket and I see a note in my diary which mentions that on June 3rd 1967 the second day of a *county* match was played on that day for the first time at Hove: there was a good crowd, but fewer members. Having once discovered that Sunday could be used for cricket, though play did not begin until 2 p.m., it was inevitable that there would be further plans to profit by the fact and 1969 produced a new one-day competition called, at first, the Sunday League, but now known as the John Player League, as it is sponsored by the tobacco firm of that name. This contest, with television largely in mind, limits play to 40 overs and is, therefore, too much of a hit or miss affair to bring forth anything of value. Sunday cricket soon had its own complications, for any man taking part in a Test was not allowed to play on the intervening Sunday and when Tom Graveney transgressed this law he was banned from the remaining Tests. After such success in the Gillette Cup it was strange that Sussex did so badly in the J.P. League; for the first two years we finished last and many seasons passed before we reached a comparatively respectable position in the table.

It was with some dismay that I greeted the new Benson and Hedges competition which began in 1972, not the least part of my dismay being caused by the fact that the county matches were now reduced to 20: this must, surely, be the minimum number of games that can properly constitute the Championship: in 1926 we used to play every other county twice. The Benson and Hedges game is run on soccer's World Cup lines with zonal groupings to play each other first and subsequently those left in to play on a knock-out basis. The original zonal system soon proved unfair to certain counties and now the groups are changed around, Sussex finding themselves in 1976, somewhat incongruously, in the same zone as Yorkshire! Now there were three competitions apart from the County Championship, plus single wicket contests, and pressure on players and public alike have become almost too great.

We were now able to evaluate the three types of limited over game which had sprung up between 1963 and 1972. Taking the Gillette Cup first — and it came first anyway — this was a welcome diversion at a time when interest in cricket was sadly on the wane and it brought a breath of fresh air to the summer sport which was greeted with pleasure by almost everyone. Since the teams play 60 overs each there is time for strategy to be employed, for batsmen to consolidate the early position and for the later batsmen to build on this. The crowds — and they included me — loved it! The John Player League lasts right through the season and, with only 40 overs available and luck and the English weather playing a large part, several teams can be battling away for first place until the very last match. This was never more so than in 1976 when the helicopter carrying the trophy was waiting at the BBC/TV centre in London, Peter Walker aboard, uncertain whether to fly to Cardiff, where Somerset nearly won, or to Maidstone where Kent *did*. Some people consider me too much of a purist over Sunday cricket and, if they do, I accept the criticism. I defend myself, if I must, by saying that this type of cricket, played by first-class cricketers, many of them with international reputations, does little credit to them or to the game. Should I wish to see a carefree, happy, friendly game I prefer to go to some small Sussex village green, where the atmosphere is peaceful, the trees large and shady, and the cricket played seriously and at the highest ability of those taking part. This is not intended to belittle what one writer has called 'the domestic cricketer' — very much the reverse. I simply think that Sunday cricket, as represented by the J.P. League is for the uninitiated, not for the genuine lover of cricket. I have often asked old-time county players for their opinion of this type of game, and, without exception, they have said that they are thankful that it did not exist in their day. I admit, however, that as 'armchair cricket' it is quite entertaining and the tea-time interviews are generally both informative and interesting. The Benson and Hedges competition strikes me as a superfluous addition to what has become a summer of bits and pieces: it is played early in the season and leaves two out of three days cricketless at a time when players need practice and spectators are hungry to see their heroes in action once more. Incidentally, it would now be virtually impossible for any batsman to get the once famous 'thousand runs in May'.

A serious aspect of one-day cricket that must be giving food for thought to the administrators is that if a new generation of supporters (as apart from players) is brought up on the one-day game, is it not possible that it will cease to appreciate a five-day Test? Should Test match gates fall as a result of this attitude it would be disastrous from an international and financial standpoint and we might be reduced to one-day Tests to the exclusion of the real thing. Even as I write I hear that many clubs of repute are adopting limited over cricket and I do not like this at all. The desire for a finish 'at any price' should be stemmed before it takes a hold on everyone: there have been many, many extremely honourable draws in the past.

Whether we liked it or not by the mid-'Seventies sponsorship had established itself as a fact, but little did we know that in a few years traditional cricket would be hit be the greatest sponsored H-bomb yet envisaged.

During these ten years Sussex was captained by four different men. Dexter continued in command until 1966 and captained England in 30 Tests, but, fine cricketer though he was, he was apt to give the impression that the county mattered less to him than England; but he is not the only man to have done this. Dexter had stood for Parliament in the General Election of 1964 and, like Marlar, had been unsuccessful: evidently the public does not picture county cricketers as politicians. Sussex suffered their first defeat in the Gillette Cup in 1965 and next day Dexter, who had deserted his red Borgward for a new Jaguar, allowed this vehicle to run backwards over his leg whilst he was manoeuvring it near the Chiswick flyover, which was a great blow for Dexter, for Sussex and for England. Soon afterwards he decided that county cricket was no longer for him and at the end of the season he asked not to be considered for the captaincy in 1966. His place as captain was taken, for one year only, by the Nawab of Pataudi, now happily recovered from his accident, but then India claimed him to captain his own country in the forthcoming tour of England. The selection of Jim Parks as the next captain did not seem ideal, for a wicketkeeper-batsman has quite enough in the way of concentration without the additional burden of bowling changes and field placings. This proved to be the case, and in mid-1968 when it was clear, even to the spectators, that all was not well either on or off the field, it was announced that Jim Parks had asked to be relieved of the captaincy. Parks appeared on 'South To-Day', our local television programme, and next day the papers all had their own version of the story. Whilst Parks was playing for Sussex in his last match as captain at Northampton the *Evening Argus* sports page had the heading 'Why I Quit' by Jim Parks. Parks, now 36, admitted that to keep wicket and captain is asking a great deal: he wrote. "My heart is in Sussex cricket, it always has been and always will be," but he explained that the captaincy had been getting him down mentally and he had reached the stage when his whole life was being affected. He thought that his batting had suffered, though he felt that he was still keeping wicket well.

There was little doubt as to who would succeed Jim Parks and the Club Secretary, Colonel Pat Williams (who had relieved Colonel Grimston in 1964), told the press on July 19th:— "Protocol and certain formalities have to be observed. That is why I cannot give you a statement now and it must wait until everything had gone through the usual machinery." There was just the hint of a suggestion that Dexter, still playing for Sussex in Gillette Cup matches, might be invited to take on the captaincy again, but I doubt if there could ever have been any question of 'Lord Edward' returning to full-time cricket. It was, therefore, understandable that Mike Griffith should be named as the new leader, though some would have backed Tony Buss, who was the senior player. I was pleased that Michael had been chosen and he must have been one of the fastest runners between wickets in the country, who, with a little luck might well have kept wicket for England, and E.W. Swanton, with whom he toured on more than one occasion, spoke very highly of him. Mike also played hockey for Sussex and only just missed going with the England hockey team to the Mexico Olympics.

"At a meeting of the General Committee held on July 18th it was decided to accept, with regret, J.M. Parks' request to be relieved of the duties of the captaincy, which were affecting his cricket. The Committee wishes sincerely to thank Jim Parks for his hard work and strenuous efforts as captain and hopes he will now quickly regain his old form. It is particularly good to know that he proposes to continue in the game for some years to come. The Committee has asked M.G. Griffith to take over the captaincy for the remainder of 1968, wishing him every possible success and he has accepted." Such was the statement issued by Colonel Williams on behalf of the Club. Mike Griffith's first match as captain was against Kent at Hastings and he was quoted as saying:- "I have been asked to do it until the end of the season. After that both sides can assess the situation. I am hoping to have 100% support from the team and I just hope we can move up a few places in the Championship." At that moment Sussex were bottom: they could only improve. Sadly, we finished last this season, but the following year Mike Griffith brought the county up to 7th and, at the time of writing, we have not held a higher position. After 1969 another of those declines set in and, although Griffith held on in extremely difficult circumstances, it was time, in 1973, to look for a new leader.

Between the start of the last chapter and the end of the present one 22 years had passed, so it is hardly surprising that I had seen yet another generation of Sussex cricketers come and go. Those whom I had witnessed receiving their caps were now receiving their benefits and even disappearing altogether from the scene. But I am bewildered by the number of names against which is written 'not re-engaged' and 'left staff'. Amongst these were Bell, Pountain, Gunn, Ledden, Cooper, Racionzer and Lewis, whilst A.A. Jones went to join Somerset (and later Middlesex) in the game of General Post which had now begun. The young man who had the largest slice of my sympathy was John Denman; too small to be the fast bowler that was inside him he found himself in and out of the first team, but even as 12th man his cheerfulness and enthusiasm were a joy to watch. About this same time overseas registrations were getting in a muddle and E.D. Solkar from India was unable to play in Championship matches because of the registration of U.C. Joshi, his compatriot. Solkar's registration was terminated after the 1972 season and Joshi, despite having been awarded his cap, was not re-engaged after 1974.

The first of the beneficiaries of the present period was Ian Thomson, whose reward came in 1963. He had flown out to Pakistan as a replacement in 1955-6 and later he played in five unofficial Tests against South Africa in 1964-65. Only once in my many years of watching first-class cricket have I seen a bowler take all 10 wickets in an innings and this was at Worthing in 1964 when Thomson took 10-49 against Warwickshire. I well remember sitting there willing the bowler at the other end (was it Don Bates or Ron Bell?) not to get the final wicket and so spoil Thomson's feat. When we were playing Yorkshire the same year I was listening to the radio and Trueman's 300th wicket in Tests, then I rushed to the County Ground hoping that Thomson would get his 100th wicket of the year, but he did not. "Monday, perhaps?" I wrote. Thomson *did* get this wicket after the week-end and so beat Tate's record of 100 wickets in 11 consecutive seasons. Even in his last full playing season of 1965 Thomson took 85 wickets and later returned several times to play in the one-day game.

Alan Oakman retired in 1968 and, after some years as a first-class umpire, became coach to Warwickshire C.C.C. He had scored over 20,000 runs, taken over 700 wickets and held 594 catches. He had played for England in 2 Tests against Australia in this country and toured South Africa in 1956-57. It was Alan Oakman, whose hair was turning prematurely grey, who founded the Sussex Cricket Society in April 1965, the aims of the Society being "to further cricket interest and enthusiasm and to provide meetings, social functions and other gatherings." How I wish that this Society had existed in my youth! Years later, in 1973, there was a crisis in the Second Test at Edgbaston, when umpire Fagg refused to come out because of displeasure shown by the West Indies at his non-dismissal of Geoff Boycott for a catch at the wicket. Alan Oakman came out instead; then, after one over, Fagg returned. A humorous note was struck a little later when Oakman kept appearing with endless balls of different ages as the bowlers were constantly unhappy with the one they had. This business of balls going out of shape was becoming a national disease and I have never discovered whether balls are really less well made in these days or whether bowlers are getting extra fussy.

Richard Langridge retired in the same year as Oakman: he played again in 1970, but after a few games in 1971 left first-class cricket for good. For several years Richard, in the wake of other Sussex cricketers, had coached at Queen's College, Queenstown, South Africa, and at length brought back a charming wife from that country. Richard's sister, Susan, went out to South Africa to be a bridesmaid at her brother's wedding and she recalls a tall, fair boy who took the collection in the school chapel. The boy was called Tony Greig.

In 1969 Bryan, himself, retired from a life spent at sea: now we could watch all our cricket together and it has been a very happy time.

1971 brought the retirement of Ken Suttle, Don Bates and Les Lenham, all of whom received benefits. The manner of the departure of the popular little Ken Suttle was almost as unfortunate as had been that of Maurice Tate 34 years before and Suttle was equally hurt. Shortly after having made a century at Nottingham he was told by the Chairman of the Cricket Committee that he was not being re-engaged the following season, a year in which he was to have a combined Testimonial with Jim Parks. What hurt Ken most of all was that he had recently made three hundreds in eight innings and now he was told that he was being left out of the next match because it would be embarrassing if he made even more runs. This to the man who had made his debut for Sussex as far back as 1949, had made over 30,000 runs, taken 266 wickets and held nearly 400 catches. On top of this Suttle had made 423 consecutive appearances for the Club between August 1954 and July 1969, so beating the record set up by Joe Vine of 399 consecutive matches. In 1968 Suttle had made 103 against our old 'enemy' Glamorgan, but the controversy over this hundred was unfortunate. Glamorgan thought that Suttle had been caught, but neither umpire gave him out and Suttle stood his ground. Parks was batting at the other end and angry words were exchanged between him and Glamorgan's skipper, Tony Lewis. The situation grew so fraught with annoyance on both sides that umpire Phillipson warned the players. Suttle tells me that there was so much ill-feeling on the field that he thought he would get himself out by slogging at every ball, but he went from 36 to 103 in half an hour! After all this we sensed that both teams were having a fit of the sulks. The Jones brothers batted as if it were a ten-day match and I wrote that "Glamorgan were so slow that it wasn't worth staying." *The Evening Argus* stated that a letter had been sent by the Chairman of Sussex C.C.C. to the Chairman of Glamorgan C.C.C., but Suttle never received an apology from anyone.

Don Bates, who had partnered Ian Thomson as opening bowler since the mid-'Fifties, had his benefit in 1968 and, like Thomson, after his retirement played several games for the county, often in the one-day competitions. Les Lenham, whose career has already been described and who also retired in 1971, is frequently seen on the Hove ground and he has a minute office in the Arthur Gilligan Stand.

Once again Sussex had new players in the offing. Tony and Mike Buss, John Snow, Mike Griffith and Tony Greig were all capped between 1963 and 1967. Others who came — and stayed awhile — during these years were Peter Graves, who gained his cap in 1969; Geoff Greenidge from Barbados; local man, John Spencer; wicket-keeper Alan Mansell; John Barclay, who made his debut when only 16½ and still at Eton, where he played in the 1st XI at the early age of 14; Paul Phillipson, son of the rector of the Sussex village of Ardingly; Roger Prideaux of Cambridge U., Kent and Northants, who joined Sussex in 1971 and Jerry Morley from the MCC ground staff at Lords.

When Tony Buss returned from his National Service he at once claimed a place in the first team, getting his cap and taking 92 wickets in his first full season of 1963. His left-hander, all-rounder brother, Mike, who is four years younger than Tony, became the Sussex opening batsman in 1966 and also changed his style of bowling from slow left arm to left medium. Mike was always a valuable member of the side, batting later at 6 or 7, but, until his retirement in July 1978, often weighing in with useful wickets or runs. During those years when I was sitting in the South Stand there was a friend of mine who was perpetually complaining about the slowness in the field of the Buss brothers. "Someone should teach them how to run," she stated day after day, match after match, year after year. I suppose she would have said the same had she been there in the days of Jim and John Langridge. Speed, however, is a matter of build and temperament and no one could ever have turned a Langridge or a Buss into a greyhound, or, more correctly, into a Tommy Cook, Ken Suttle or Mike Griffith. Yet 'Trolley' and 'Omni' Buss, as they have been called, have served their county well, with a quiet competence which is unusual in these days of blatant exhibitionism in so many sports.

There were others who were not so dedicated to the job in hand. A player had sustained an injury which was keeping him out of the game for several weeks. One day I met this man on the ground and, somewhat naturally, commiserated with him on his bad luck, but his reply staggered me. "Oh, I don't care," he said, "I get paid just the same." All I know is that I was left speechless. Never would I have heard such words from Bowley, Tate or Cornford, Wensley, Cook or 'old' Jim Parks. This was a very small and unimportant episode, but it shocked me and showed me how greatly the world of sport had changed. Money now comes before pride and has done so increasingly with every year that has passed. No longer is there even pride in appearance and players have grown more and more scruffy, with the long hair of the next chapter adding to the general impression of 'couldn't care less.'

Of all the players on the Sussex staff as I write Peter Graves, born in Hove, must be considered the most selfless and the most unlucky. Selfless, because he always puts the team first, never stops trying and will bat wherever he is most needed; unlucky, because in his early days with the Club he suffered first illness and then frequent injury: had things been otherwise I am sure that Graves would have represented England. In days when smiling has become a rare occurrence it is nice to get a cheerful 'Hullo' from Peter Graves when one comes onto the ground. His fielding, especially in the gully, or, indeed, anywhere near the bat, has never been less than all he can give and some of his catches have been little short of miraculous. With Graves, Greenidge, Greig and Griffith in the side it was becoming increasingly difficult to put the names in alphabetical order.

John Snow, though born in Worcestershire, was educated at Christ's Hospital at Horsham and his father was, until recently, rector of Bognor Regis. John has been one of the characters in the game whom many people have loved to hate, yet he has always seemed supremely indifferent to their opinions. He came to Hove as a batsman, soon developed into a speedy bowler and, having made his county debut in 1961, was given his cap at the end of 1964, playing in the first of his 49 Tests the following year. In

## One-Day Cricket Is Born 1963 – 1972

1966 against the West Indies in the last Test at the Oval, Snow and Higgs of Lancashire put on 128 for the last wicket; Snow made 59 and Higgs 63, both career best scores, and England won by an innings and 34 runs. Next day there appeared in the press one of those memorable pictures showing the elated young pair of cricketers each brandishing a cup — of tea! It was only years later that we learned that they had been compelled to leave the slightly more heady drink which they had been enjoying, for the sake of the cameras! There were times when Sussex suffered from having Dexter, Parks and Snow in the England side, just as later 'Snowy' and 'Greigy' were said to be 'on England duty', although I never thought of it as a duty, but rather as an honour.

Before the advent of Lillee and Thomson for Australia John Snow was generally recognised as the fastest bowler in the world and it is curious that the *Playfair Cricket Annual* does not describe him as RF (right fast) until 1970, though there must have been many who played against him who found him fast before that. During the Second Test in 1968 Bill Lawry, the Australian captain, had the little finger of his right hand broken by a ball from Snow; the next year Boycott had his hand broken by a rising ball from the same bowler, who, the following day, was taken off for bowling bumpers.

Soon the Sussex fast bowler became the problem child of cricket and was dropped by Illingworth from the First Test against New Zealand in 1969 as a disciplinary measure: John had not obeyed Illingworth's instructions and the captain, quite rightly, felt that his authority should not be undermined, but Snow, who, on his own admission had not always co-operated with Colin Cowdrey's requests during the previous winter's tour of Pakistan, was once again forgiven and was a member of the 1970-71 side that went to Australia, brought victory to England and the Ashes back to this country. It was a triumph slightly marred, however, by the incidents in the final Test at Sydney and, once again, John Snow at the centre of them. On February 13th I recorded:— "When the Test came on the air at 8.15 there was a near riot. Snow had just hit Jenner on the head with a bumper (Benaud says it wasn't his fault): umpire Rowan warned Snow: Illingworth remonstrated and waved his arms and Snow went to the boundary where he was man-handled and beer cans were thrown at him. Illingworth took England from the field, followed by the umpires, but not the batsmen. Illy was told that his team would forfeit the game and he returned." In the wee small hours a few days later we had the final stages of the final Test on Radio 1 and 2. I tuned in at 2 a.m.

and it was thrilling. It took just another hour to get the last five wickets and England had won by 62. Illingworth, so often criticized, was chaired from the field and was later awarded the C.B.E. in the New Year's Honours List of 1973. (With all this excitement I had hardly noticed that the U.K. had adopted the Decimal System of Currency on February 15, 1971.) Now we were to witness these incidents over and over again on T.V. and on seeing the film I felt that Snow had acted with considerable restraint in what was a very provocative situation: he showed no retaliation and, indeed, looked more surprised than angry as he tried to free himself from the clutches of those behind the fence.

The First Test against India in England in 1971 brought with it the now famous Gavaskar incident. Snow, in a dive for the ball, knocked Gavaskar, the non-striker, flying and then threw his bat to him. Later it was announced that the TCCB in the shape of Billy Griffith had requested Snow to apologise, which he did— but in his own good time. More and more I was bewildered by Snow's personality. He has never been a publicity-seeking man and yet he has done the most unaccountable things: in this case the throwing of the bat to Gavaskar only intensified the error already made. Then came another trial by television which every sportsman must now undergo and if we saw the Gavaskar incident once we must have seen it twenty times in the next few days and on future sports programmes for weeks to come. Snow had been top scorer with 73 and it was sad that he had laid himself open to criticism yet again. Michael Melford wrote concerning the fact that anyone can make a mistake on the spur of the moment, but added that "the spur of the moment wears rather blunt when things keep happening on it. Other fast bowlers, however fiery, do not send small Indian batsmen flying . . . . ." And so on. Soon after this Snow was dropped again. I was sorry, but it really was his own fault. I always wanted to stand up for John Snow, but there were times when he made this very difficult. He was restored for the last Test at the Oval, but India won. I wrote:— "The Indians, players and spectators (of whom there were hundreds from their own country) were overwhelmed with joy and it was a delight to see their happy faces and how wonderful it is that we encourage this sort of thing in England!"

We had a distinctly disgruntled Snow playing for Sussex during 1971 when he was exiled from the England side. At Hove, against Surrey, we could see that he took a much shorter run than usual and only a few of his balls were really fast, which was one of Snow's forms of 'not trying' for which Sussex dropped him more than once. Another and almost equally infuriating form was that of making no effort to save a boundary; I have seen him run over the rope *accompanying* the ball, rather than making any attempt to stop it, which must have made him a great trial to any captain, especially as he was capable of doing so much better. The dropping of Snow made headlines in the newspapers and one of these put its piece on the front page, next to an article about the Common Market negotiations. I wonder if Snow ever read Prince Ranjitsin jhi's *Jubilee Book of Cricket,* which is dedicated to 'Her Majesty the Queen-Empress'; if so he must have found comfort in the Prince's comment that "it is necessary to husband one's strength when one is engaged in continuous first-class cricket." But at this point Snow had grown disenchanted with cricket and was saying that he intended to give it up as he was dissatisfied with the conditions under which professionals had to play.

Spectators were beginning to sense the strange nature of this enigmatic man, who, as Alan Ross wrote in *The Cricketer,* appears to switch off completely. "Others," continued Mr. Ross, "can look distracted or detached — Dexter for one — but Snow, in some curious manner that seems almost a Zen or Yoga technique, manages to become non-apparent." As Snow generally fielded at that time at third man in the S.E. corner of the ground we had plenty of opportunity, sitting as we did in the cowshed, of studying him at close range. He always fascinated me by the way he would stand, utterly motionless, between balls being bowled: you would think that he was hardly breathing: as the bowler ran up there might be the slightest twitch of an eye-lid, little more; neither hands nor feet moved, then, unless the ball were propelled towards him, he would relapse into his self-imposed trance. All who saw him will remember how well Snow, at his best, could field, for he had the long stride of the cat family and he was moving much more quickly than most people realised.

John Snow was — and is — a man of many moods and interests — poetry, music, art, writing and fishing. Having met him away from the County Ground I always felt that he was happiest when not talking about cricket: this is so very different from every other cricketer I have known. During the 1971 season I had asked him to sign his first slim volume of poems entitled *Contrasts* which had just been published. This was my initial encounter with the man whom few people understand and I wrote in my diary that night that "he is rather uncommunicative." Some might call this an understatement. I do not profess to be a judge of poetry, least of all of modern poetry, but the more I read these poems the more I realise the depth of feeling which must lie within that gaunt, spare frame, with its (then) leonine mane of hair. Gone is the fast bowler who hates batsmen; here we have the sensitive human being who is deeply distressed on seeing the poverty of India and Pakistan and is also distressed, in a totally different way, at being dropped from the England side. John's use of words is colourful and the poem dedicated to Len Bates, his old coach at Christ's Hospital, is imaginative and moving. Speaking of himself Snow writes:—

> Young I was
> yet to your wrinkled hawkish eye bountiful
> and so I was garnered with farmer's care
> to the barn kept ever empty waiting.

But then John Snow was always several people wrapped into one and I am glad that I was able to meet the non-cricketing side of him.

Michael Buss succeeded Richard Langridge as coach at Queen's College and one day suggested to one of his pupils that this good young cricketer might like to come to England for a trial with Sussex. I doubt if Tony Greig needed asking twice; he paid his own fare, arrived at the ground at Hove and from that moment it looked as if he had struck gold. Having been born in South Africa he was not available for Championship matches until 1967, but soon the 6ft 7½in giant with the long arms and legs which appeared at times to be completely uncoordinated became a familiar figure, easily picked out by all who saw him. I first watched him play against Cambridge University in 1966. These matches sometimes tend to lack interest, mainly because the counties so often rest their best players, but on this occasion I remarked that "at least I saw the South African, Tony Greig, bowl." In the same match Greig's mentor, Mike Buss, completed his maiden century of 136. Greig got his 1,000 runs and took 65 wickets in his first full season and was, therefore, awarded his county cap which is some indication of his almost meteoric rise to fame. In his first county innings against Lancashire he made 156, after which it rained solidly for two days as if to show the young man from the sun just what the English climate could do. By 1970 Greig was on top of the world and when Sussex beat Kent at Canterbury in the Gillette Cup he made 54 runs and took 5-42, so that Freddie Brown, who was the adjudicator, had no problem about making him Man of the Match. The cricketer with the blond hair, and the cheerful, yet combative, approach to the game, was making an impression wherever he went; everything was going right for him and the name 'Tony Greig' was on everyone's lips. People who normally took

## One-Day Cricket Is Born 1963 – 1972

no interest in cricket would ask me what I thought of his prospects. Was he a future Sussex captain? Was it possible that he might captain England? Tony had all it needed to hit the headlines and he never denied his South African upbringing; often, before the cameras, he was quizzed about the situation in his home country, but he always dodged these questions skilfully. Later, when browsing through some old *Wisdens*, I found him quoted as saying that he was lucky in having two countries and we should leave it at that, and so we did.

From now on a still young and largely inexperienced stranger to our shores was exposed to every sort of publicity and was lauded by the cricketing fraternity in a way that could only bode ill for the future. Short of being a god (and there were times when he was almost deified) no ordinary mortal could have withstood the adulation that was heaped upon him. Whenever I spoke to Tony Greig he was charming and courteous, but from 1972 onwards I thought that the publicity was going too far and now I feel that we, in this country, must bear some responsibility for what happened in 1977.

Throughout the period of 1963-72 Sussex had little success in terms of the Championship, the only reasonably good season being that of 1963 when, under Ted Dexter, we tied for 4th place with Warwickshire. Apart from this year and 1969 Sussex have remained firmly in the lower half of the table, but at least we had beaten the West Indies in 1966 and the Australians 1972. The poor showing of Sussex against Yorkshire in a Championship match at Bradford inspired 'Jon' of *The Daily Mail* to show an oddly-dressed female returning to her seat with two cups of tea, whilst her husband tells her, almost angrily as if it is her fault, "you've missed Oakman, Suttle, Dexter, Parks and Langridge." These players had made respectively 0,0,3,0,0. At one point Sussex had 5 wickets down for 4 runs and yet the game was drawn.

1972 was the Centenary of the Hove County Cricket Ground and before the Sussex v Northants match Mayor Lovegrove, accompanied by Arthur Gilligan and the Chairman, D.W. Wilshin, unveiled a plaque at the Tate Gates to commemorate this event. A few weeks later we were playing the Australians and the celebrations were continued. A John Player League fixture should have been played on the Sunday, but rain decreed otherwise. The outstanding happening of the afternoon was, therefore, Arthur Gilligan's presentation of his portrait, by Juliet Pannett, to the Duke of Norfolk, representing the Club. In the early evening I went to a small gathering at the home of George and Stella Grimston: also

*left to right: The Duke of Norfolk, Arthur Gilligan, Juliet Pannett*

there were Arthur Gilligan and his wife Penny, Juliet and Rick Pannett, and that man who, until to-day, had been but a voice to me, Alan McGilvray.   How often I had heard the Australian commentator's tones coming out of the air over thousands of miles as I drank my tea and ate my ginger nuts! I found him delightful to talk to and in 1955 Arthur Gilligan had said that he was "the best commentator in the world to-day." The time was all too short before we had to pile into cars for the official party in the Arthur Gilligan Stand at the County Ground, where the Australians were our guests.   The man who had burst upon the English scene this summer was Dennis Lillee, who probably deposed John Snow from his position of "fastest bowler in the world," and at the end of the tour he had taken 31 Test wickets and 53 altogether.  Penny Gilligan asked me if I would like to meet Lillee and, of course, I was thrilled.  We discussed Western Australia, from which state he comes and where relatives of my mother still live, then I laughingly said, "You don't look a bit fierce." Lillee replied with a smile, "I'm not. I'm not a bit fierce really."  I am not sure that England batsmen would agree with Lillee's assessment of himself and one article which I read amused me a lot.  It was by Michael Parkinson and part of it ran as follows:- "Quite simply the lowdown on Mr. Lillee is that he was developed at a secret weapons establishment near Canberra which had been doing research work on a robot kamikaze soldier for charging through minefields, barbed wire installations and the like. He is operated by remote control from the dressing-room, the Australian masseur being an electronics expert in disguise." There were moments now, and in the future, when we could almost have believed this to be true.

Before the start of the 1973 season the AGM had to hear the sad news of Jim Park's departure from his old club. The Committee wanted to bring in the young wicket-keeper, Alan Mansell, but Jim Parks, now 42, had no wish to hand over the gloves to a successor. The upshot of this was that Parks left Sussex to join Somerset, to which county his uncle, Harry, had gone many years before. It was not until I read 'James Michael ("Jim") Parks' under Somerset in the *Playfair Annual* that what had happened really sank in and I felt grieved that the honoured name of Parks should be listed under any county other than Sussex. It must have been a great blow to Jim Parks, senior, himself one of the soundest of players and staunchest of supporters that Sussex has ever known, who, though far from well, follows Sussex wherever and whenever he can, fearful, he told me, of ever missing a day's cricket. In 1971 I talked one day to old Jim and grandson, Bobby, then about twelve years old and already keeping wicket in adult village teams, so that I had eagerly awaited his appearance in the county. Bobby joined Sussex for net practice and played some cricket for the Sussex Young Cricketers, but after rumours that he was to join Somerset he finally went to Hampshire. In 1973 I 'watched' the John Player League match between Sussex and Somerset on television, but although Sussex won, I hated to see Jim Parks playing against us. Where were the Sussex martlets which he had once worn so proudly on his chest? At the time of leaving Sussex Parks had made 34,709 runs, made 50 centuries held 1,052 catches and made 93 stumpings.

I had seen Mike Griffith play his first game for Sussex and throughout the succeeding years he had been making himself a valuable member of the side getting his cap in 1967 — the same year as Greig. No doubt Griffith would have preferred to keep wicket, but with Jim Parks *in situ* this was not possible, so Mike had made Jim's old position at cover his own and an excellent fielder he was. The story of how Griffith took over the captaincy from Jim Parks has already been told, but he looked less and less happy, so that when we heard that he had been appointed to lead again in 1971 we hardly knew whether to be glad or sorry. Yet, in 1972, Mike Griffith was to lead Sussex to victory over the Australians by 5 wickets, a thing that had not happened since 1888, but at the end of the season he let it be known that he did not wish to to be considered for the captaincy in 1973.

No story of cricket during these past years would be complete without mention of South Africa. Because of the South African Government's policy of apartheid there had been doubts as to whether the 1960 tour would take place, but all had gone well. MCC toured South Africa, unofficially, in 1964—65 and the following summer South Africa returned the compliment. But the political situation was getting no better and, whilst most cricket lovers deplore the theory of apartheid, there have always been disagreements about the best way of dealing with the problem. In 1966, the Cape-coloured Worcestershire batsman, Basil D'Oliviera, made his first appearance for England at Lords. He was so proud — and in the right way. When the Queen shook his hand he could hardly believe it was true.

England were due to visit South Africa again in 1968 and Billy Griffith, as Secretary of MCC, went to that country to assure himself that whatever team he picked would be welcome. The assurance he sought was not forthcoming. Then D'Oliviera made that now historic 158 against the Australians at the Oval and was, eventually, chosen for the MCC tour, but D'Oliviera was not acceptable to the South African Government, and so the tour was cancelled and none has taken place since. Probably the most disappointed man of all was D'Oliviera himself: above everything he had wanted to walk onto South African cricket grounds, where he had been segregated as a 'coloured boy', as an equal with the white man. Now this would never be. The 1970 tour by South Africa was subsequently called off, the leaders of the 'Stop the 'Seventies Tour' campaign including David Sheppard and Young Liberal Leader, Peter Hain.

Instead of the South African tour a series of games entitled England v The Rest of the World were played in 1970, but to the chagrin of those who took part they were never recognised as first-class. Snow played in all five matches and took 19 wickets, Greig played in three. From now onwards it was predictable that South Africans would seek to play their cricket here during the English summer and each year more and more have been joining English counties. If it were not for the South African policy of apartheid would Tony Greig ever have considered playing for Sussex ? He would almost certainly not have played for England.

Perhaps I may be permitted a brief personal story which is very appropriate at this point. During 1963 I spent much of my time travelling in the *R.F.A. Fort Sandusky*, with Bryan in command.

In the spring I was in the Mediterranean, mainly in Malta, but we exercised with Greek and Turkish navies off Crete and Greece. Back home I paid a fleeting visit to Scotland to see Nanny, thus missing the Gillette Cup Final and Sussex's first win. I had been torn in two, as in childhood, by conflicting desires, but, since Nanny died the following Februrary I was glad that I had made the right decision, for had I gone to Lords I should never have seen her again. Directly I got home from Scotland I was off again, on a voyage round Africa, but it is only the South African part of the voyage that concerns us here. We did more exercises, this time with the South African navy, off Cape Town, and found them friendly and hospitable, but we had a Seychellois crew, of various shades of skin, and these had been given strict instructions not to become involved in any sort of discussion on religion or politics in South Africa. As soon as we docked at Cape Town I went ashore and was taken by taxi all about the city, including the area known as 'District Six'. Next day I wandered on foot up the beautiful Adderley Street, buying Christmas cards in the sunshine. I was seeing bi-lingual signs everywhere — at taxi ranks and at 'bus stops — all saying 'Whites Only' or 'Blacks Only' in English and Afrikaans. Although this was extremely alien to the British way of thinking I suppose I was not altogether surprised: that surprise came later when I went to look at the fine new railway station, built on land reclaimed from the sea. Others may describe this station with more accuracy, but one thing that remained firmly in my memory was the left luggage department. I saw a cubby-hole marked 'White Luggage Only'; how stupid, I thought; my eye travelled along the line and I saw 'Black Luggage Only'; well, to my mind having admitted the first, that is at least logical: then I saw the third compartment. Here were written the words that appalled me *"white luggage left by blacks"*. For a moment I stared, not knowing what this meant, then light dawned. If I, as a white person, sent a 'coloured boy' with my luggage to the station, he would, naturally, wish to leave it with other 'white' luggage, but being a non-white himself he could not queue up with other white people and must, therefore, take my cases to a completely separate compartment. I have never forgotten (what seemed to me then and still does seem) the insanity of this and it returned to the forefront of the mind with striking clarity in 1968 at the time of 'The D'Oliviera Affair' and made me aware of how deeply this philosophy is ingrained in the South African mind.

CHAPTER NINE

## OF THIS AND THAT

Perhaps we should now stop this scamper down the post-war years and take a moment to 'stand and stare' at a few aspects of cricket that were not on the field of play. Although my main interest has always been in the game itself I realise that no cricket would exist without the numerous activities behind the scenes, which, all combined, help to constitute the County Club.

In 1950 Billy Griffith's place as Secretary was taken by Colonel George Grimston, who had been in the Winchester XI in 1923 when he had headed the school bowling averages: he made his first appearance for Sussex the following season and played 17 innings during his army career: he was also an accomplished hockey player, who had represented Sussex. George Grimston remained with the Club for the next fourteen years throughout a time when cricket was having to decide where it was going next, and he saw it into the one-day era before he left. Colonel Grimston was of the old school of secretary who, as an army man, expected orders to be obeyed and for the most part they were. No doubt awkward moments occurred in the administration of the Club, but there were none of the violent upheavals which we have experienced in recent years. George Grimston was succeeded by Colonel Pat Williams, previously an officer in the Royal Corps of Signals, whose hobby was painting and he made a picture of the Hove ground which he presented to the Club. After six years Colonel Williams handed over to Brightonian Arthur Dumbrell, a truly Sussex man who had served in the Sussex Yeomanry and who is never happier than when ferreting out some obscure, but intriguing, piece of cricketing history and he has done much good work as the tireless honorary secretary of the Sussex Cricket Society. Mr. Dumbrell was followed, in 1974, by Commander Ian Stoop, D.S.C., R.N., but as the years went by it was apparent that the secretaryship demanded the experience of a business man rather than the qualities of leadership. The days of Lance Knowles, Billy Griffith, George Grimston and Ian Stoop had gone and all county secretaries are now confronted with forms and legal documents which are completely foreign to the soldier or the sailor. In due course Stanley Allen, M.B.E., a local solicitor, was appointed, but it was not the secretaryship I had known of old and when I heard Mr. Allen describe the Club as 'an industry' I realised just how much things had changed.

The idea of parking behind the pavilion, where players' cars now jostle for position, is but a memory of long ago: each year more and more spaces have been labelled for Secretary, Captain, Chairman, Coach, Committee and two spaces marked 'Umpire'. In 1956 I had tended to take up my car position to the north of the Harmsworth scoreboard, because, with the road behind, I could leave when I wished without disturbing anyone. At the beginning of 1958 I found a board which said that I must not park here, because 'Nursery Turf' had been laid and ten years later there was still being a hoo-ha, as I called it, about parking at this spot. Once more I moved, this time to a site near the Tate Gates, convenient for where I now sat in the South Stand (cowshed) and easy for getting out ahead of the crowds. After a while, however, parking by the gates was not for the likes of me and this space was reserved for Committee Members, the Honorary Medical Officer, Hotel Manager etc., and I was on the move again. For a while I parked behind the Arthur Gilligan Stand, but then, in 1977, members in cars were instructed that they could no longer enter by the Tate Gates, but must use the tiny, narrow entrance in Palmeira Avenue, which leads straight onto the car park. By now we were sitting on the pavilion roof so it hardly mattered, but I do rather resent being pushed around, never able to park where I wish.

The tennis courts at the north end of the ground have long since disappeared and now half their space is used for county nets and half for overflow car parking: often, as one looks round the sparsely filled ground, it would seem that there are more cars than people.

The pavilion at Hove is not large by modern standards, the seating is adequate, if not particularly comfortable, and the refreshment facilities are somewhat cramped. When I went to sit in the South Stand it was easier and quicker to get tea and sandwiches at what is called the 'Chalet' than to return to the pavilion. This Chalet was not, as is so often stated, built for the Home Guard during the last war: it was there when I was a child and, being anxious to discover its origins, I visited the Building Controller's Office at the Hove Town Hall, where Mr. Ravenhill showed me the plans which prove that it was erected between April and July 1923 as a 'temporary tea pavilion'. During the 1939-45 war it was used as a *Silver Lady* canteen for the Home Guard who were training on the ground and Messrs. Burchell and Beach, as well as others

'The Chalet'. Built as a temporary tea pavilion in 1923

working there, were able to get lunch at 10d per head — less than 5p in to-day's money! The chalet is a large glass-fronted structure which is used as nets in the winter, and in summer gives plenty of room to enjoy tea, coffee or what you will, either inside or on the small lawn near by. For years the chalet was under the supervision of Mrs. Leaney and her late husband, Fred, who, with Esme Straw, Nancy, Jean, Phyl, Mabel and the others, have looked after us so well over the years that I should like to pay special tribute to them: their friendliness and help have added so much to our pleasure on 'cricket days'. That this chalet is still rendering valuable service 55 years after being put up is a compliment to its builders and it will be a sad day when it, like the cowshed, is demolished to make way for yet another horrid up-dated construction.

After Tom Burchell, Beach and Prior retired I had not known the groundsmen, except as figures in the distance mowing the grass, rolling the pitch, marking out the wickets, or, less happily, racing for the covers when the rain came down. For some time Charlie Holden was head groundsman, but in 1967 Len Creese, the old Hampshire player, who had been in charge of the Hastings ground, came to Hove and he made the place very beautiful with flowers and newly-planted trees and was also devoted to his alsatian, Nikko, the only dog allowed to roam the ground freely, but which met a sad end when it picked up some sort of poison and died: its master was heart-broken. Creese erected poles above the Welfare buildings and from these flew the flags of all the cricketing countries — a nice touch this, I thought, but, unfortunately, the flags were left up night and day and in due course they began to look pretty tattered. The Indian flag was in such a deplorable state that when the tourists came to this country we felt thoroughly ashamed and a message went through to the Indian High Commission for a replacement which was brought by road from London as speedily as possible. In 1974 the Pakistan flag was stolen during the night and now the flags have disappeared altogether, except for the county flags and, during the Queen's Silver Jubilee Year in 1977, the Union flag. Len Creese was followed by his pupil, Peter Eaton: not a great talker like his predecessor, he is a hard worker and in the sun-drenched summer of 1976 won the Watney Mann Challenge Trophy and £150 for his efforts on the Hove pitches that season.

The groundsmen are still in the dug-out under the Committee Room from which Tom Burchell brought out the Sussex flag which he gave me all those years ago. Not so the umpires. First they came out ahead of, but through the same gate as, the players, and shared the dressing-rooms. Then it was generally agreed that they should have separate accommodation and, at Hove, they shared the dug-out with the groundsmen, which must have made it pretty cramped. Now, I am glad to say, umpires have been rewarded for their long hours in the field with their own quarters, next to the dug-out, but completely private and they eat at a separate table, with the scorers, in the dining-room, which enables them to leave when they will, for if any man is not in position when the luncheon interval ends it must not be an umpire or a scorer.

John Langridge, as an umpire, could once be distinguished easily by the white cap he wore, but now so many umpires have these caps that recognition is more difficult, though Sussex followers will never fail to know which is John. Now white *hats* and even straw hats are worn by some umpires and the long old-fashioned white coats, which, if the umpire were a trifle short almost reached to his ankles, has given way to a smart, rather dapper short coat, which makes people like David Constant and Ray Julian look like ultra-efficient dentists. These coats have a loop in the side through which can be slung the bowlers' sleeveless sweaters which had been the bane of all umpires in the past: the long-sleeved sweaters had posed no problems as the umpires always tied them, by the arms, around their waists. During the tremendous heat of 1977, when *The Daily Telegraph* headlined the amazing news that 'MCC Remove

Jackets at Lords' with a temperature of 93° (34C), umpires were allowed to leave off their white coats, provided they kept on their ties — the Englishman's last bastion of respectability. John Langridge declared that he did not mind the heat and insisted on keeping on his coat, saying that he would not know where to keep his bowling counters without it. Incidentally, it is surprising the amount that is kept in those capacious pockets — anything from new and replacement balls to screw-drivers and safety-pins, and now light-meters!

At the start of 1930 a fine new scoreboard in memory of Sir Hildebrand Harmsworth was erected on the eastern side of the ground; it was surmounted by a three-faced clock (it has since lost its two side faces) and was universally acclaimed, E.W. Swanton praising it as one of the clearest in the country. In the late 'Fifties it became the first board to have an extension made to allow for all the additional figures required by the new and complicated method of scoring which arose. The scoreboard on the western side was built in 1934 in memory of Ranji and in 1955, when the Welfare buildings were opened, a new complex was created consisting of Secretary's Office, Welfare Association, scoreboard, scorers' box and press box, a general purpose cubby-hole, as well as the printing office and — to-day — the Library. In 1975 we were advised that the grand old Harmsworth scoreboard must have a drastic overhaul and would be given a new look. I wrote to the Secretary, as did others, expressing a hope that none of the clarity would be lost although we knew that the inner workings of the old board had had their day. Commander Stoop replied telling me of the Harry Tate mechanism which was now rusting away, and assuring me that the Club had gone to a lot of trouble to make certain that the new board would be as simple to read as the old one had been: he also expressed the gratitude of the Club to the sponsors, the Sussex Mutual Building Society. I wish I could say that Commander Stoop's optimism had been fulfilled, but the new board is far less clear than it was before and the figures are half the size. The new workings had their teething troubles as regards manipulation and, having examined the inside with Harold Beardsmore, who helps to work the thing, I wondered who had thought up such an intricate affair. If the old board were Harry Tate, surely the new one is Heath Robinson. A man from Leicester — I think — kept coming to see it through its fits and starts, but it has remained slightly temperamental. The old board had the advantage of the fact that when a batsman's runs went up the total went up as well: now I have visions of little men running from one tin box (which works each section) to another, trying wildly to keep up with themselves. No wonder, when wickets fall quickly, they are all at sixes and sevens. Would it be a good idea to have a standard scoreboard facia for the main grounds? If so, I would suggest our old board should be used as the basis for any new design.

I could not begin to enumerate the various points systems which have been in vogue in the last fifty years, but in 1952 the attempt to get it right was continuing and this brought about a curious situation in the game against Warwickshire at Hove which had resulted in an exciting tie. Because Sussex had lost on the first innings they were awarded only 4 points, whereas Warwickshire took 8. Many Sussex people were dissatisfied, claiming that a fairer apportioning of the points would have been 6 each. In 1957 things were little better and I wrote that "Gloucestershire lead Sussex on the first innings, but with the new complicated scoring system nobody seems to know who gets what." I can only quote a book of reference which says that "points were awarded to the side scoring at the faster rate measured in runs per over when the first innings lead was taken." Stop watches and slide rules were needed by scorers and the only man not confused that day was Don Smith who was busy making his mammoth onslaught on the Gloucestershire bowling. In 1968 the first innings points were abolished and bonus points given for batting and bowling in the first innings of 100 overs only.

Scorers, like the rest, have come and gone: I remember Messrs. Gaston, Isaacs and Killick in pre-war days; later W. Locke scored for several years and his son, Derek, now looks after our car. After Mr. Locke had left George Washer must have scored for Sussex for nearly twenty years until his death in 1974. Apart from travelling many thousands of miles in the Land Rover put at the disposal of the Club by the late Norris Rothwell (who also acted as Honorary Librarian) George Washer compiled an invaluable book of statistics of Sussex County Cricket from 1728 until 1957. This is, indeed, a bedside book for Sussex members and others and I hope that it will be brought up-to-date by someone who has the mind for these matters — and the time. After George Washer's death W. Denham, young John's father, scored for most of the Sussex matches, but he began to suffer ill-health and now the scorer is Geoffrey Saulez, who uses the same scoring system as that master of figures, Irving Rozenwater. Mr. Saulez, who has watched Sussex cricket since the mid-'Thirties, has been scorer for many Test sides on tour and he was the official scorer in the Centenary Test Match at Melbourne in 1977.

The scorers' box is next to the scoreboard on the western side of the ground and is, therefore, out of sight of members sitting in the pavilion. Before the number of overs was put on the scoreboard a coloured disc would be displayed to show when the new ball was due; the number of overs, like everything else, varying with the years. Never having seen this signal at Hove I was mystified when it appeared at the Oval. The disc was lemon-coloured and at the same time drinks were brought out, so I imagined that this must be a signal for refreshment. I believe it was an amused John Langridge, sitting nearby, who put me right!

During the 'Seventies Irving Rosenwater came to visit me, so that he might see my 'cricketana'. Later, when I wrote my article on Tommy Cook, I had assumed that 'T.E. Cook', playing for N.E. Transvaal, was the Sussex Cook, but Irving Rosenwater delved back into the past and wrote to me that "someone out there has sought out Xenophon Balaskas, the old Test player, who played in the North Eastern Transvaal match v MCC of December 1938 and he says that the player concerned in that match was Trevor Cook, described as a local boy. This same Trevor Cook played after the war as well. I think Tommy was in Cape Province before the war, and so *prima facie* was not likely to turn out for N-E Transvaal — but a great many people were confused. Trevor Cook's initials were T.E. Cook and his entire first-class career consisted of two first-class games." This has taught me not to take anything for granted and I can see that any errors I have made in this book will be quickly snapped up by Irving Rosenwater.

The Sussex Cricket Society celebrated its tenth birthday in 1975. The first chairman was C.G. Gerrard, the tireless honorary secretary Percy Edwards, and the first President, A.E.R. Gilligan. The Society has grown beyond all expectations and has over 600 members, some living as far away as South Africa and Rhodesia; it is a member of the Council of Cricket Societies and contact is kept with those who join by means of a monthly news letter. Regular winter meetings are held, generally at the County Ground Restaurant, and speakers have included famous cricketers, journalists, county secretaries, BBC television and radio sports commentators, photographers and an artist, the last being Juliet Pannett, who made a quick charcoal drawing of George Cox, which she presented to the Society. There is an Annual Dinner and the ladies of the Society hold 'Bring and Buy' coffee mornings to raise funds and to help the Sussex Young Cricketers; they also vote for the 'Sussex Player of the Year', who is given a cup. Coaches are run to away matches and these are well supported and help to give the players the encouragement which they need.

Recently all cricket grounds have been seeking new ways to make money in addition to the members' subscriptions and the gate. Apart from the activities of the Welfare Association we now have squash courts which have been built at the north-west corner of the ground and for some years there has been a Donkey Derby on Easter Monday, whilst the lastest venture was a Beer Festival in the spring of 1978. A permanent eyesore is that of the vast amount of advertising boards that have sprung up all around every county ground throughout the country, ours no less than any other, which invite you to bank with a certain bank, buy your house through a certain building society, put special petrol in your car, soothe your inside with a particular patent medicine, paint your house with a well-known brand of paint or keep out the cold with the help of a famous double-glazing firm: now that we have the Schweppes County Championship it is necessary to be advised of the fact. When these boards were first put up people complained bitterly to the Secretary, but later they found that they acted as a windbreak and the complaints died down. One of the gimmicks at Hove has been the request that spectators bring egg-boxes of a firm of egg-marketers and put them in a gadget that looks like a 'Dr. Who' telephone kiosk, except that it has only a small slit instead of a door: the Club is allowed 2p (it was originally 1p) for each box deposited and in the early days of this scheme Tony Greig's smiling picture decorated every poster for eggs — fortunately hen's eggs, not ducks! Four huge eggs in egg-cups stand at each corner of the field and a reward is offered to the batsman who can successfully clout one of these: so far as I know this has not happened yet and the only use an egg has served has been as a leaning post for a tired John Snow! A country-wide wine firm has put up its own tent near the Arthur Gilligan Stand and this is hired out to visiting business houses, which makes it something like a commercial version of the private boxes at Lords.

The Club Shop has been one of the most welcome of the money-making devices of recent years. It was started in 1975 by Richard Sharpe, first in a caravan, presented by the Chairman of the Welfare, Reuben Levenson, then, as trade expanded, in a larger, more solid wooden structure beneath the flagpole. Every sort of souvenir of a visit to the Sussex H.Q. is on sale and a large amount of clothing ranging from woollen pullovers with the martlet badge on them to tee-shirts, ties, caps and sunhats. There is a first-rate book department and every new cricket book appears quickly on the shelves; many players sign their book when they come to the ground, and the Sussex players sign their photographs, these now adorning my almost creaking album.

The small Library which Norris Rothwell collected some time ago soon outgrew the tiny room in which it was housed and he moved it to a much bigger room above the Welfare Office. This is a wonderful place in which to browse and the big table in the centre enables the reader to do some detailed study. After Norris Rothwell's death the Librarian was Maurice Farncombe and when he, too, died H.A. Osborne took over and has put in a lot of hard work as new volumes pour onto his over-crowded shelves. In 1978 an exhibition of photographs and other cricketana, including Ranji's blazer, was mounted at the Hove Museum.

In 1974 came the downfall of that male stronghold at Hove, the Men's Pavilion. Now women are admitted, but although I see no objection to this I have never wanted to sit amongst the beer and smoke and we prefer our lofty seat on the roof, where we shall probably remain.

At the AGM in 1973 Frances Mannings, a maths teacher, proposed that the word 'male' be deleted from the rule concerning those eligible to stand for the Committee or Council. Rather predictably her motion was defeated and I could almost feel the shudder of disapproval at the mere thought of a woman's influence on the Sussex Club. The following year Frances, quite undaunted, returned to the attack, but failed to get the required majority by just seven votes. Then, in 1975, she gained a sweeping victory of 113-31 votes in her favour, though George Cox voted against and I wondered why. Frances told me that the first man to congratulate her had been Arthur Gilligan and a few days later he said that he and Billy Griffith were delighted that the women had achieved victory, whilst Commander Stoop was quoted as saying, "It's a sign of the times. In any case, we are aware that it is International Women's Year." Frances wrote to me:— "It was so kind of you to come last night. What a victory! I never expected such a majority. I think Poona got quite a few votes." There were still a lot of diehards and Poona had been a bit worried about the 'facilities' for Committee members, which, if a woman were present, would have to be altered! But every hurdle can be overcome, this no less than any other.

Shortly after the AGM the Committee invited Frances Mannings to form a five-woman Advisory Committee, the terms of reference being:— "To help the Club Committee in the running of the Club in whatsoever manner the Club may approve." This was a cautious statement and there was still a long way to go, but Frances knew what she wanted and persevered until she got it. The first meeting of the Ladies' Advisory Committee was held at the County Ground, those present being Miss F. Mannings, Mrs. E. Luccock and Mrs. I. Stenning. About this same time Bishop David Sheppard's wife, Grace, was saying that she had come to agree with her husband that women could and should be ordained.

It is never easy to get a new venture off the ground and the Ladies' Committee had its early problems, but the season ended with a party which showed what could be done. This was held in the Arthur Gilligan Stand on the last day of the Kent match in September and was organized by the ladies in the form of a wine and cheese evening which was attended by nearly 300 cricket-lovers and their friends who paid 75p each. It must have been largely due to Tony Greig's 'captaincy' that all the Sussex players turned up — as guests, of course — and I think that everyone enjoyed the occasion. I saw Jerry Morley and Jerry Groome handing round plates of 'eats'; Spencer and Phillipson operated as wine-waiters; Peter Graves appeared to have put himself in charge of the cheese and others were just tucking in. John Snow was as remote and detached as ever, but Tony Greig had brought his lovely wife, Donna, and members and players mingled happily. We had a chat with Tony and Donna, the latter having been speaking on 'Woman's Hour' earlier in the day when she had been explaining the difficulty of keeping Tony supplied with enough spotless white trousers to carry him through the season. I asked if she were keen on cricket, but no, on the whole she preferred tennis! It was a really happy gathering: for almost the first time I can remember players and spectators were joining together as friends — no longer 'them' and 'us'. £101 was raised and the money handed over to the Welfare Association to be used to improve the kitchens in the Arthur Gilligan Stand.

Frances Mannings stood for election to the Committee/Council in 1975 and was defeated at this first attempt, but she succeeded in the year that followed. It had been a long battle, but the determination of this young woman had reaped its reward at last and she was the first lady member of the Sussex C.C.C. Council. We were not the first county to have a lady on Committee or Council for already Somerset and Leicestershire had taken this step and Yorkshire were to follow. In August 1977 Sussex members were summoned to a Special Meeting in order to hear the proposition to reconstruct the Committee, which, with its accompanying Council, had become an unwieldy piece of machinery. The suggestion was to abolish the Council and have one main Committee, a move which, it was hoped, would make the running of the Club easier for everyone. The new plan was put to us by S.C. Griffith, who had been the Chairman of the Structure Committee which had drawn it up. There are few people in the cricket world to-day who know more about cricket administration than Billy Griffith, so that when he recommended us to accept the scheme for the new committee I, and a large section of the meeting, voted in favour. Elections for this new Committee took place in December and Miss Mannings and Mrs. Eileen Cotter became the first women on the main Committee, which would take up its duties on April 1st 1978. I never wanted to be on any Committee myself, but if the ladies can come forward with useful ideas and can help to carry them through their presence can only be beneficial to the Club.

The old Committee Room had become too cramped for the number of sponsors who now have to be entertained at different times and early in 1978 the room was enlarged and a presentation balcony included. This was the gift of Mr. Spen Cama, who, ever since my childhood, has been an ardent supporter of the Club. He, himself, took me to see the extension and in the wall above the balcony there is a small plaque which reads:-

> The extension of the Committee Room and the provision of
> the Presentation Platform were the gift of
> MR. SPEN CAMA
> who particularly wishes these additions to be
> dedicated to the memory of his boyhood hero —
> that great man of Sussex cricket
> ARTHUR (A.E.R.) GILLIGAN
>
> April 1978.

Cricket grounds, however attractive and however many people come to watch or to help with the administration, have little meaning without the players. Nowadays they like to be called 'entertainers', though I prefer to think of them as sporting competitors. One is liable to be called a fuddy-duddy if one offers any criticism, yet, if anyone has watched cricket as long as I have done, he is bound to make comparisions. I have already mentioned the slovenly attire of *some,* not all, of the modern players and I do not intend to pursue the matter: it may be just a fashion and I hope it will soon change. What worries me more is that cricketers of to-day all look so strained and miserable. They almost fall out of their cars and disappear into the pavilion with no inclination for a word to passers-by: they are obviously tired and certainly were, until recently, underpaid. The latter problem has been dealt with by the TCCB, the former is one which might be considered at county level. I voiced my opinion on this unfriendliness to John Snow and he replied, laconically, "It's all this rushing about." When we discussed the subject further John explained that "The game is much more professional to-day." But then there are so many meanings of 'professional' and if those who come to watch feel less welcome, cricket as a county game is going to suffer. Yet I have some sympathy with the county professionals in the amount of travelling they have to do in one first-class season and I should like to see more clubs adopt other means of travel than the private car. Players may howl in disapproval, but one moment of inattention on a long journey, perhaps after a wearisome day in the field, could be so disastrous that it makes one shudder. Derbyshire C.C.C. have a large and very comfortable coach in which their team arrived at Hove, and I was greeted with a cheerful 'Good morning' by men I had never seen before. An arrangement of this nature would save Sussex money and, perhaps, the players' lives. One feels it is only a question of time before misfortune strikes — as it struck Colin Milburn years ago. One player told me that often, especially in a Sunday League match, it is the team which is most awake on the day that wins the game.

A nasty habit which has crept into modern cricket, probably as a result of televised football, is that of the show of feelings expressed on the field of play. Harold Larwood, when he came to England from Australia in 1977, was disgusted by all the hugging and kissing that went on. "When we got a wicket," he said, "we just sat down." The picture conjured up in the mind of Maurice Tate hugging Ted Bowley or 'Tich' Cornford is as laughable as it is inconceivable. I still find it unsporting to gloat at the downfall of a rival, but then times have changed and the exhibitionism is, I fear, all part of being entertainers. Still more do I deplore the 'dissent' which is often shown when a man disagrees with the umpire's decision: these umpires already have a difficult enough task and it is up to all players to give them their full support.

There are, naturally, changes which are not controversial and one of these is the capabilities of those who bat at 9, 10 and 11. In my early days of watching cricket these later batsmen were bowlers pure and simple, even if this sounds a little Irish. They were not expected, still less relied upon, to get runs, and their job was to 'throw the bat', connect if they could and if a flukey six or four resulted this was a bonus and one greatly appreciated by the crowd, who would let out a great roar whilst the bowler-turned-batsman would grin a little sheepishly. To-day you will find men batting at the tail-end who are far from 'rabbits' with the bat, but are, in fact, no mean performers, who are often called upon to take on the unenviable role of night-watchman. The era of the all-rounder is with us: batsmen can bowl, bowlers should bat and all are expected to show speed and agility in the field.

The question of first-class registration for counties is much in the mind of the TCCB as I write and before this reaches the reader much of what I say now may prove to be overtaken by events: all the same I offer a few thoughts of my own.

It is understandable that cricketers who, at the end of a long and distinguished career, cannot retain their places in their county side, should ask to be released to play for another county which can assure them of a regular place. We should be dogs-in-the-manger if we denied them this right, but I do not like to see players hopping about from one county to another as the whim takes them: I find it all very confusing and it must, surely, destroy the county spirit. If I dislike seeing our English — and Welsh — cricketers changing counties still less do I care for the influx of overseas players that has come about in the last ten years. Yet Sussex invited the most famous overseas cricketer of them all, K.S. Ranjitsinjhi, to play for them in 1895 and his nephew, Duleepsinjhi, came to Sussex in 1924. But Ranji and Duleep, like D'Oliviera and Greig later, were overseas players who, after qualification, were eligible to play for England and these men come into a different category. I, like most other cricket-lovers of these islands, have obviously delighted in great players like Mushtaq, Lance Gibbs, Mike Proctor, Barry Richards, Gary Sobers, Asif Iqbal, Engineer, Kanhai, Andy Roberts, Clive Lloyd and host of others: the public has, no doubt, been grateful for the opportunity of seeing so much of these men, be it in the flesh or on T.V., but each one has been debarring a young English player from his county side and, consequently, diminishing the number from which an England team can be potentially chosen. Surely it is time we put our cricket house in order! The situation had reached such a crisis that, during 1977, the TCCB decreed that only two overseas players would be permitted in a first-class County match at the same time.

It may be of interest to follow the history of membership tickets over the years. The first three I had — 1926, 1927, 1928 — were indentical and told me that I had free admission to Ground and Enclosure to all county matches in Sussex and that I might in-

*Of This and That* 129

troduce one lady or gentleman to the Enclosure. Then, 1929, although the price did not change, my ticket was called a 'Lady's Ticket', much to my disgust! The following year the subscription went up to £1.0.0. — quite a considerable leap and in 1934 there was the additional information that I must live within seven miles of the County Ground. No difficulty there. In the spring of 1936 when I acquired my little car I had to buy a different ticket so that I could bring this beautiful vehicle into the ground. Surprisingly, this cost only £1.11.6 and included various extra privileges for introducing friends into the Pavilion. It also said that I could practise at the nets *without* professional bowlers! I smiled at this at the time for I had been practising *with* professional bowlers for years. What makes me smile even more to-day is the last paragraph of this ticket which admits 'Carriage or Motor Car Free, with Coachman or Chauffeur in Livery.' I think that this delightful sentence remained in force until the Second World War.

I should have been unlikely to have a carriage with or without 'Coachman in Livery', but instead of a car I nearly had a horse. Next to cricket, riding was my greatest passion. I thought that I would buy a horse, allow the riding stables to use it in exchange for its keep, then I could ride after school and at week-ends. The idea fell through, partly because we could not settle the insurance problem, but even more because I did not see the Club allowing me to tether a horse behind the pavilion, where, in those spacious days I eventually parked my car. Sadly, the little Singer car broke down after a year or two and my mother refused to pay for any more expensive repairs, so I was demoted to a Lady's Ticket again for the seasons of 1938 and 1939.

During the war we all paid whatever we could: all my tickets until 1943 were signed by Secretary W.L. Knowles, that of 1944 by Sir Home Gordon, Bart., and that of 1946 by Colonel S.C. Griffith, who had become secretary — captain that year. After the war the Lady's Ticket remained at £1.0.0., but a full member paid £3.0.0. From 1951 to 1971 there was no price on the tickets, but in 1972 I was paying £8 as a full member and in 1975 this was raised to £12: in 1977 the price for the same ticket became £16 and in 1978 I was required to pay £18.50. Such has been the rate of inflation!

CHAPTER TEN

# THE CAPTAINCY OF TONY GREIG
## 1973 – 1977

Tony Greig was never at a loss for words and one of his first utterances after his appointment as captain of Sussex was to the effect that he wanted to get rid of the 'gin and tonic image' which he had found at Hove, though whether this referred to the Committee Room, the Members' Bar or the Hotel (surely not to the players!) I never quite made out, but this indicated that the new leader was ready to attack from whatever angle he felt suitable. A few days later the extrovert young man was saying that if he did not do his job he would expect the sack and that he would not mind forgoing his Test career if he could get Sussex to the top. Brave words, but life as a star was probably more exacting than he ever thought possible, nor, I imagine, did he expect his cricketing career to erupt with the speed of an especially violent volcano. And we all know what disasters volcanic eruptions can bring.

Meanwhile Greig was one of the MCC side which toured India and Pakistan in the winter of 1972-73, where he topped the batting and was second in the bowling averages. Michael Melford seemed almost bewildered by the hero-worship which was lavished upon the Sussex captain-elect. He wrote that:— "Tony Greig's passage through India has been one of the most extraordinary features of the tour." *The Times of India* said:— "Not since Barrington has any cricketer captured the hearts of our cricket-crazy masses as Greig has done." He had captured most Sussex cricket hearts too.

But gin and tonic or no gin and tonic Greig's five years as captain brought Sussex little success and not until 1977 did we find ourselves in the comparatively respectable position of 8th, and, apart from 1973 when we were beaten Gillette Cup finalists, we showed up poorly in limited over cricket as a whole. Certainly Sussex tied for 2nd place in 1976 and were 4th in 1977 in the John Player League, but these were the only glimmers of light in what was a disappointing era. In 1973 the team looked well balanced between experience and youth, for with Greig there were Mike Griffith, Tony Buss (who was made vice-captain this year), Michael Buss, John Snow, Peter Graves, Geoff Greenidge and Roger Prideaux, though the last of these emigrated to South Africa at the end of the year: on the side of 'youth' we had John Barclay, Mark Faber, John Spencer, Alan Mansell, Uday Joshi, Paul Phillipson and Jerry Morley, but despite this Greig stated that in his opinion Sussex needed several years to reach the top.

In that first year Greig awarded caps to Spencer and Morley and a 2nd XI cap to the red-haired Old Carthusian fast bowler, Roger Marshall, whom a friend of mine had termed 'the atomic carrot'. The Test Trial of 1973, held at Hove, was between the side that Tony Lewis had taken to India and Pakistan, and Illingworth's XI, called The Rest. Greig was in the former, Snow in the latter; Roope made a century, East did the hat-trick and later Greig took 4 wickets and Amiss made a century. When Greig and Prideaux came together in the Sussex game against Gloucestershire in early June I felt that I had not seen such batting for years: it was the first Sussex victory of the season and little did we realise that we should have to wait until we beat Glamorgan at the end of August for the next.

New Zealand and the West Indies came to England this summer: Greig played in all six Tests, Snow in all those against New Zealand, but only in the first against the West Indies. Congdon, the N.Z. captain, received a nasty blow off a ball from Snow in the First Test, but went on the make 176. When Snow was dropped from the England side by Ray Illingworth this summer he did not play again in Tests until 1975, but Snow's absence from the national side gave him a chance to captain Sussex when Tony Buss was unavailable and when Greig, himself, was playing for England or having treatment for a chipped rib which was causing him a good deal of trouble this year. When Snow captained his county side against Hampshire he obviously revelled in it and looked as happy as a sandboy: Hants were all out for 178 and Morley scored his maiden hundred. Snow writes that in the early 'Seventies there had been a suggestion of his taking over the leadership and I have often wondered how things would have worked out had he done so, for it was with Snow as captain that Sussex achieved the second win of the season over Glamorgan. John Snow consistently refused to let himself become part of any accepted norm and for some reason best known to himself always remained aloof and remote, even when engaged in play. But if someone had been able to capture his fertile mind at an early age, this mind might well have been used for the betterment of the game he has made his profession, for he is not lacking in ideas.

During our match with Surrey this year I met, after what seemed like a lifetime, that fine old Sussex batsman, Ted Bowley: he was sitting in the pavilion with old Jim Parks, and to see these two men together brought back many happy memories. Bowley, who had spent the years between 1934 and 1954 as coach at Winchester College, was now 81, but he was very alert and far more talkative than he had been when I was young. He asked about Juliet Somers not knowing that she was now Juliet Pannett, the artist, who had painted the portrait of Arthur Gilligan, Bowley's old captain, which he had been admiring shortly before. He was thrilled. "She drew *me*, too," he said, proudly, and, indeed, he had been one of the series which Juliet had drawn for the *Sussex County Magazine*. We talked for a while of olden days, of Tate and Tommy Cook and of others we had known so long ago, as cricket-lovers will. I was glad to have had this short conversation with Bowley, for he died the following year.

Whilst watching the Sussex v Middlesex game this summer, when John Murray made a century, I turned on my tiny transistor to hear the Third Test v West Indies at Lords, only to find that there was a bomb scare and the ground was being cleared. The Test wicket was covered, but as thousands of people milled onto the centre I wondered what had happened to the pitch for the Gillette Cup final. Music was played on the radio, but after 89 minutes the game was resumed: one could only assume that nothing had been found. Colonel and Mrs. Grimston were at Lords and they told me later that no one bothered very much: what a phlegmatic race we British are! This was all part of the Northern Ireland 'troubles' when the I.R.A. turned their attention to this side of the Irish Sea. My concern for the Gillette Cup final wicket was by no means disinterested for we were once more in the final, only to be beaten by Gloucestershire by 40 runs, when Sussex had a certain amount of bad luck in having to face the full fury of Mike Proctor's fast bowling after 7 o'clock in a fading light. Roger Marshall had the remarkable figures of 12-3-29-1, but I felt sorry for Tony Greig, who had set his heart on winning the Cup.

During this summer I had bought John Snow's second book of poems entitled *Thoughts and Moments* and he was much more friendly when he signed it for me. Later in the year Snow was on the carpet again for not getting clearance from the Secretary which is obligatory on all cricketers who write articles and I feared another row was brewing. Snow was complaining that he did not know whether he would be touring the West Indies under Mike Denness in the winter ahead: with his benefit due in 1974 he had plans to make and it was reasonable that he should want to know.

## The Captaincy of Tony Greig 1973 – 1977

In fact, Snow did not go on this tour: instead he went on a brief visit to South Africa and then settled down to arranging his benefit in earnest.

Sussex finished 15th in 1973 and although it looked as if we had some promising players nothing had gone right. The only reason we kept away from the bottom of the ladder was that we gained 67 very valuable bowling points. Only Greenidge reached his 1,000 runs, whilst Snow topped the bowling averages though Mike Buss and John Spencer took more wickets. It was worth noting that the Sussex 2nd XI were 4th in their own competition and, as ever, one could only hope.

If John Snow did not go on the MCC tour of the West Indies, Tony Greig did. His success in batting was patchy, but he headed the bowling averages largely through his twin-pronged attack of seam and spin. In the First Test at Port of Spain there was another of these ever-growing 'incidents' when Greig ran out the non-striker, Alvin Kallicharran, as he left the field after the last ball of the day. There was the usual furore in the English papers which included accusations of racism because of Greig's South African birth, but in the West Indies, I understand, the reports were factual and restrained. I studied the series of film clips in *The Cricketer Spring Annual* of 1974 and two things emerged clearly from these: firstly, that Greig had his back to Knott (who was removing the bails and pulling out the stumps) and the other players who were already wending their ways to the pavilion; secondly, that Kallicharran, backing up in the usual manner, just went on walking and made no effort to ground his bat within his crease before leaving the field. What else could Umpire Sang Hue do but give him 'out' on Greig's appeal? That this decision was later reversed and that the West Indian was allowed to resume his innings next day is now history. Was Tony Greig over-enthusiastic or was Kallicharran far too careless? This was a happening on a par with the Snow-Gavaskar collision of 1971 in the sense that both actions were obviously unpremeditated and, in retrospect, I believe that both were blown up out of all proportion to their importance and *I* am a stickler for good behaviour both on and off the field. Ted Dexter wrote that Greig had been "shamefully treated" over this run out, but although on the evidence available one would be prepared to give Greig the benefit of the doubt he would certainly have to watch his step in future. I am sure that neither Greig not Kallicharran bore each other any malice, but the very posed and 'matey' picture of the two men together made me feel slightly sick.

Back at home in the spring 1974 John Snow's benefit was getting

*Peter Graves Hove 1977*  *Ian Greig – Paul Parker*

under way. He was sponsored at the rate of £2 per run and at once made 73 v Northants: by the end of the season he had notched up 543 for Sussex and the idea of Snow as a batsman was not entirely a pipe-dream.

On the whole, however, 1974 was another disappointing year for Sussex. Greig seemed to have shot his bolt for the moment and he made only 399 runs for the county, whilst Graves and Greenidge were the only two to reach the coveted 1,000 runs. One bright spot was the Sussex victory over Middlesex at the end of August: this was helped by the batting of Greenidge, Graves and Mark Faber, who made his maiden century, and the bowling of John Snow. Faber and Barclay were two of the young players on whom the county was pinning its hopes: both had been at Summer Fields Preparatory School at Oxford, though Faber is four years older than Barclay; next they both went to Eton, after which Faber went up to Oxford University, gaining his Blue in 1972. On leaving school Barclay decided to play cricket and was vice-captain of the English Schools Cricket Association team in India in 1970-71, after which he captained the England Young Cricketers in the West Indies in 1972.

This August I was writing:— "The Test team for Australia will be chosen tomorrow. I doubt that Snow will go." Snow did not.

## The Captaincy of Tony Greig 1973 — 1977

A cutting from *The Brighton and Hove Gazette* has pictures of Snow, Greig, and Mike Griffith, captioned respectively, 'Snow Snubbed'; 'Greig Deposed'; 'Griffith Goes'. These comments referred to Snow's omission from the England side, Greig being replaced by John Edrich as vice-captain to Mike Denness and, finally, Mike Griffith's decision to give up first-class cricket. Possibly disconcerted at losing the vice-captaincy Greig is alleged to have expressed his views on the team selection on the telephone as far as we know to the Australian newspapers. For this he was called before the TCCB in mid-October, but he denied having made the statements attributed to him: the Board regarded these views, as printed, as totally unacceptable, but did accept Greig's explanation and a few days later the team flew off to Australia.

The last match of the Sussex season was at Eastbourne, but the weather was not up to normal Saffrons standard. There was a Force 8 gale and later we heard that Edward Heath's yacht 'Morning Cloud' had been lost in the English Channel and life-boats had been out all around the coasts. Sussex moved up two places in the Championship finishing 13th and once again bowling points were well in excess of those for batting, whilst there were some who were already questioning Greig's captaincy.

This autumn Snow, who was seldom out of the news for long, was disgruntled at being left out of the team for Australia and was saying that the only way he would be picked would be to shoot the selectors! He felt that even if the whole 17 in the group broke down no one would send for *him*. Being a bit of a philosopher he soon shrugged off this mood and realised that there were a lot of ends to tie up with regard to his benefit which was to bring him in about £18,000. *The Daily Mail* asked if Snow was the 'black sheep' or the 'bad lad' of cricket and Snow, nothing if not honest, said he would explain in his own time. Now he has done so and it is up to those who read his book to decide for themselves whether or not they agree with his own accounts of what has occurred in his somewhat controversial career. During October I watched Juliet Pannett as she did a portrait of John, who is wearing his England touring sweater and has the Sydney pavilion in the background. This was his father's gift to the fast bowler, who, we thought at the time, might be coming to the end of his first-class career. The painting was the centre-piece of Dr. Snow's next art exhibition in his church hall, but strictly 'Not for Sale'.

During the winter of 1974-75 whilst Bryan and I were watching Brent Geese at Pagham and Chichester Harbours, grebe and other ducks at reservoirs and a kingfisher at Weirwood, the English batsmen were in almost complete confusion before the attack of Dennis Lillee and his new fast bowling partner, Jeff Thomson. Then, in New Zealand, came the near fatality of a different kind when Ewan Chatfield was hit by a ball from Peter Lever and needed mouth-to-mouth resuscitation before being taken to hospital. Once again the question of bumpers arose and in December 1975 Tony Greig, speaking from Australia, was suggesting that some form of helmet should be designed before someone was killed. Tony Lewis, in *The Daily Telegraph Supplement,* had an article which went even further and showed an entire outfit of cricketing armour. The first man to use a helmet in this country was Mike Brearley, who, in 1977, appeared in what one could only describe as an object more suited to a horror film. Surely modern technology could have devised something a little less unbecoming! The ICC debated bouncers and umpires were made more responsible for controlling bowlers; it was suggested that bouncers should not be bowled at tail-enders, i.e. non-recognised batsmen and much mirth was caused by the idea of 'NRB' emblazoned on sweaters as a badge of incompetency.

The 1975 cricket season was remarkable for many things, not the least of which was that the sun shone for weeks on end and the receipts from the big matches must have surpassed the estimates of the most optimistic. Those from other countries who in past years had gained the impression that, on an average, 25% of the time of any cricket match in England is spent in the pavilion playing cards, watching television, reading, doing crosswords or just gazing out at a rain-sodden ground, must, in 1975, have had the surprise of their lives.

This great 'Summer of Cricket' as Tony Lewis has called it was also my fiftieth season as a member of the Sussex County Cricket Club and my old friend Arthur Gilligan wrote in my ticket:— "Warmest congratulations on your 50th year of membership. You have always been a terrific supporter of Sussex cricket — from an old 'un. Arthur Gilligan. June 23rd. 1975." But my golden jubilee brought little success to my county team for Sussex faded early from the Benson and Hedges Cup, were beaten in the first round of the Gillette Cup, were 11th in the John Player League and last of all in the County Championship. Mark Faber, Greig and Graves reached 1,000 runs, but Faber was not given his cap and midway through the next season he asked to be freed from his contract. Tony Buss, now county coach, stressed that most young cricketers need at least five years to mature in first-class cricket and this was supported by John Barclay who agreed that he had found the

## The Captaincy of Tony Greig 1973 — 1977

transition from 2nd to 1st XI very difficult.

There were, nevertheless, plenty of good young players only awaiting the call. Against Hampshire I saw Giles Cheatle, coached by Charlie Oakes at Stowe, take his first county wicket — and it was that of Barry Richards — on a day when John Snow was having dreadful trouble with his run up and was being constantly no-balled. Cheatle, who bowls slow left arm, forced himself into the side in 1977 at the expense of Chris Waller, bowled extremely tidily and took 23 wickets.

This year I watched another interesting young player when, standing on the secretary's balcony with Commander Stoop, I admired an exciting batsman whom I had never seen before. Commander Stoop told me that this was the 18-year-old Javed Miandad from Pakistan, who was playing his first game for the 2nd XI. And what a game it was! He hit 227 in 255 minutes and shared a 3rd wicket partnership of 220 with Peter Kirsten from South Africa, who later joined Derbyshire. At this time Miandad was engaged by Daisy Hill, a club in the Lancashire League, and was only available for Sussex in mid-week, but in 1976 he made his debut for the county and the following year became an established member of the side, playing some outstanding innings and fielding with great agility. Miandad scored 163 in his Test debut for Pakistan v New Zealand in 1976 and followed this up with 206 in the Third Test, thus becoming the youngest player to have made a double century in Tests, for he was still only 19 and a bit. Then in the winter of 1977-78 Miandad took his exploits still further when, against the England side in Pakistan he topped his country's batting with an average of 131.00! After this he was an obvious choice for the 1978 tour of England and Sussex had to reconcile themselves to being without him for the early part of the season. Miandad and the Colombo-born Gehan Mendis, who was educated at the Brighton and Hove Grammar School and is therefore not registered as an overseas player, have been almost indistinguishable from one another on the field, looking like tiny twins under their enormous white sun hats.

Twice in the early part of 1975 I saw Selectors Alec Bedser and Ken Barrington at Hove. I longed to know whom they were watching: was it Peter Graves, who had been playing so well — or could it be John Snow? Throughout May and the first part of June there had been demands in the press for Snow's inclusion in the 'squad' (which the England side is now called) for the Prudential Cup, with headlines such as 'Snowy is England's Man for the Pru' and 'John Snow — the People's Choice'. Someone must have listened for Snow played in all the Prudential matches except that against New Zealand and in all four Tests against Australia. It was this year that he recorded his best bowling performance to date when he took 8-87 against Middlesex at Lords.

England was beaten by Australia in the semi-finals of the Prudential Cup and the final was between Australia and West Indies. Through the kindness of Mr. Kenneth Gilkes, a member of the Sussex Committee for many years, who gave us tickets, Bryan and I were privileged to witness this great game. On arrival at Lords we found a microcosm of what we used to call the British Empire: brightly clad and noisy enthusiasts from overseas, waving all manner of favours, contrasted with the more conventionally dressed and club-tied crowd mingling behind the pavilion during intervals and talking and behaving as I am sure they have done ever since Lords came into existence. In the public seats below us sat two West Indians, one small, tidy and clean; the other large, untidy and uncouth. It was difficult to know why the latter was getting so annoyed, for the West Indies, put in by Australia, and through the fine batting of their captain, Clive Lloyd, were doing extremely well. This rather loutish man continued to shout for most of the day, finishing up by telling us that it was "no good blaming it on the Irish." How the Irish got into a cricket match between Australia and the West Indies we shall never know! But it was fascinating to see how Lillee and Thomson could be tamed by really confident batting, and the West Indies emerged triumphant.

Two events apart from the cricket stand out in my memory of this day: firstly, the pollen count in London was 411, which was abnormally high and must have been the reason for my horrid snuffling: and secondly, that we read in our evening paper that a son, Mark Alexander, had been born to Donna and Tony Greig the day before.

Hard upon the Prudential series came four Test matches against Australia and the Ashes were at stake. 'Aussies Fear Snow Storm' stated *The Evening News*: how true this was I do not know, but at last Snow was on the Test match scene again. These four games were notable for several things, all of a very different kind. First of all poor Mike Denness, for whom nothing had gone right since he took over the England captaincy in 1973, put Australia in to bat in the First Test at Edgbaston: "Either the bravest or the most foolhardy thing that Denness has ever done," commented Ted Dexter on television; Australia made 359 and England could only reach 101, followed on and lost by an innings. The head of Denness was bound to roll and the very next day, with what Michael Mel-

## The Captaincy of Tony Greig 1973 – 1977

ford called 'merciful promptness', his successor was announced. One could not help thinking that this haste was almost indecent, but there was so much speculation that some positive action had to be taken.

On the morning of Tuesday, July 15th, Commander Ian Stoop, the Sussex Secretary, arrived early at his office at the County Ground at Hove. Almost at once the telephone rang. It was Alec Bedser, Chairman of the Selectors, and he asked to speak to Tony Greig. The Secretary informed him that Greig was not yet on the ground, but that he would see to it that he rang back. At 10 a.m. Tony arrived in the outer office to pick up his regular and considerable fan-mail. The Secretary asked him to come into his office and shut the door. "Now," he said, "telephone Alec Bedser." Tony did so and during the course of the conversation which followed it was clear to the Secretary that he was being offered the captaincy of England and that he was accepting. At length Greig put down the receiver and turning to Ian Stoop, said, "Well, that's it, mate. I am now captain of England." The Secretary congratulated him and suggested that he might like to make a few 'phone calls. "Yes, thank you," replied Greig, "and may I first ring Donna?" Having given the good news to his wife Tony was asked, "Who next?" Commander Stoops tells me that Tony's reply was that he wished to commiserate with his captain on the recent Australian tour, Mike Denness. "Now Tony," went on the Secretary, "who next?" "Would it be possible to 'phone my father in South Africa?" Commander Stoop had already met Tony's father, Sandy Greig, and was only too pleased to let him have a three minute call on the Club. When Tony's father heard his son's voice his first reaction was to say, "And what have you done now?" On hearing the news he was as delighted as the new captain himself and later Tony told us on television that his little sister, always inclined to be emotional, had burst into tears. Finally Greig telephoned his agent.

The very day after Greig's appointment to the England captaincy Sussex found themselves engaged in a game with the Australians, this coming about because we had lost in the first round of the Gillette Cup and had a spare three days on our hands. The Australians made 402-7 dec. and Sussex replied with 401-6 dec., Greig and Austin Parsons from New Zealand getting centuries. The game ended in a futile draw because Greg Chappell, deputising as captain for his brother Ian, batted throughout the third day for 354-5 without declaring. No captain takes any action without his own reasons, but in this case it was hard to find any good ones: we could only assume that the Australians were annoyed at the good batting of Sussex. The crowd grew more and more incensed and people said that they had already seen Greg Chappell leaving the ground. Tony Greig, with the backing of the Sussex Committee, issued a statement about the Australian tactics:— "Cricketers the world over play to win. Fair enough. And if you cannot win then we all appreciate there are no prizes for coming second, and I go along with that. But I feel that the people who have paid to keep the game going have a right to expect proper treatment. It does seem a great pity that what had been such a fine match for the first two days has had to end to-day in such an anti-climax."

When we played Glamorgan the hot summer had become, if possible, even hotter. Almost every cricketer was wearing a wide-brimmed, floppy, white sun-hat, which, over some very long hair, made identification something of a problem. We had a talk with George Cox, who said that the media had lauded Greig to the skies and now could only knock him down: I doubt if any of us thought that Tony Greig would, before long, do the job himself. Just then Commander Stoop gave out that Greig was about to leave the ground for Lords and the Second Test and that all wished him well. There was a round of applause from the not very large crowd, but John Snow wrote a year later that he hoped at the time that the new responsibility would not take its toll too early. This was a shrewd piece of observation which might be borne in mind in view of future events. Next day Greig won his first toss as England's captain and proceeded to make 96. Torn in two I rushed back and forth between the County Ground and the T.V. Sussex lost to Glamorgan and the Test at Lords was drawn. We had our usual day at Eastbourne this year; the weather returned to its usual good form and a cool wind kept us from roasting. "How lovely the Saffrons is!" I wrote when I got home. These words of mine have echoed down the years. But Sussex lost.

Shortly after Greig's accession to the England captaincy I was given a photograph of a young Greig being clapped off the field at Tunbridge Wells in 1971 after he had taken 8-42 against Kent. As I turned away from accepting this gift who should be before me but Tony himself. He looked very busy, with a black portfolio under his arm, and he was heading for the Secretary's office: I was hesitant of worrying him, but it was too good a chance to miss. "Please, would you mind signing this for me?" I said. The captain of England and Sussex halted immediately and smiled. "I'll do anything for you, my dear," he said. I felt that time had rolled back and here I was, just where I had begun.

## The Captaincy of Tony Greig 1973 – 1977     141

The majority of cricket followers were pleased with the choice of Greig as England captain, but others objected to a man who, ever since his arrival in England, had been declaring his South African connection. Yet, so often the moment produces the man and so it appeared now. The fair 6ft 7½in giant with the engaging smile and plenty of charm, had also the belligerent approach to the game that has become so necessary to-day when cricket has to be a money-spinner whether it likes it or not: he seemed to be the ideal person to instil heart into a side which was thoroughly depressed by the disastrous time it had had in Australia. Greig certainly made mistakes, but in those early days he was always ready to listen to advice and to acknowledge his errors.

From now on the press, television and radio treated Tony Greig as little less than a 'pop' idol; the whole thing was deplorably over-

*Tony Greig, Kent v Sussex, Tunbridge Wells June 19th, 21, 22nd 1971*

done. The final extravaganza of the year was introduced on Radio Brighton and BCC's 'South To-Day', which informed us that 'a headless body' was to be brought in a coffin to the County Ground during the Lancashire match, but we need not worry as this was the wax effigy of Greig, which he was to unveil before it was taken to Madame Tussaud's in London. During the luncheon interval this somewhat macabre drama was played out in front of the pavilion, except that, thank goodness, the coffin did not appear and the body was covered with silvery plastic sheeting and the head was in a box. Not until the effigy was properly assembled did the original come to stand beside it. The yellow waxen image bore little resemblance to the rosy-faced real-life character, though we were assured that under artificial lights it would look more natural. A rather embarrassed Greig was plied with questions about South African cricket to which he gave his stock reply that he was a professional entertainer and not a politician. Cameras, including that of the present author, were being let off like wild-fire, but at last it was all over and Greig escaped to eat the roll which we had heard John Barclay ordering for his lunch. Meanwhile, the head of the effigy was removed and carefully put back into its box and the thought went through my mind that one day the real owner's head, like that of Mike Denness, might be struck from its shoulders. The ultimate horror came when the Secretary announced that "the wake will now begin." Although I knew he was having a dig at a certain Committee member who made a habit of attending such functions, a cold shudder went down my spine.

The furore over Tony Greig brought him what the trade unions would call 'fringe benefits' and Arthur Gilligan told me that Greig had been asked to give more time and thought to Sussex cricket and less to these side lines. At the end of the summer we learnt that Greig had obtained a lucrative post as captain-coach to the Australian club, Waverley, which is in the district of Bondi Beach. After a brief visit to South Africa for a double wicket competition Tony, with his wife and their children, Samantha and Mark, flew to Australia: the 'plane was late, Greig's luggage, with his cricketing gear, got left behind and on his first appearance for his new club he was dismissed for 0 and 1 — on the same day! When asked how he felt about this Greig was reported to have said, "They've seen a Pommie out twice for one run, so what more could they want?"

By now Sussex had begun to join the free for all in the registration stakes. The most bizarre idea of all was that Colin Cowdrey, captain of Kent and one-time captain of England, who was about to retire, should join his neighbouring county for a few years in order to

## The Captaincy of Tony Greig 1973 — 1977        143

encourage and advise their young players. In his autobiography Cowdrey says that this came to him as a complete surprise and he considered it a 'huge compliment', but during our game against Kent those concerned put their heads together with the result that Cowdrey declined. The thought of his exchanging his Kentish horse for the Sussex martlets made the mind boggle. There are so many 'ifs' and 'buts' in cricket and *if* Cowdrey had joined Sussex in 1976 it is just possible that some of the unfortunate events of the next few years might never have come about. Jeff Thomson and Gary Gilmour, the Australians, were two more who turned down our offers, and then attempts were made to persuade Fred Titmus to come a little further south, but, again, there was a negative reply. In the end the signings that did take place were those of Roger Knight, late of Gloucestershire and Surrey, and Arnold Long, the Surrey wicket-keeper, who, we were told, was to replace Alan Mansell. Sussex also took on Kepler Wessels, a South African of outstanding brilliance, and Javed Miandad, whom I had already seen performing for the 2nd XI.

The summer months of 1976 were even more remarkable than those of the year before from the point of view of the weather. Week after week went by without rain: water was rationed in parts of Wales and stand-pipes were set up in the West Country. At Hove a notice outside the County Ground Hotel requested that patrons be 'dressed above the waist'! On August 24th Denis Howell was declared Minister of Drought (in February 1979 he was Minister of Snow) and four days later it rained — for the mini-Test at Lords. The farmers were happy and even groundsmen allowed themselves at gentle smile. In September we had the nearest thing to a monsoon that anyone had seen in Britain, but cricket was over and we just got out our 'wellies' and macs.

Michael Buss had his benefit in 1976 and the new players, Roger Knight and Arnold Long, were given their Sussex caps and were a considerable asset to their new county, several sports writers tipping Knight for England. John Barclay, and Chris Waller (another ex-Surrey player) were also capped and of the new generation Paul Parker, of Collyer's School, Horsham, and Cambridge University, Javed Miandad and Kepler Wessels all did well, Miandad and Wessels being two of the most forceful players we had seen for some time, with Parker not far behind. Miandad made his first Championship hundred against Hampshire at Hove, and 69 in front of a 10,000 crowd in the Gillette Cup against Warwickshire. Not speaking much English Miandad thought he had been made 'Man of the Match' and had to be pulled back by John Spencer. Sussex had lost and it was the only smile we had during the day. Against Essex, Paul Parker and Miandad had a fine partnership and Wessels (not qualified to play for Sussex until 1977), reached his 1,000 for 2nd XI.

In 1976 Sussex were 10th in the County Championship, with Knight, Graves and Barclay getting their 1,000 runs, whilst Spencer took 79 wickets and Snow 59, including Tests. After a grandstand finish in the John Player League with five teams ending up on 40 points (Sussex among them) Kent were placed first since they had more away wins. Peter Graves was captain in the last J.P. match and later the Sussex Committee wrote to congratulate him on his season and on his handling of the side in Greig's absence. Peter had done a first-rate job and it was good to see it appreciated.

Tony Greig, who in the spring had returned from Australia where he had helped the Waverley club to win the Premier Cup in Sydney and had bowled a lot of spin, experienced a summer he will prefer to forget. It began, after he had been named England's captain for the series against the West Indies, with what became known as 'the infamous grovel speech', made at Hove, when Greig, with great vehemence and, in my opinion incredible lack of tact, stated that England intended to make the West Indies grovel. But it was England, not their opponents, who did the grovelling, for two Tests were drawn, the West Indies won the other three and also all three of the one-day games. England were all out for 71 at Old Trafford and this brought forth yet another of those cartoons showing Greig telephoning golfer, Tony Jacklin, who had just completed a round of 76, with Greig saying, "Hey, Jacko! how about changing scores?" Greig said that this had been his worst day since he became captain. For much of this summer he looked far from well and suffered, in turn, from a pinched nerve under a rib, a boil, a recurrence of an injury to his right arm and a growth on his toe, which was removed: the growth, not the toe! Chairman of Selectors, Alec Bedser, stood by Greig throughout his lack of form and Greig stated that he would have tennis balls thrown at him in the nets from 16 yards to get used to the bounce. This paid off for he made a century at Headingley: but the general impression was that he was not really fit and was badly in need of a rest.

During these last four years a large number of players joined the ranks of the 'not re-engaged' or 'left staff'. First Roger Prideaux, one of those whom I call the 'strolling players', decided to emigrate to South Africa and Ken McEwan, a South African whom Tony Greig had hoped to have playing for Sussex, went to Essex because

## The Captaincy of Tony Greig 1973 — 1977

Sussex had no room for another overseas player, whilst the following year Mike Griffith gave up first-class cricket. In 1975 Geoff Greenidge, who had been with the county since 1968, returned to his native Bardados for good: Greenidge had played in 5 Tests for the West Indies and had scored 1,000 runs for Sussex on five occasions. Alan Mansell, whom the Club had wished to replace Jim Parks behind the stumps, was himself replaced by the more experienced Arnold Long and there were some of us who felt that Mansell had been treated rather badly. Tony Buss retired in 1975, having received a benefit of £8,000 in 1971, but he has continued to serve the Club in a variety of capacities, never more so than when both Secretary and assistant secretary, Frank Matthews, were taken ill at the same time. 1976 saw a flood of departures: Alan Wadey was discarded, so, although capped, was Jerry Morley: Austin Parsons returned to New Zealand; and Roger Marshall left the playing staff to become assistant coach.

It would seem that a great many cricketers depart this life almost as soon as the cricket season ends. This was true in the case of Arthur Gilligan who died, suddenly, on September 5th 1976. I had never known cricket without A.E.R. and could hardly imagine such a thing. A.E.R. Gilligan and R.E.S. Wyatt were the two senior England captains, and when I met Bob Wyatt a few weeks later, when Juliet and I had lunch with him and his wife, Mollie, in Horsham, he told us how he and Arthur had planned, during the Oval Test match, to accept the Australian invitation to the Centenary Test match in Melbourne in March. Now, for Arthur, this would never be.

Life was seldom dull when John Snow was around. In 1976 he produced a baby daughter, Katherine ("He's nutty about her," said John's wife, Jennifer), wrote a book, played against the West Indies, opened the batting for Sussex with some success and then spoilt it all, first, by wearing what is called 'advertising insignia' on his clothes during a televised match, and then by showing dissent when given out by umpire 'Cec' Pepper. The TCCB recommended that Snow be suspended from a vital John Player League game against Warwickshire at Edgbaston, but Sussex openly defied Lords and Snow played, but he was required to apologise to Mr. Pepper, which he did. Snow's *'Cricket Rebel'*, which he and Jennifer would have preferred to be called 'The Summer Snowman' was launched on the occasion of the Gillette Cup final and Juliet Pannett's charcoal drawing of him appeared in Peterborough's column in *The Daily Telegraph* shortly afterwards. "I've never seen the awkard side of him," she said, tactfully. In John's book there is the story of how he began to show dissent at a very early age, in garden games at home. His sister, Rosemary, not approving of such behaviour, once hit him over the head with a watering-can. When I told a Yorkshireman about this, he said, "Perhaps that's what is wrong with him." But *I* wondered if it would be a good idea to issue umpires with watering-cans in future to damp down unruly batsmen: it would save endless meetings of Committees and Councils and instant punishment is always the most effective.

But the mind of the TCCB does not work that way and in mid-September they asked Sussex what action they had taken over Snow's misdemeanours. A fortnight later the Sussex Committee met and reprimanded Snow for both offences and also Jerry Groome for wearing advertising material. This did not satisfy the TCCB and at the end of October Lords was still discussing Snow's misbehaviour, but delayed taking any action until they had seen him in person. Now Snow was saying, with injured innocence, that he was at a loss to know why the business was dragging on: he thought Sussex had handled it very fairly. With the Sussex Secretary and his solicitor Snow appeared before the disciplinary Committee of the TCCB and was suspended from the first three one-day games of 1977 for 'public dissent of a most blatant nature.' This was not without precedent for Geoff Arnold of Surrey, soon to join Sussex, had suffered the same penalty for the same offence. Whilst in no way defending the county's lack of action where Snow was concerned, I find it interesting to note that Sussex won all three games from which Snow was banned. Meanwhile Mr. Allen described the whole thing as unfair, because one of those who had given judgment against Snow was a Worcestershire member and one of the matches which Snow would miss was against that county! It is more to the point that two Old Blues (Christ's Hospital), Tom Pearce and Dennis Silk, had pronounced against their fellow Old Blue, John Snow — but Mr. Allen did not mention this. In the end Snow put aside his idea of an appeal; Sussex were severely censured by the TCCB, but the ruling body agreed to allow advertising on one garment only, preferably the shirt: had Snow gained a Pyrrhic victory?

Throughout this time nothing much had been heard of the Sussex captain, but in September Denis Compton wrote in *The Daily Express*:— "It is crisis time for Tony Greig this coming season in India. His leadership and record so far cannot be regarded with optimism for the future. The appointment of Mike Brearley as vice-captain indicates to me that Brearley is breathing down Greig's neck as captain for next summer's confrontation with the

Australians." Surely Denis Compton could not possibly have foreseen how prophetic this short paragraph would be, or in what manner his forecast would be fulfilled!

As yet unaware, presumably, of his fate, Greig set out for India with the last team to be called 'MCC'; in future, since MCC no longer has direct responsibility, it would be called 'England'. Before the end of the year Greig had won his first Test in what was his ninth match as captain. Then followed victories in the 2nd and 3rd Tests and the series belonged to England.

Before the winter tour of India was over Sussex was negotiating with Imran Khan, the Oxford University, Worcestershire and Pakistan all-rounder, who was saying that he was unhappy at Worcester and, since John Snow had always been his fast bowling hero, wished to come to Sussex to open the bowling with him. Sussex announced that they had agreed terms with the 24-year-old Imran and although this move would create a precedent, since no overseas players had ever changed counties before, Stanley Allen denied that it would bring about a soccer-style transfer system. Yet, in May, the TCCB turned down the Imran plan, saying that his reasons for the move were not strong enough. The case was taken to the appeals committee of the Cricket Council and the TCCB's decision was reversed, with Imran being given permission to play for Sussex in county matches from the end of July. As a result of this Wilf Wooller resigned from the registration sub-committee, calling it a 'toothless bulldog'. The TCCB accepted the decision of the Cricket Council, but the powerful Cricketers' Association felt that it was not in the best interest of competitive cricket, and several clubs threatened not to play Sussex. This same week Tony Lewis wrote in *The Daily Telegraph*:- "Sussex refused to discipline Snow last season when requested to do so by the TCCB, and the fact that Tony Greig is never far away from these disturbances hardly leads one to think of Sussex as loyal members of the first-class Board." And again, with Imran in mind, Tony Lewis said:- "It has cheapened club loyalty, diluted county identity and created a money-market with all the attendant unpleasantness." I, myself, would claim that 'county identity' disappeared long before we ever heard of Imran Khan. Imran, not yet qualified to play in county matches, played for Sussex against the Australians and also against Ireland at Pagham, the latter being a game in which Greig's younger brother Ian, reading Law at Cambridge, was also included in the side. One day, perhaps, we may see a cricket match including Tony and Ian Greig, and Ian and Greg Chappell.

This would, indeed, be a commentator's nightmare.

Greig, a triumphant winning captain in India, took his successful team to Australia for the Centenary Test at Melbourne on March 12th. Of the 244 old Test players and officials invited 218 accepted and it would have been wonderful to have been the famous 'fly on the wall' to overhear the conversations of those few days! What memories were stirred in the minds of the old cricketers we shall never know, but it must, surely, have been a memorable occasion for all who saw Australia beat England by 45 runs — exactly the same result as 100 years before. Everyone cheered the Queen as she and Prince Philip drove around the ground and they cheered Derek Randall's 174 and went home delighted. Within this setting it is almost unbelievable that Tony Greig should have been in conclave with an Australian television tycoon called Kerry Packer, who owns Australia's Channel 9, about a future series of matches to be played during the winter of 1977-78.

Soon the England side was home again and it was time for the Sussex AGM. We had spent the early part of the day watching Princess Anne and Captain Mark Phillips competing in Horse Trials at Liphook: we were tired when we arrived home and as the AGM looked like being uneventful we decided to give it a miss and turned on the television. To our amazement we found that the subject of Eamonn Adrews' 'This is Your Life' was no other than Tony Greig! Later we heard that when the meeting at the County Ground was told the reason for the captain's absence there were cries of "Oh!" and directly the business was over people rushed to the nearest T.V. set. Stanley Allen and the Chairman, Tony Crole-Rees, had been invited to the studios, but had declined, saying that they must put the AGM first. At this meeting S.C. Griffith, who had been President for the past two years, gave way to his old friend, Hugh Bartlett.

In April the Australians arrived — with Thomson, but without Lillee. They had their warm-up against Lavinia, Duchess of Norfolk's XI at Arundel Park, where the Friends of Arundel C.C., with Billy Griffith as Chairman and Secretary, was fast becoming an important centre for cricket in southern England. The Christ's Hospital School Band played 'Sussex by the Sea' and, as a compliment to the visitors, 'Waltzing Matilda'. It was another beautiful day, with a cloudless sky, but Tony Greig and John Barclay were the only two Sussex players on view and the Australians won by 20 runs. Tony's small daughter, Samantha, in kilt and jersey,

# The Captaincy of Tony Greig 1973 – 1977

THE REST OF THE WORLD ( v AUSTRALIANS) 1977
BACK ROW: (left to right): W.L. Budd (umpire), K. McEwan, A. Kallicharrran, R.W. Taylor, R.G.D. Willis, Imran Khan, Zaheer Abbas, R Knight (12th man), John Langridge (umpire)
FRONT ROW (left to right): D.L. Underwood, E.J. Barlow, M.J. Proctor, Lavinia, Duchess of Norfolk, Sadiq Mohammad, Mushtaq Mohammad

rolled down the slope where the Duchess's daughters had rolled when they were very young: when Samantha tired of this she came along the front row offering us cans of beer and was a bit put out when they were refused by the slightly embarrassed members. In an interval I met her with her father: "She's been offering us South African beer,' I laughed. "She's not supposed to do that," said Tony, almost curtly and moved on. This was so unlike him that I was surprised, but realising that he must have other things on his mind I thought no more of it. How much he had on his mind at this time, I had not the slightest idea.

Ten days later the Australians came to play Sussex at Hove. The cricket was almost completely rained off and all that happened was that the visitors made 111-1: I enjoyed Greg Chappell's batting and was impressed by Imran's bowling, but that was all. Thoughout the Monday there were rumours of talks which had taken place at a party which had been held under a marquee on Greig's lawn, which had been given for the Australians on Saturday night. Whether it was intended that the news should break at this time I do not know but we soon heard that Greig, Snow, Knott and Underwood had signed to play for the Rest of the World in a series of matches in Australia which would automatically make it impossible for them to play in the forthcoming tour of Pakistan and New Zealand in the winter of 1977-78. "It will mean the end of Test cricket," I wrote, in shocked horror, that night. Greig held a press conference on the County Ground at which he announced that there was a massive cricket project involving most of the world's top players due to commence in Australia during the coming winter and that he was part of it, along with a number of other English players. Packer had made Greig and Greg Chappell captains of the ROW and Australia respectively and had told them to pick their own teams. Greig said that he had considered asking Lords for advice, but had decided against it, knowing that they would say no. When the ICC, united as seldom before, expressed their disapproval Greig's reply was, "These games will go on, come what may, unless there is a compromise," and he later told the TCCB that they should "be sensible".

On May 11th there appeared in *The Times* the following notice, inserted by three Australian journalists:— "In affectionate remembrance of international cricket which died at Hove, May 9th, 1977. Deeply lamented by a large circle of friends and acquaintances. RIP. The body will be cremated and the ashes taken to Australia and scattered around the studio of TCN 9 Sydney. NT. JC.BM."

Two days later Tony Greig was relieved of the England captaincy and Commander Stoop's 'wake' had begun. I doubt if Greig was exactly surprised at losing his position of trust and Alec Bedser, Chairman of the Selectors, said, "It is sad. I am very sorry." John Woodcock of *The Times* wrote:— "There was always this danger that, for some reason or other, this impulsiveness or his commercialism or the strangely insensitive streak, which exists within a normally charming and considerate person, might be his undoing." This was the most perceptive and fairest description of Greig that I had yet seen — and there had been plenty.

After his sacking Greig issued another statement:— "Obviously I am sorry my reign as England captain has come to an end just as we were beginning to put things together. From a personal point of view the only redeeming factor is that I have sacrificed cricket's most coveted job for a cause which I believe could be in the interests of cricketers the world over. I should like to put on record how I cherish the truly magnificent support I have been lucky enough to enjoy from the players who have played under me for England. If I am selected to play for England again I will give my all to whoever the new captain may be and to the team." This Tony certainly did. *The Daily Mail* asked readers for their views on the sacking of Greig and John Arlott wrote in *The Guardian* that "the plot begins to unfold; but this is not a seven days wonder nor even a short story; it is a historical novel of conflict and its end is still far distant."

The reaction on members at Hove was distinctly mixed and it would be unfair to Greig not to say that he had many supporters — and some of these remained. But the adjective I heard most often in the May and June of 1977 was that which Alec Bedser had used — sad. We had all admired and like Tony Greig and many of us felt bitterly let down by what appeared to be his lack of loyalty to the county and the country which had made him famous, and, above all, there was the manner in which the transaction had been brought about. But Stanley Allen, ever sticking by Greig, insisted that the County Committee had every faith in him as the Sussex captain and Alan Edge, from Leamington Spa, wrote to *The Daily Telegraph,* saying:— "In Greig's own words every one of England's cricketers who toured India and Australia last winter would have walked under a 'bus for him. I wonder how long it will be before another captain can induce such loyalty and devotion." But Maj. Gen, E.A.E. Tremlett wrote:- "Sir — whatever the proposed international circus call themselves, it will not be cricket they play."

On the last day of the Gloucestershire match Kerry Packer came to Hove. I did not see him for, after a brief introduction to the Secretary, he was whisked away to Greig's captain's room and was kept well away from the Sussex Committee. A day or so later there was a David Frost programme on television in which Packer, Robin Marlar and Jim Laker faced each other in argument. This was disastrous, in part because Marlar was so infuriated at having to sit in the same room as Kerry Packer that he looked like blowing up at any moment, thus giving the suave, cool and assured tycoon the best of the discussion: Jim Laker remained calm and talked a lot of sense, whilst David Frost, for once, was almost dumb.

Mike Brearley was appointed England's new captain for the Queen's Silver Jubilee Test at Lords: Jeff Thomson — and later West Indian Alvin Kallicharran — disentangled themselves from the Packer contract, but Bob Woolmer and Denis Amiss joined: Sussex went on — somehow — whilst Paul Parker and Ian Greig, both of Sussex, played for Cambridge U. in the 'Varsity match: Wessels, Barclay and Parker all got maiden centuries for Sussex, but then Wessels had to return to South Africa. Before his departure he was given his county cap, which, after playing only nine matches, I regarded as rather premature. Javed Miandad was also capped in 1977, but he *did* get his 1,000 runs and played throughout the season. The county had a certain amount of success, but as Greig was playing for England for a great deal of the summer it was left to Peter Graves to hold Sussex together: although he had a relatively poor season himself, he led the side well and in July was told that he had been awarded his benefit in 1978 although in cricket-playing terms Greig was his senior. We all wished Peter well.

Away from the mainstream of worry there was a most interesting match at Arundel Park between England under-19 and Australian under-19 sides. The sole Sussex representative was Old Harrovian, Tony Pigott, a fast bowler who had been playing for the Waverley Club in Sydney the previous winter. The Young England cricketers won by 32 runs in a game reduced to 45 overs because of early rain, but I am keeping the scorecard carefully to see which, if any, of these twenty-two players reach the top. At the same time Greg Chappell's senior side was being severely rated by the Australian press for "no application, pathetic batting and fielding, and sloppy dress."

We were trying our best to forget Tony Greig and Kerry Packer, but then Greig published an article in criticism of the Old Trafford pitch and Sussex were in trouble again. Stanley Allen had given Greig the necessary clearance — over the telephone, but Lancastrians were understandably angry. Ten days later the disciplinary committee of the TCCB, which must have been working overtime this year, reprimanded Greig for 'derogatory remarks' and Sussex were fined £500 for passing the article. There was a suggestion of an appeal, but in the end Mr. Allen and Greig shared the fine between them. Tony Lewis, whose lack of love for Sussex was growing, wrote:— "In many ways (and Sussex have explored most of them) it (the TCCB) is not strong enough. Last season Sussex ignored a disciplinary decision concerning John Snow. This year they broke the registration rules when everybody knew they could be easily disrupted. Others were happy to stick to the spirit in which they were made and now, most sadly of all, Sussex have been fined £500 by the Board."

On the brighter side John Edrich, recently awarded the M.B.E., made his 100th hundred this summer as did Geoff Boycott, the latter now back in the England side, and he did it at Headingley in the 4th Test.

On July 16th whilst the ICC was holding its long drawn out meeting about Packer 'pirates' as they were called, Sussex were beating Warwickshire at Hove by an innings and 98 runs. News was expected to come through from Lords at any moment and as the

## The Captaincy of Tony Greig 1973 — 1977

Sussex players took the field for the last session of the match the T.V. cameras were everywhere. Greig passed them quickly and unsmiling, Snow, in playful mood, grabbed Roger Knight and held him in front of the lens, little Miandad jumped on someone's back like a footballer who had scored a goal, but this was all a very forced hilarity: play was a bit unreal, and although some credit must go to Giles Cheatle who took 5-9, one felt that all the players wanted to be out of sight before details of the meeting were made known. The game was over soon after lunch and I stayed to help put notices in envelopes to be sent out to members about a special meeting in August, which was to discuss the new Committee formation. Meanwhile the BBC were, very glumly, dismantling their equipment which they had set up on the roof of the Welfare Buildings and betaking themselves to the Players' Entrance behind the pavilion. In the Library we went on with our work like beavers, but from where I sat I kept glancing at a highly-enlarged picture of the 1968 Sussex team, which, with Jim Parks as captain, included the grey-haired Alan Oakman on his right and the tall, lanky figure of the young Tony Greig, resplendent in his new county sweater in the row behind. How happy he looked. And how bright his future was then!

The cameras waylaid Greig and Snow as they left the dressing-room. The usually talkative Greig signed autographs grimly and when a woman's voice said, "B.B.C." and a camera was pushed in to his face he refused to comment. Snow was affable, but completely detached, merely saying, "Yes, I've accepted Mr. Packer's offer," and we knew that anyway. When I left the ground Greig's familiar white Jaguar was standing at the foot of the steps leading up to the Secretary's office. Were he and Mr. Allen — and perhaps others — waiting for a 'phone call or radio announcement? If so they had a long wait. The meeting at Lords had occupied seven hours and it was not until 6.20 that Jack Bailey, Secretary of the ICC, appeared on our screens to tell us that it had been decided to ban all Packer men from international cricket from October 1st unless they withdrew. For weeks many of us had thought that this was the only outcome and so, when the facts were made known, they came almost as an anti-climax. It only remainded to be seen whether, at their meeting in August, the TCCB would ban all these men from domestic cricket as well. On August 10th the TCCB banned all those who took part in Packer's World Series cricket from domestic cricket for two years after they last played in an unauthorised match, but this could not be put into effect until after the High Court hearing which was pending.

On August 18th the Rest of the World met the Australians in a game at Arundel Park in aid of the Queen's Silver Jubilee Fund. Greig was conspicuously absent and Mike Proctor, the South African captain of Gloucestershire, now captained the Rest of the World. The ground had been flooded the night before, but the ROW won on a cold, bleak day, which suited the mood of the cricket establishment world. The Australians, looking disgruntled and untidy, refused to join in the group photograph with Lavinia, Duchess of Norfolk, so we all just shrugged our shoulders and the pictures were taken without them. Roger Knight, 12th man for the ROW, was the only Sussex player in sight. Shortly afterwards Knight made 100 not out in what was to be his last game for Sussex — and it was against Surrey!

In this eventful year Sussex finished 8th, which was a considerable improvement on previous years, but Greig made only 509 runs for the county and took 28 wickets. Barclay and Miandad were the only batsmen to reach 1,000 runs: Spencer took 48 wickets and Snow 43.

All through the summer there had been rumblings about the Packer Affair and, eventually, on September 26th came the High Court hearing of the case in which World Series Cricket Pty Ltd. (Packer's company), with Tony Greig, John Snow and Mike Proctor, sought injunctions on the ICC and TCCB to prevent their ban on Packer players from Test and other first-class cricket. It is not my purpose to go into this lengthy case, but I could not help being amused at the description of the Court on the first few days.

"Next to him" (Mr. Packer) "wrote *The Daily Telegraph* reporter, sat Mr. Greig, wearing a dark pin-stripe suit and sporting his MCC touring tie," whilst "Mr. Snow stood at the back of the court, in a blue velvet jacket and polo-neck sweater." I did not need to be in court to picture these two men. First the exuberant, golden-haired, highly-complexioned and extrovert Tony Greig, attired for all the world as a successful business man, full of confidence, and, as ever, the star of the show, sitting in front with Mr. Packer: then John Snow, as retiring and aloof and unconventionally dressed as ever, standing in the background and surveying the scene with detachment and even, maybe, disdain. Snow said little during his time in court, his most reported speech being when he stated, with regard to his future employment, that he had had nightmares at the thought of having to become an umpire on his retirement! Was his conscience beginning to smite him a little? The case went on for 31 days, but the judge delayed the findings until November 25th when he took 5½ hours

## The Captaincy of Tony Greig 1973 – 1977

to read out 211 pages of foolscap. He ruled that "to ban cricketers from playing county or Test cricket because they had signed with World Series Cricket would be an unreasonable restraint of trade and an inducement to them to break their Packer contracts." Costs were awarded to Packer and these were estimated at about £250,000. Later the Sussex C.C.C. Annual Report disclosed the Sussex share of this being £9,240.

Whilst the case was in progress I wrote to ask Madame Tussaud's what had happened to the wax effigy of Tony Greig. I was informed by the press officer that it was "still in the Exhibition, in the Conservatory. Tony Greig remains very much in the public eye as a cricketer even though he is no longer captain of England."

On December 6th Greig was re-appointed as captain of Sussex with an official statement which said that he commanded the loyalty of the players, but Stanley Allen also said that it was time people stood up and were counted. Forthwith Billy Griffith announced that he would not be standing for election to the new Committee and George Cox resigned from the cricket sub-committee as an act of protest, although he was prepared to stay on the main Committee if re-elected. I wrote to both Billy Griffith and to George Cox to say how much I supported them in the stand they had taken. Billy replied that he was almost completely overwhelmed by everything that had happened, but felt that there might be a powerful reaction against current (cricketing) moralities and standards accepted at Hove. George Cox wrote explaining that it was not only on the Greig issue that he and Billy Griffith had resigned: they had both been shocked at events of the past two years and George said that he refused to lower his standards, even at the cost of being called 'old-fashioned' or 'out-of-date'.

The Packer Affair was a tragedy for international cricket, for cricket in England and for cricket in Sussex, but, above all, it was a tragedy for the man who had helped to bring it birth – Tony Greig. It may have been a personal sorrow for Greig that he should have lost the England captaincy, but sadder still was it that he had also lost his fair name in the cricketing world. His behaviour had always been upredictable and there had been times when I had felt that perhaps he had taken on more than he was fully able to bear for there had been times when he had looked mentally and physically exhausted. Packer was all about money and Greig claimed from the start that his own 'sacrifice' would benefit professional cricketers in the future. Cricket followers are a fair-minded lot – on the whole – and I never heard any criticism of John Snow for joining WSC: Freddie Trueman even said that he must regard

Kerry Packer as a sort of Father Christmas, for John's England career must almost certainly have been at an end and the way in which he earned his living in the winter was his own affair: but it was quite mystifying to know how an England captain could defect in such a way and could also persuade such established members of his own side as Knott and Underwood and Woolmer to go with him. When I spoke to two of the Sussex cricketers' wives one day of the secrecy which had upset everyone so much I was told, "That's the way Packer wanted it. That was why Tony had to do it."

It is not for me to predict the outcome of Packer's WSC adventure for only the first chapter of John Arlott's historical novel has yet been written, but the authorities who run the game in this country had been working for some time on improved conditions for professionals, helped ever more by sponsorship; perhaps they had been moving too slowly; certainly Tony Greig moved first and in the winter of 1977-78 half the Sussex side was to be found leaving like lemmings to join the Packer coaching scheme in Australia; but, as in the case of Snow, no blame should be attached to them, except that the very name of Packer was beginning to put many people's teeth on edge. This country is under no obligation to compromise with Kerry Packer or any other cricketing entrepreneur, but I possess no crystal ball. Perhaps the day will come when we shall find Mr. Packer pouring money into English Test and County cricket; then Tony Greig may once again be hailed as the saviour of English cricket. Stranger things have happened in the history of the world.

CHAPTER ELEVEN

## TWO MEN WHO LOVED CRICKET

1.
### Bernard Marmaduke Fitzalan-Howard, 16th Duke of Norfolk

No story of Sussex cricket would be complete without reference to the Duke of Norfolk, who had been President of the County Club for one year in 1933 and later for 25 years between 1949 and 1975.

The Duke's heart was in Sussex cricket and the dreadful AGM of 1950 must have been a bitter blow to him. I always thought that he showed the sort of man he was when he again accepted the Presidency after the vote of 'No confidence' at the Royal Pavilion. Others might have said, "If that is how your members behave, they can do without me." But not Duke Bernard. He was President, too, not only in name but in fact, and he missed few AGMs over the years, always enlivening what could be a boring evening with some light-hearted comment or story; his familiar car with the 'N' registration and the Earl Marshal's pennant flying was a frequent sight on the Hove ground. He found supreme relaxation in the game and contributed to it in whatever way he could. Even after King George VI died in 1952 and the young Queen Elizabeth returned sadly from Kenya with her husband and when the Duke, as Earl Marshal, must have been fatigued with all the arrangements for the King's funeral, he was still in his place in the chair as President at that year's AGM. At the following year's meeting I remember that we all stood in silence in memory of Queen Mary, who had died the night before: it was a sorrow to many that she did not live to see the splendour of her granddaughter's Coronation, so magnificently managed by the President of Sussex.

After 1950 AGMs were held at the Hove Town Hall for several years, but were later transferred to the Ralli Hall, Denmark Villas and later still to the County Ground itself. I recall how, one evening, the Duke arrived late — a most unusual thing for one who was such a stickler for punctuality — and he was complain-

*Bernard, 16th Duke of Norfolk by Juliet Pannett*

ing vigorously about the traffic on the A27; this was before the Shoreham by-pass was built and long before the widening of the road into Hove. One had to cross the River Adur by the old wooden toll bridge which was so narrow that two vehicles could hardly pass and which, during the rush-hour, could cause the most frustrating delays. This year the Duke had just returned from a winter overseas when he had taken a team to the West Indies: he looked tanned and fit as did Sussex captain, Mike Griffith, who had been a member of the side. It was not the first time that the Duke had taken his own team abroad for in 1957 he had travelled with a side to Jamaica which had included several Test players and they had returned undefeated.

The Duke of Norfolk was never a mere figurehead: he was forthright in his speech either when criticizing the Australian press for its treatment of the MCC touring team or when Sussex refused to release Tony Greig to play for MCC in a Test Trial in 1972. Always thinking of cricket first the Duke told the Sussex Committee that he would resign if such an action were repeated. The Committee and players met at the County Ground and issued a statement saying that they supported the Duke and promising that it would not happen again. Duke Bernard did not have to speak twice. Later this same year at the Annual Dinner of Sussex C.C.C. held at the Hotel Metropole in Brighton, it was the Duke who thanked Mike Griffith for all he had tried to do and told Tony Greig that he had the full support of the Committee and all the people in the county, but added, "I have been here a long time — too long, but, by God, I am fed up with some of the things that have happened in the past years. We want to get together, support the team, and knock out all the nonsense — knock it all out, bang, smash, finish!" One almost trembles at the thought of what the Duke would have done had he lived to see the events of 1977. One of the things he loathed was the appearance of betting shops on cricket grounds and he told his audience:- "I would like to sit outside with a pea-shooter or water pistol and have a crack at everyone going into them. And if I didn't hit them, then I'd get them on the way out." The Duke, a keen racing man, would have been pleased to find that the life of these betting shops was very short.

In 1973 he accepted the Presidency for the 25th and, he said, for the last time. I felt very sad and somehow I knew that part of Sussex cricket history would be going with him. He left early, but before he went he had been faced with the 'Parks row' and he dealt gently, but firmly, with some of the less than generous remarks made from the floor. He was something of an autocrat and there were those who stood in awe of him, but you only had to see that twinkle in his eye or hear some of his dry humour to be completely won over.

So the members at the AGM said good-bye sadly to the Duke of Norfolk as he completed his Silver Jubilee with Sussex. He was presented with a silver salver and loudly cheered: my sense of sadness was lessened to a certain degree because he was being succeeded by A.E.R. Gilligan.

It was not only at the County Ground that the Duke exercised his influence on cricket. There can be few more delightful places to play or watch the game than his own ground at Arundel Castle and few places where the bowling is described as being from the 'Castle' or the 'Park' ends. Here, in a clearing amidst trees typical of Southern England is a well-kept, level, circular playing area. Grass slopes for seats have been formed on two sides of the arena and a cutting in the trees to the east opens up a glorious view across the River Arun from which the town gets its name. In the spring there is a carpet of daffodils and all around there are squirrels and singing birds. The atmosphere is that of country house cricket with (in those early days) the strawberries and cream which always put me in mind of Wimbledon — cricket and tennis being so much a part of any English summer. When some big match was to be played an early start was necessary if we wanted deck chairs, for these were limited and the alternative of the hard ground on the bank, however attractive to look at, was for youth rather than middle age. The Duke's enthusiasm was infectious and everyone was happy to see him get his runs, which, in his playing days, he usually did. Everything about Arundel has always been well-organized, as one might expect, but at the same time there are few restrictions and, apart from a small enclosure that was fenced off for the special friends of the Duke and Duchess and for the players, the public might wander at will, the only request being that they leave the place as tidy as it was when they arrived. It would be criminal to despoil such idyllic surroundings.

In 1951 the Sussex County Cricket Club awarded George Cox a well-earned benefit and my subscription card was full of matches in aid of the man whom I had first watched play in 1931. There was a large variety of games, but perhaps the greatest day of all was when the Duke of Norfolk arranged for a game to be played for 'young' George on his own ground. This was billed as 'The Duke of Norfolk's XI v George Cox's XI' and the Duke's team

## Two Men Who Loved Cricket 161

included Hugh Bartlett, G.O. Allen, Derek Shackleton, John Dew, J. Crapp, E. Eager, Colin Cowdrey, Hubert Doggart, Learie Constantine and film star Trevor Howard. George Cox led a truly Sussex side of Jim and John Langridge, Oakman, Bates, Don Smith, Ted James, Charlie and Jack Oakes and Rupert Webb. It is probably fair to say that the cricket was secondary to the occasion and the outstanding feat was performed by a member of the public, an 18-year-old plumber's mate, called Arthur Hounsome, who caught an almighty six hit by the powerful Don Smith: during the interval the Duke presented the embarrassed young man with the ball. I am sure he has it still.

From now onwards the Duke invited a 'Sussex XI' to play his own side nearly every year, the proceeds going to the beneficiary of the season or, if none, to the Sussex C.C.C. Funds. After Cox, Jim Langridge, Smith and James all had games at Arundel.

Soon after the Sussex matches at Arundel Castle began a new fixture appeared in the lists. This was the Duke of Norfolk's XI versus the current touring side, a game played at the end of April which soon became recognised as the first appearance of our summer visitors. The Duke always put out a team worthy of the opposition and anyone invited to play deemed it an honour. The Duke dearly loved a close finish and I am sure that he did not mind who won provided the cricket was good. In 1956 David Sheppard captained the Duke's side against the Australians. He had planned with the visiting captain, Ian Johnson, that the visitors must not lose, but Alec Bedser and Doug Wright bowled so well that the plan nearly went awry, but the day brought a bumper £4,000 which must have been a record for such a match at the time.

The South Africans came to Arundel in 1960 as already told and then in 1962 Pakistan began their tour on the ground when the Duke's XI batted first and made 204-6 dec. with the attractive Hampshire batsman, Roy Marshall, the most entertaining. Pakistan made 173–6 and the game was drawn. In 1963 the West Indians beat the Duke's XI by 3 wickets and the following year the Australians came again. The Duke had in his side Dexter, Cowdrey, Sheppard, Marshall, Alec Bedser and Fred Titmus. The Queen Mother, staying at the Castle, came to the ground at 11.20 and the teams were presented to her. I won a 'Jim Parks' scarf (this was his benefit year) — the first and only time I have had any luck with all the raffle tickets I have bought in fifty years. This time the crowd was estimated at 7,000 and the fixture was growing in importance with every year that passed. The West

Indians made a return visit in 1966 and the anticipated warm-up was just that, but the unusual strength of the April sun gave me such a headache that I made no notes, contenting myself by writing that the West Indians won by 4 wickets. In 1968 the game with the Australians was marred by rain; when they came back four years later it was a sunny day, but with a cold north-easterly wind: Tony Greig made 96 and it was yet another of those glorious festival occasions which Sussex folk had by now come to expect as a prelude to the cricket season. It may have been on this day — I am not quite sure — that, having been in search of refreshment, I was returning to my seat when I found a large and smiling Colin Cowdrey, completely surrounded by a hoard of small boys with autograph albums, bearing down upon me on a narrow pathway. Cowdrey gave me a charming smile. "Make way for the lady," he said to the boys. If only I could have explained to him that 'the lady' he saw was not the real me at all; I was really one of those youngsters who would have been just as pleased to have his autograph to-day as would the child of nearly fifty years before. The Duke's side won by 18 runs.

As far back as 1953 Prince Philip, Duke of Edinburgh, and the Duke of Norfolk each captained a star-studded side in aid of the National Playing Fields Association, a cause always dear to the Prince's heart. Play did not start until 2 p.m. for Sunday cricket was still frowned upon by those of an earlier generation and David Sheppard always refused to play, yet when the Prince attended morning service at the old flint parish church of St. Nicholas in Arundel the vicar, the Rev. H.A. King, told his congregation that "Sunday to the Christian is a holiday as well as a holy day and a holy day as well as a holiday." On the Continent this has been known for years, but the British used always to have that streak in them, left over from the Puritans, which made them feel guilty when they enjoyed themselves on the Sabbath. On the ground this day a small boy asked Prince Philip for his autograph, but the Prince, smiling, declined, saying, "Not to-day." The boy, on holiday from Oldham, was disappointed. "I didn't have any difficulty getting Randy Turpin," he is reported to have said, "I just went into his dressing-room." Prince Philip won the toss and put the Duke's side in to bat: his own side consisted of many Test players, whilst the Duke of Norfolk's side was mainly a Sussex one, but it also included Bill Edrich and Young of Middlesex. One item on the scoreboard was impressive — "Duke of Norfolk, b. Duke of Edinburgh 4." Prince Philip made 18 runs as well, but the Duke of Norfolk's side won by 7 runs. Later, speaking through the announcer's microphone, the Duke of Norfolk thanked the Duke of Edinburgh for playing, but said, with the utmost gravity, that he had no intention of thanking him for deciding to bowl! In 1957 there was another ducal contest: this time the Duke of Norfolk bowled Prince Philip for 2, but the latter retaliated later by taking 4–60. The heat was terrific, but the crowd of 25,000 was thrilled.

The Duke of Norfolk did not content himself with the big occasion only and as time went on the Sussex 2nd XI and the Young Sussex Cricketers played on his ground. In 1975 the first John Player League fixture took place at Arundel.

In 1957, too, the Duke showed his sportsmanship when he played at Hove for David Sheppard's XI against a side captained by Robin Marlar in aid of the Brighton and Islington Boys' Clubs. It had been announced that there would be 20,000 children present and no cars were admitted, but these numbers were somewhat exaggerated. There was, however, a big crowd and the game itself was good fun. Robin Marlar's XI made 329, with Don Smith getting 95, reserve wicket-keeper, Mantell 69, and the Duke of Norfolk 28, including a 6. "He is a grand person," I wrote that night. David Sheppard's team won by 7 wickets; both he and Denis Compton getting centuries and 659 runs being scored in 4½ hours!

The Duke of Norfolk was President of MCC in 1955-56, this being the highest non-playing honour which cricket can bestow, yet I believe that the 'honour' which pleased him most was his appointment as manager of MCC's tour of Australia in 1962-63 when Dexter, whom he greatly admired, was England's captain. The series was drawn, but all who have written about it have spoken about how happy the team had been. The Duke had given up much to be away from home for so many months and probably only cricket would have drawn him. Two things stand out in memory, apart from the cricket: one, that the Duke had to return, secretly, to conduct a rehearsal of Sir Winston Churchill's funeral for which he would be responsible; the other that the Australians, not renowned for their love of what people call the 'establishment', took the Duke to their hearts from the start; they promptly called him 'Dukey' and he loved it!

Amongst the many cricket cartoons which are in my cutting books is one of Emmwood from the *Daily Mail,* drawn on the occasion of the Investiture of Prince Charles as Prince of Wales at Caernavon Castle. Both the Prince and the Duke are seated, in full regalia, and each is holding a small radio transistor to his ear, whilst an official is whispering to the Duke, "Would you mind turning the Test Match down a bit, Your Grace; His Royal Highness is trying to listen to Wimbledon!"

On January 31st 1975 the cricketing world and Sussex in particular was grieved to hear of the death of the Duke of Norfolk. Bernard Marmaduke Fitzalan-Howard, 16th Duke of Norfolk, Earl Marshal and Hereditory Marshal of England had succeeded his father when he was only nine. He had seen Sussex County Cricket Club through good times and bad and he had been an ardent supporter of the game in so many ways. As Earl Marshal the Duke had arranged the Coronation of King George VI and Queen Elizabeth II as well as the funerals of King George VI and Sir Winston Churchill. In 1963 he was the Queen's representative at the Coronation of Pope Paul in Rome. In 1971 the Duke and Duchess of Norfolk had moved out of Arundel Castle to the newly-built Arundel Park in the grounds of the Castle: this was both for comfort and economy, but it was always the Duke's wish that cricket should go on where he had spent so many happy days.

The Requiem Mass in the Cathedral of Our Lady and St. Philip in Arundel was celebrated by Bishop Bowen, now Archbishop of Southwark. The Queen was represented by Princess Alexandra. It is most unusual for a member of the Royal Family to be present as a private individual at any funeral other than one for a member of their own family, yet Prince Charles was there, no doubt with his Investiture still in mind, for the late Duke had been Chairman of the Committee which had masterminded that successful day.

When one thinks back to the great occasions of state for which the Earl Marshal had been responsible his own funeral seemed a simple one, but it was very moving. The Heralds in their tabards were resplendant on either side of the altar steps, whilst in the centre aisle stood the coffin draped with the Duke's personal banner on which lay his ducal coronet and baton as Earl Marshal: there was also a large cross made from his favourite flowers, carnations, from his widow. At the end of Mass the gold-laced state trumpeters sounded a fanfare and Garter Principal King of Arms proclaimed the Duke's styles and titles from the steps of the sanctuary. A single piper played 'The Flowers of the Forest' as the procession moved slowly from the Cathedral to the private Chapel a short distance away. This was, indeed, our final 'goodbye'.

As I left the Cathedral I spoke to S.C. 'Billy' Griffith, a great friend of the late Duke and one of many cricketing personalities who had come that day in memory of one who shared their love of the game. He told me that he had seen Duke Bernard very shortly before he died and that he had been cheerful, but still very concerned that cricket should continue to be played on the Castle ground. His heir was able to assure him that this would be so and now the Friends of Arundel Castle Cricket Club has been formed by Lavinia, Duchess of Norfolk, in her husband's memory. Billy Griffith was its first chairman-secretary and Colin Cowdrey vice-chairman.

The AGM of 1975 was prefaced by a two minutes silence for the Duke of Norfolk and then Arthur Gilligan said, "His love of Sussex cricket was a great part of his life. Cricket was a game he loved dearly and deeply."

## 2.
## A.E.R. Gilligan

Early in the morning of September 6th 1976 I heard, with great shock and sorrow, of the sudden death the day before of Arthur Gilligan at his home in Pulborough.

I first saw Arthur Gilligan play cricket in 1921, he a young man, myself a small child. Down the years we had always greeted each other and exchanged a smile or a few words either at the AGM or on the County Ground. With Maurice Tate, he had been one of my earliest cricketing heroes and so it was with considerable excitement and pleasure that I learnt, at the beginning of 1972, that Juliet Pannett had been commissioned to paint a three-quarter-length oil of Arthur to be hung in the Committee Room at Hove. When the arrangements for the portrait were made he had no idea that the artist was to be the little girl who had once made sketches of him and the other members of the Sussex team in, what was now, the distant past. In March there was to be a break in the sittings during which the indefatigable Arthur and his wife, Penny, went on their annual ski-ing holiday. When they returned the sittings were resumed and Juliet asked me to come over to Angmering to watch her at work and to talk to our childhood friend. It was a great reunion and cricket talk endless; I could tell how much Arthur enjoyed going back over old times and speaking of the men with whom he had played. Over our drinks before lunch he looked at the article I had written for *The Journal of the Cricket Society* about the old days at Hove: he insisted that I take this to Secretary Dumbrell so that it might be included in the forthcoming *Sussex Centenary Handbook*. After some swift work on this to bring it up-to-date it was just in time for publication.

This was the first year that the AGM was held in the Arthur Gilligan Stand and as we went into the room we found the portrait standing there with the subject near by, so that everyone could see what a good likeness Juliet had achieved. In this picture the old Sussex captain is wearing a dark suit against which the splash of colour from his I.Z. tie stands out vividly. He was very proud of this tie, which, as most cricket followers know, is black, red and gold, the colours symbolizing "an ascent out of darkness, through fire, into light."

Two years later Arthur Gilligan celebrated his 80th birthday and Bob Wyatt told me that he had written to congratulate Arthur and had advised him to "get the next 20 in singles". I, too, had written and had wished him well, receiving the following reply:-

> Cherry Trees,
> Pulborough,
> Sussex.
> 27. XII. 74.
>
> Dear Letty and Bryan,
> How very kind of you to send me such a lovely greeting for my 80th. I did appreciate your very nice thought for the "young" Old Un. Penny joins in sending all kind wishes for 1975.
>
> Yours ever
> Arthur Gilligan.

When I wrote to Arthur twelve months later for his 81st birthday he replied, "I've completed my 2 years as President of the XL Club. They've made me an Hon. life member and I'm very bucked." Here was the 'Young Old 'Un' as excited as a schoolboy about yet another honour bestowed on him by cricket throughout his long life.

After Sussex had lost that Gillette Cup Final to Gloucestershire in 1973 letters had been exchanged between Arthur Gilligan and the Duke of Beaufort, Master of the Horse. A.E.R. had congratulated the Duke on Gloucestershire's victory at Lords: he always addressed the Duke as 'Master' and the Duke signed his reply in similar fashion, regretting that Sussex had had to bat in such a poor light. One can only hope that such courtesies will continue to be exchanged between true devotees of the game.

A.E.R. Gilligan never lost his interest in Sussex cricket and the words he used of the Duke of Norfolk could equally well be said of him. When he became President of MCC in 1967 the President, Past Presidents, Vice Presidents and Committee of the Sussex County Cricket Club presented him with a fine silver tray on which is written, in their own handwriting, the names of all the donors: this is one of Penny Gilligan's many treasured possessions. At the time of his death he was Patron of the Club, combining this with the position of President after the retirement of the Duke of Norfolk in 1974; he had also been Chairman of the Cricket Committee for several years. At Dulwich College, as a boy, he had been a first-class gymnast, helping the school to win the schools shield for which they then competed. Later, apart from cricket, ski-ing and golf were his main recreations and he was President of the English Golf Union in 1959 as well as Presi-

*A.E.R. Gilligan by Juliet Pannett*

dent of the West Sussex Golf Club and numerous other clubs and of the County Cricketers' Golfing Society. Arthur actually played a full round of competitive golf on his home course at West Sussex the day before he died.

This September morning I could hardly believe that A.E.R. would not be at the County Ground to greet us when cricket came again. He had seemed indestructible and though he had been hit on the hand by a golf ball earlier in the year and had had a fall in the bathroom of his home, he had made light of these mishaps. Only a fortnight before his death he had been at the final Test Match against the West Indies at the Oval and had been planning with Bob Wyatt to accept the invitation from the Australians which had been sent to all who had played Tests against them, to go 'down under' for the Centenary Test in March. A.E.R. Gilligan and R.E.S. Wyatt were the two most senior captains and they had been anticipating the trip with undisguised excitement.

Apart from playing cricket Arthur wrote about it, broadcast, toured the county on the lookout for young players, spoke at cricket dinners and encouraged all with whom he came in contact. E.W. Swanton's obituary of one who will go down in cricket history was headed 'Arthur Gilligan, the Friendly Captain', and it ended with the paragraph, "His record as an all-rounder is notable enough, but off the field I judge his endeavours to have been of even greater value to cricket." One day I had asked Arthur why he had not written his autobiography for he was always so full of stories and anecdotes. His reply was, "No, I might say something that would hurt someone and I should not like that." Such was the nature of the man. He was deeply grieved at some of the events taking place in the cricketing world and, towards the end, I fear, just a little disillusioned. I am thankful that he never saw the Packer upheaval which would have broken his heart.

The Memorial Service held at St. Mary's Church in the Causeway at Horsham, only a few yards from the ground where he had played for Sussex so many years before, was crowded with cricket-lovers and with golfing friends, all of whom had come to pay tribute to a fine man. The address was given by Maurice Allom, President of Surrey C.C.C. and a Past President of MCC. With Penny was Arthur's brother, Harold, whose daughter, Virginia, and son-in-law, Peter May, were also present. S.C. Griffith and ex-Secretary Ian Stoop, Ronnie Aird, Colin Cowdrey, E.W. Swanton, Tony Buss, John Langridge and George Pearce were all in the congregation, the last of these a Horsham man himself, who had played as far back as 1928.

Whilst Mr. Allom was speaking it was hard not to think of A.E.R. as he had been in his cricketing youth. Now he was united with his old bowling partner, Maurice Tate, and I could just imagine the talk that would be going on. There is no doubt that the spirits of these two great Sussex bowlers will frequent the County Ground whenever play is over — or even before — and they will take the field and bowl as they did in their prime, doing battle with other old cricket warriors who are not with us any more. This thought makes me happy and I hope it will make others happy too.

It seems appropriate to end with the prayer spoken at the start of the Memorial Service for the one-time Sussex and England cricket captain:-

> We are gathered this day to remember Arthur Edward Robert Gilligan; to give thanks to God for his life; to recall to mind the great sporting talents with which God blessed him and the faithful use made of those gifts to promote friendship and happiness in so many parts of the world.

CHAPTER TWELVE

THE PHOENIX RISES

No one would have expected that the breaking of Mike Brearley's arm in Pakistan, painful though it must have been to its owner, would have had such repercussions on the Sussex C.C.C. Boycott took over the England captaincy and soon Greig was commenting from his Packer lair in Australia on "Boycott and his cronies" and accusing the Yorkshireman of always managing to be where the fast bowling was not. There was swift reaction in England with Lancashire and Notts (with whom Sussex had shared the County Championship in 1875) even wishing to have Sussex banned from the Championship. Shortly before this episode the Club had put themselves into bad grace with the other counties because they wished to swap Roger Knight, who was taking up a new teaching post at Dulwich College and wanted to join Surrey, for the Surrey and England fast bowler, Geoff Arnold. Since this would be the first exchange of players between counties the arrangement would need the sanction of the TCCB and in the new year permission was given, but what price soccer-type transfers now? Later Worthing-born Stuart Storey, who had retired from Surrey in 1974, was recruited onto the Sussex staff and we were in danger of being called 'Surrex'!

Not all Sussex members were happy to have Greig as captain in 1978. Perhaps the Boycott article was fortuitous, for others had written on the same lines before; in any case, the Committee called an extraordinary meeting on January 30th and requested Greig to resign the captaincy, although there was still a year of his contract to run. Arnold Long was invited to lead the side for the coming season, with Peter Graves as vice-captain, thus leaving Peter more free to concentrate on his forthcoming benefit.

I had expected something of an explosion at the AGM this year and it was probably due to the diplomacy of the Chairman, Tony Crole-Rees, that this did not happen: all the same I was disappointed that more questions were not asked and felt that the administration had been let off lightly. Arnold Long, sitting on the platform as captain for the first time, spoke quietly and well, not making wild promises, but saying that he would do his best. He had a warm reception and I was glad, for if ever a man had a confused and difficult season ahead of him that man was Arnold Long.

Tony Greig, back from Australia, faced the disciplinary committee of the TCCB on April 3rd and was banned from playing first-class cricket in England from April 22nd until June 16th for his 'derogatory' remarks about Boycott in the Sydney *Sun:* instead he and his brother, Ian, were granted permission to play League cricket for Brighton and Hove. Before this happened Greig and his family flew off to America to discuss the possibility of a cricket match in the United States and it crossed my mind that Greig was getting through his continents at great speed and would soon have only the Polar Regions to conquer.

Apart from being the wettest summer for ten years 1978 was 'The Year of the Helmet' and also of a sudden sprouting of beards and incipient moustaches, which, all combined, produced some rather horrific sights: the craze for necklets continued, although these ornaments must be extremely aggravating during a tiring day in the field. Discarded helmets created yet another problem for umpires and could be worn on a belt at the back of their coats, or, as by David Constant on at least one occasion, by the umpire himself, whilst his partner, Tom Spencer, held Constant's hat! A long-suffering twelfth man was sometimes responsible as armourer and he would be seated at the ring-side with helmet at the ready for immediate need. These helmets were derided by the old hands and laughed at by the spectators, but one Sussex cricketer, who never indulges in any form of head protection, told me that when you are fielding very close to the bat it is terrifying, as the bowler runs up, to think that this may be your last day on earth, and he defended, vigorously, the right of any man to use a helmet should he so wish. Fashions were also exhibited in the variety and shape of the sun-hats which have become the vogue, from the normal large, floppy sort and the 'beany' kind worn by Keith Fletcher, to the shallow type with green-lined brim upturned which is sported in such debonair style by Phil Edmonds. It must be difficult, to-day, to know whether to present a man with his county cap, hat or helmet: perhaps he might be allowed to chose!

Two of my old cricketing heroes died early in 1978. First Herbert Sutcliffe of Yorkshire, who had partnered Percy Holmes for his county and Jack Hobbs for England in the happy days of my youth; then A.H.H. Gilligan, youngest of the three Gilligan brothers, who died on May 5th. Having toured New Zealand as captain in 1929-30, he later represented that country at meetings of the ICC. Later in the month when Sussex played Gloucestershire at Hove, we found the county flag at half-mast in memory of the former Sussex captain.

John Snow, like Greig, was now home from his Packer winter, which he told me he had thoroughly enjoyed, but he had damaged a hand in an accident with a plate-glass window in Melbourne and would take a while to be fit. It was something of a blow — though not, perhaps, a surprise — to learn later that he had not been re-engaged by the Club; many Sussex supporters were sorry to see Snow go for they felt that he had much still to offer and, in conjunction with Imran Khan, would have been a force to be reckoned with. Instead Snow was to be found playing for Pudsey St. Lawrence in the Bradford League and also for East Grinstead.

Arnold "Ob" Long, as he is called in the dressing-room, is the exact opposite to Tony Greig, being self-effacing, quiet and undemonstrative. Perhaps the burden of the captaincy made his wicket-keeping a little less than perfect at times, but for the most part he was efficient and led the side wisely and well. In a pre-season interview he was asked what would happen at the end of June when Greig, Wessels, Miandad and Parker all returned to Sussex and his reply was that he would see when the time came and there might be injuries to be taken into consideration. How right he was!

The fates which had dogged Peter Graves throughout his cricketing life pursued him relentlessly into his benefit year. He broke a finger early on and did not play again the whole season. At the Saffrons I saw not only the fire damage to the Eastbourne club's new pavilion, but also the damage to Peter's left hand, the forefinger of which was still badly swollen. He explained that he had to have another operation soon and was hoping to be fit for 1979. Thus Sussex was robbed of one of her most loyal of modern players and I only trust that the public rallied round Peter Graves in the way that he deserved.

Most of the regular first team players, except Arnold Long, suffered some sort of injury during 1978 and at one point it was necessary to call upon Paul Parker, though the University term had not yet ended; Roger Marshall, now bearded, was enlisted, whilst Simon Hoadley (with another beard) from Uckfield and Colin Wells, from Newhaven, were hastily registered. One of the unluckiest of the 'walking wounded' was Gehan Mendis, who broke a finger not once but twice, in the semi-final and the Final of the Gillette Cup, a catastrophe which left him just 21 runs short of his 1,000 for the first time, and he was bitterly disappointed. Still hanging over the Club was what was called 'The Sussex Dilemma' since we would ultimately have three overseas players available — Imran, Wessels and Miandad — with only two permitted to play at one time. Problems enough for any captain one would think.

The season could be fairly divided into three parts: pre-Greig, Greig and post-Greig. During the first few weeks it was difficult to field a well-balanced team because of injuries and absentees, but Sussex battled through the early rounds of the Benson and Hedges Cup only to be beaten in the semi-finals by the powerful Somerset side. Gehan Mendis made his maiden hundred, followed soon afterwards by another and on this second occasion George Cox, on behalf of the Sussex Cricket Society, presented the smiling Mendis with a tankard for his *first* century and as we gathered on the grass in front of the pavilion to watch we heard a voice say, "I *think* he's George Cox. I *believe* he once played for Sussex." *Tempora mutantur!* Later in the season Simon Hoadley received a similar award for *his* first century, whilst Old Harrovian, Tony Pigott, who had been making quite an impact this summer, received a tankard for his hat-trick against Surrey, the first time that the Society had recognised a bowler in this way.

Tony Greig returned from his suspension to play for Sussex against Hampshire on June 17th. He came out to bat complete with helmet and circling his arms like the sails of a windmill: his reception was very mixed for there were cheers, boos and jeers. Sadly for Greig he was bowled first ball by Andy Roberts and a man in the crowd called out, "Go back to Brighton!" The TV cameras, which could never resist Greig if he was within reach, interviewed him on the roof just behind where we were sitting: I could hear the odd phrase about 'compromise' and 'the cheque book talks', then Greig removed himself, almost thankfully I thought, from the onlookers' gaze and that evening the back of Bryan's head appeared for the first time on the small screen.

On July 11th Bryan and I had attended an 80th birthday luncheon for Rick Pannett at Angmering, but on our return to Hove we looked in at the County Ground to see how Sussex were faring against Essex. For a few moments we stood at the back of the public seats and watched Greig bowling from the sea end: he looked exactly the same, with his high-stepping, pony-like action, as he had done when I first saw him more than ten years before in his first game for the county. To-day Sussex were obviously going to lose and we went home to tea. It was with utter amazement, therefore, that we heard on the TV news about an hour later that Greig had asked to be freed from his contract *at once*.

I can think of many reasons why Greig should have wanted to go, but to decide which of these swayed him most would be pure conjecture and so valueless. I had known of Greig's disability for the past six years and when he fell at London Airport in 1975 I had received a frantic telephone call from a well-known journalist who asked me if I knew what was the matter with Tony Greig. I admitted that I did know, but although neither of us named the complaint the caller stressed that it was vitally important that I should not share my knowledge with anyone. He need not have worried. The information I possessed had immediately been stored away in my mind like a cabin trunk 'not needed on the voyage'. There had obviously been an agreement amongst cricket writers — and members of Sussex C.C.C. — never to mention Greig's epilepsy for fear of endangering his career, yet only 36 hours after the end of the 1978 season — and while I was engaged on this chapter — it was made known in a Sunday paper. My personal opinion is that, since Greig had by now left England for good, it would have been fairer and kinder to have let him tell the story in his own way and in his own time. Since I have never mentioned the matter to anyone at the ground I do not know how many people were aware of the situation, but I hope that when Greig comes to write his autobiography he will take note of the loyalty of both the Committee and members of Sussex who *did* know, but, because he wished it, kept their counsel. On the other hand, *had* the public known more of the handicap under which Greig lived he might have received more understanding and also greater admiration for his courage in the face of what must have been no small anxiety for him, living as he did in the constant glare of publicity.

I may well have been the last person to speak to the one-time Sussex and England captain in the precincts of the Sussex County Cricket Ground. The match against Leicestershire had been ruined by rain, but on a chill, grey 1st of August I wandered along just to see what was going on. As I approached the Tate Gates on foot a large white car was coming out and both it and its occupant were at once recognisable. The greyness of the day was at once lightened by the golden hair, pale blue pullover and friendly smile of Tony Greig, who had his tiny son, Mark, on the back seat. He had just said farewell to a gateman and as I passed he waved and called out, "Good luck!" "Good luck," I called back, "and to your family." Tony pulled up his car and stretched out a hand. We exchanged a few words and as I moved away he said, "I may be back to watch some cricket again one of these days." These were almost the identical words that Tommy Cook had used on practically the same spot 41 years before. I hate all good-byes and as I turned to walk into the ground much of my anger at what Greig had done to cricket melted away. I just regretted, more than ever, all that had happened since March 1977.

After the match against Surrey Michael Buss announced his retirement, saying that he had not intended to play at all in 1978, but had carried on to help out until Greig returned. Buss came back to play in the quarter-final of the Gillette Cup and then left to set up a small business, which includes a Post Office, at Battle. And so another senior player had vanished from before our eyes and with Greig and Snow gone as well it was time to start anew and for the young ones to take their places.

The television cameras went to the Central Ground, Hastings, for the first time when Sussex played Glamorgan in the John Player League and during the tea interval Doug Insole, as chairman of the TCCB, presented John Langridge, who was umpiring, with a silver coffee pot and a cheque to mark the completion of his fifty years association with the first-class game. John looked almost embarrassed at being the centre of attention, but I am sure that he was pleased for he wrote to me, saying, ". . . I appreciate the Test and County Cricket Board honouring me in this way. Fifty years is certainly a long time to have been involved in cricket but I have been so fortunate to have had a very happy and rewarding career in the game I love. I am sure if I had my time over again I would do exactly the same, for I have enjoyed every minute of it."

It was untypical of Greig to have walked away leaving the Club at the bottom of the Championship Table, but it was not long before an improvement set in and then, just as we were climbing from the depths, Sussex were fined £100 and had 6 points deducted for playing Miandad (after the Pakistan tour) before he had been registered. The Secretary called this 'an administrative oversight', but it just shows the complications of running a county club to-day, when an already capped player has to be re-registered before he can be legally accepted.

Throughout August and early September Sussex continued in their winning ways and it was as if a cloud had been lifted. The ex-Surrey players, and especially Arnold Long, had helped the Club through what might well have been a disastrous spell and we should, indeed, be grateful to them. Geoff Arnold finished up as the leading bowler, closely followed by Chris Waller. The workhorse was, as ever, John Spencer, out briefly with back trouble, but who captained the side when Long stood down and gained a couple of useful victories for his team. In these matches young Tim Head, educated at Lancing College, kept wicket and from what I saw he acquitted himself well and is extremely agile. Imran Khan was probably the most consistent player and, like most all-rounders, could swing a game either way, but before the season ended he looked worn out. Kepler Wessels, obviously out of form and suffering from a post-operative cartilege condition, lost his place to Javed Miandad, who had had a wretched tour with Pakistan, but who showed much of his old brilliance when he came back to Sussex and headed their batting averages. The really bright spot, from the point of view of one who is truly Sussex at heart, was the forceful batting of Paul Phillipson and Paul Parker, the former bowling less, but batting with a new-found zest; the latter one of the players whose future must surely be bright. Then there was the excellent batting of the cheerful little Mendis and the fine slow bowling of Giles Cheatle. Here we have four of our own players, any one of whom could go to the top. I hope that they will be given the encouragement they need.

Sussex finished up exactly mid-way in both County Championship and John Player League, the 2nd XI were top of their own competition, whilst the under-25 side reached the semi-final. But who would have thought that in this year of all years Sussex would win the Gillette Cup! Perhaps we were a trifle lucky in the early rounds to draw Suffolk and Staffordshire, but we scraped through by only 2 runs against the latter and then won a 10-over, rain-affected bash-about against Yorkshire. The defeat of Lancashire, however, was no fluke and on the eve of the Final at Lords the Sussex cricket sub-committee gave a unanimous vote in favour of the re-appointment of Arnold Long as Sussex captain for 1979 and expressed their thanks to him for "his exemplary leadership and conduct both on and off the field."

So Sussex went to the Final at Lords with their heads held high and Long, winning the toss, took his courage in both hands and put Somerset in to bat. Sussex defeated Somerset with Ian Botham, Viv Richards and all, and though Botham, the new England all-rounder, might have felt slightly aggrieved that his good innings of 80 did not bring him the Man of the Match award, I had already made my own decision — as impartially as possible — in favour of Paul Parker and Ken Barrington agreed

SUSSEX GILLETTE CUP WINNERS 1978
Back Row: Imran Khan, B. Storey, G. Cheatle, P. Phillipson, J. Groome
G. Arnold, P. Parker
Front Row: G. Mendis, J. Barclay, A. Long, J. Spencer, Javed Miandad

with me. Barclay and Mendis in an opening partnership of 93 gave Sussex just the start they needed, but then three wickets fell with alarming rapidity, so that had Paul Parker failed all might have been over in the battle between the martlets and the wyvern, but he kept his head, batted with the confidence of a veteran and, with Paul Phillipson playing an invaluable part, saw Sussex through to the end. It was just the boost that the Club wanted, both morally and financially (since the winners took £20,000), and this was final proof that Sussex were once again on the march. Robin Marlar, who had rated Sussex so soundly earlier in the season now said that Arnold Long must be "the miracle-worker of the season."

Just as a bonus to what had suddenly become a memorable year the Gillette Cup holders, Sussex, met the Champion County, Kent, in the last match of the season at Hove — and Sussex won. On the new presentation balcony Kent were given a vast cardboard cheque by Schweppes, whilst Sussex were photographed with the Gillette Cup and, for a fleeting moment, Bryan and I held the coveted trophy in our hands. After all the trials and tribulations it was rather like a dream and I keep pinching myself to see if I am awake.

My last memory of 1978 is of Jim Parks, senior, whose 93-year-old mother had died at the beginning of the year, and whose grandson, Bobby, had recently presented him with a great-grandson, climbing gingerly down the steep pavilion steps. There was a glint in his eyes which had not been there two months before.

And so the phoenix rises from its ashes, and here, alas, my odyssey must end. For the most part it has been a very happy journey, though there have been many changes on the cricket scene since I came to my first match as long ago as 1921 and, no doubt, there are more to come; more in the way of sponsorship, stricter laws about bouncers, firmer rules about the registration of overseas players and even, perhaps, changes in the structure of the three-day game, though these I shall regret. I am delighted, however, to finish my story on a note of triumph for it is time to put past anxieties behind and look forward to the future and to the days when Sussex will again hold the honourable place which the Club has always held in the past, the place it held when I was but a child and my heroes were Arthur Gilligan and Maurice Tate.

## INDEX OF NAMES

| Name | Page | Name | Page |
|---|---|---|---|
| Aird, R. | 169 | Chapman, A.P.F. | 14 |
| Allen, G.O. | 26 | Chappell, G. | 139 |
| Allen, S. | 117 | Chappell, I. | 139 |
| Allom, M.J.C. | 169 | Cheatle, R.G.L. | 137 |
| Amarnath, L. | 63 | Chichester - Constable, Maj, R.C. | 18 |
| Ames, L | 47 | Compton, D. | 38 |
| Amiss, D. | 131 | Constant, D. | 119 |
| Arlott, John | 34 | Cunstantine, Lord | 26 |
| Armstrong, W. | 6 | Cook, T.E. | 12 |
| Arnold, G. | 171 | Cook, R. | 24 |
| Asif Iqbal | 128 | Cooper, G. | 57 |
|  |  | Cornford, J. | 12 |
| Bailey, J. | 153 | Cornford, W.L. | 12 |
| Bakewell, A.H. | 38 | Cotter, Mrs. E. | 126 |
| Barclay, J.R.T. | 105 | Cowan, S. | 50 |
| Bardsley, W. | 17 | Cowdrey, M.C. | 161 |
| Barrington, K. | 130 | Cox, G.R. (Senior) | 12 |
| Bartlett, H.T. | 47 | Cox, G. (Junior) | 21 |
| Bartlett, J.H. | 63 | Crapp, J. | 161 |
| Bass, D. | 45 | Creese, L. | 118 |
| Bates, D. | 68 | Crole-Rees, A. | 171 |
| Bates, L. | 110 |  |  |
| Beach, A. | 7 | d'Arch Smith, T. | 90 |
| Bedser, A. | 58 | Davies, E. | 45 |
| Bedser, E. | 58 | Dempster, C.S. | 37 |
| Bell, R. | 87 | Denham, J. | 121 |
| Benand, R. | 92 | Denness, M. | 135 |
| Blake, P.D.S. | 63 | Dew, J.A. | 63 |
| Botham, I. | 177 | Dexter, E.R. | 86 |
| Bowes, W. | 36 | Doggart, A.G. | 59 |
| Bowley, E.H. | 12 | Doggart, G.H.G. | 59 |
| Boycott, G. | 171 | D'Oliviera, B. | 96 |
| Bradman, D.G. | 8 | Douglas, J.W.H.T. | 14 |
| Brearley, M. | 171 | Ducat, A. | 26 |
| Brinckman, Capt. T.W.E. | 43 | Duckworth, G. | 16 |
| Browne, The Rev. R.B.R. | 12 | Duleepsinjhi, K.S. | 12 |
| Bruce, The Hon. C.N. | 26 | Dumbrell, A.A. | 116 |
| Burchell, T. | 7 | Durston, J. | 26 |
| Buss, A. | 76 |  |  |
| Buss, M. | 89 | Eager, E. | 161 |
|  |  | Eaton, P. | 29 |
| Caillard, Z. | 18 | Edinburgh, Duke of | 162 |
| Cama, S. | 126 | Edrich, J. | 152 |
| Campion, Sir William | 70 | Edrich, W. | 162 |
| Carew, Dudley | 48 | Engineer, Farouk | 128 |
| Carmody, K. | 60 | Enthoven, H.J. | 22 |
| Carr, A.W. | 14 |  |  |
| Chaplin, H.P. | 20 | Faber, M.J.J. | 131 |
|  |  | Fagg, A. | 47 |

|  | Page |  | Page |
|---|---|---|---|
| Farncombe, M. | 124 | Herbert, P. | 41 |
| Farnes, K. | 47 | Higgs, K. | 107 |
| Farrell, R. | 20 | Hoadley, Simon | 173 |
| Feltham, R. | 35 | Hobbs, J.B. | 11 |
| Fender, P.G.H. | 27 | Holden, C. | 118 |
| Fletcher, K. | 172 | Holdsworth, R.L. | 22 |
| Ford, F.G.J. | 48 | Hollingdale, R.A. | 18 |
| Foreman, D.J. | 88 | Holmes, A.J. | 32 |
| Frankau, Gilbert & Susan | 59 | Holmes, E.R.T. | 26 |
| Fry, C.B. | 79 | Hopwood, L. | 45 |
| Gadsby, Daisy | 19 | Home, A.B. | 26 |
| Gaston, A.J. | 26 | Howell, H. | 14 |
| Gavaskar, S. | 108 | Hulme, J. | 38 |
| Geary, G. | 16 | Hunt, R.G. | 69 |
| Gerrard, C.G. | 122 | Hutton, L. | 48 |
| Gibb, P. | 47 |  |  |
| Gibbs, L. | 128 | Illingworth, R. | 107 |
| Gibson, C.H. | 12 | Imran Khan | 147 |
| Gilkes, W. | 138 | Insole, D.J. | 176 |
| Gilligan, A.E.R. | 5 | Issaacs, A. | 121 |
| Gilligan, A.H.H. | 12 |  |  |
| Gilligan, F.W. | 12 | James, A.E. | 68 |
| Goddard, T.W. | 47 | Jardine, D.R. | 26 |
| Godfree, C.S. | 45 | Javed Miandad | 137 |
| Gordon, Sir Home | 69 | Jenner, T.J. | 107 |
| Gover, A. | 58 | Johnson, Ian | 161 |
| Grace, W.G. | 11 | Johnston, Brian | 21 |
| Graveney, T. | 92 | Jones, A.A. | 103 |
| Graves, P. | 105 | Joshi, U.C. | 103 |
| Greenidge, G.A. | 105 | Judge, P.F. | 59 |
| Greig, A.W. | 86 | Jupp, A.L. | 53 |
| Greig, I. | 147 | Julian, Ray | 119 |
| Griffith, M.G. | 89 | Kallicharran, Alvin | 133 |
| Griffith, S.C. ('Billy') | 58 | Kanhai, Rohan | 128 |
| Grimston, Col. G.S. | 12 | Khan, Mansur Ali (Pataudi) | 91 |
| Groome, J. | 125 | Kidney, E.H. | 52 |
| Gunn, T. | 103 | Killick, E.H. | 121 |
|  |  | Killick, E.T. | 25 |
| Hammond, H.E. ('Jim') | 36 | King, The Rev. H.A. | 162 |
| Hammond, W.R. | 47 | Kippax, A. | 38 |
| Hardstaff, J. | 47 | Kirsten, P. | 137 |
| Harmisworth, Sir Hildebrand | 120 | Knight, R.D.V. | 171 |
| Hartley, N. | 78 | Knott, A. | 156 |
| Harvey, R.N. | 65 | Knowles, W.L. | 26 |
| Hassett, L. | 92 |  |  |
| Head, Tim | 177 | Laker, J. | 86 |
| Heane, G.F. | 39 | Langridge, James Mr & Mrs | 12 |
| Hearne, J.W. | 26 | Langridge, John Mr & Mrs | 36 |
| Heasman, Dr. W.G. | 30 | Langridge, Richard | 87 |
| Hendren, E.P. | 16 | Langridge, Susan | 87 |
| Henley, H.J. | 21 | Larwood, H. | 16 |

|  | Page |  | Page |
|---|---|---|---|
| Leaney, F. Mr & Mrs | 118 | Newham, W. | 58 |
| Leconfield, Lord | 72 | Noble, M.A. | 11 |
| Ledden, P. | 103 | Norfolk, 16th Duke of | 69 |
| Lee, F.S. | 26 | Norfolk, Lavinia, Duchess of | 149 |
| Lenham, L. | 86 | Northway, R.P. | 38 |
| Le Roux, G. | 110 | Nunes, R.K. | 26 |
| Levenson, R. | 103 | Nye, J. | 63 |
| Lewis, A.P. | 131 | | |
| Lewis, E. | 103 | Oakes, C. | 46 |
| Leyland, M. | 27 | Oakes, J. | 21 |
| Lillee, D. | 68 | Oakman, A.S.M. | 67 |
| Lillywhite, F.W. | 89 | Oldfield, W.A. | 38 |
| Lloyd, Clive | 128 | Osborne, H.A. | 124 |
| Locke, W. | 121 | | |
| Long, A. | 37 | Packer, Kerry | 148 |
| Long, G. | 67 | Palmer, G.A. | 22 |
| Luccock, Mrs E. | 125 | Pannett, Juliet | 13 |
| | | Pataudi, Nawab of | 63 |
| Mais, S.P.B. | 46 | Parker, P. | 173 |
| Mann, F.G. | 50 | Parkinson, Michael | 112 |
| Mann, F.T. | 26 | Parks, H.W. | 16 |
| Maltby, E.R. | 72 | Parks, J.H. | 12 |
| Mankad, V. | 63 | Parks, J.M. | 67 |
| Mannings, Frances | 124 | Parks, R. | 102 |
| Mansell, A. | 105 | Paynter, E. | 19 |
| Marlar, R. | 68 | Peach, A. | 26 |
| Marshall, John | 34 | Pearce, G. | 35 |
| Marshall, R.P.T. | 131 | Pearce, T.N. | 146 |
| Marshall, Roy | 161 | Peebles, I.A.R. | 26 |
| Mathews, J.K. | 5 | Pepper, C. | 145 |
| Mathews, F. | 6 | Phillipson, P. | 105 |
| May, P.B.H. | 169 | Pigott, A. | 152 |
| McCarthy, Cuan | 17 | Price, W.F. | 26 |
| McEwan, K. | 144 | Prideaux, R. | 105 |
| McGilvray, Alan | 112 | Prior, Bert | 28 |
| Meades, R. | 50 | Proctor, M. | 128 |
| Melford, Michael | 108 | Pountain, F.R. | 103 |
| Melville, A. | 39 | | |
| Mendis, Gehan | 137 | Quaife, W.G. | 15 |
| Merchant, V.M. | 63 | | |
| Miandad, J. | 137 | Racionzer, T. | 103 |
| Milburn, C. | 127 | Randall, D. | 148 |
| Miller, Hallett, A. | 45 | Ranjitsinjhi, K.S. | 27 |
| Miller, K. | 60 | Raymond, Ernest | 47 |
| Moore, R.H. | 39 | Relf, A.E. | 21 |
| Morley, J. | 105 | Relf, R. | 21 |
| Morris, A.R. | 65 | Rhodes, W. | 16 |
| Morris, H.M. | 27 | Richards, B. | 35 |
| Murdoch, Richard | 44 | Richards, V. | 177 |
| Murray, J.T. | 132 | Riley, W.N. | 45 |
| Mushtaq, Mohammed | 128 | Rist, T. | 35 |

|  | Page |  | Page |
|---|---|---|---|
| Roberts, A. | 128 | Twinning, R.C. | 51 |
| Robins, R.W.V. | 26 | Twinning, Rosalind | 51 |
| Root, F. | 14 | | |
| Rothwell, R. Norris | 124 | Underwood, D. | 156 |
| Rosenwater, Irving | 122 | | |
| Ross, Alan | 109 | Verity, H. | 47 |
| Ross, Gordon | 97 | Viljoen, K.E. | 65 |
| Rowan, Lou | 107 | Voce, W. | 36 |
| | | Waghorn, L. | 35 |
| Sandham, A. | 14 | Walcott, C. | 90 |
| Sang Hue, | 133 | Walker, P. | 100 |
| Saulez, G. | 121 | Waller, C. | 137 |
| Saunders, Sir Alan | 20 | Washbrook, C. | 38 |
| Scott, R.S.G. | 32 | Washer, G. | 121 |
| Semmence, D. | 76 | Waters, R. | 91 |
| Shackleton, D. | 161 | Watson, Col. A.C. | 12 |
| Sharpe, R. | 123 | Webb, R.T. | 88 |
| Sheppard, Bishop David | 68 | Webb, S.J. | 20 |
| Silk, D. | 146 | Wensley, A.F. | 12 |
| Smith, D.V. | 67 | Wessels, K. | 173 |
| Snow, J.A. | 89 | White, F.G. ('Poona') | 51 |
| Snow, Dr. W.G. | 135 | White, F.G. | 78 |
| Sobers, Sir Garfield | 128 | Whitfield, E.W. | 41 |
| Spencer, J. | 105 | Whittome, Hylda | 77 |
| Spencer, T. | 172 | Wickham, H.T. | 5 |
| Stainton, R. | 63 | Willes, John | 25 |
| Stapleton, Bryan | 47 | Willes, Christina | 25 |
| Stenning, Mrs. I. | 125 | Williams, Col. C.P. | 102 |
| Stevens, G.T.S. | 16 | Williams, L. | 12 |
| Stone, Christopher | 46 | Wilshin, R.W. | 111 |
| Sloop, Cmdr. Ian | 116 | Wilson, F.T.K. | 71 |
| Storey, S. | 171 | Wood, J. | 46 |
| Street, G. | 37 | Woodfull, W.M. | 17 |
| Strudwick, H. | 16 | Woodley, F.E. | 15 |
| Sutcliffe, H. | 16 | Wooller, W. | 90 |
| Suttle, K.G. | 67 | Woolmer, R. | 156 |
| Swanton, E.W. | 72 | Woolston, Mrs | 78 |
| | | Worsley, W.A. | 16 |
| | | Wright, D. | 47 |
| Tate, F.W. | 21 | Wyatt, R.E.S. | 17 |
| Tate, M.W. | 16 | | |
| Tate, Mrs. M.W. | 58 | | |
| Tate, M. ('Jimmy') | 64 | Yardley, N. | 82 |
| Tate, Michael | | Young, R.A. | 12 |
| Taylor, A. Chevalier | 23 | | |
| Titmus, F. | 161 | | |
| Thomson, J. | 37 | First page number given for each name only. | |
| Thomson, N.I. | 68 | | |
| Trueman, F. | 155 | | |
| Tuppin, A. | 35 | | |
| Twinning, R.H. | 26 | | |

*County Ground, Hove, Sussex v Gloucester, 1978. From roof of Arthur Gilligan Stand*